Introduction to International Legal English

A course for classroom or self-study use

Teacher's Book

Jeremy Day

with

Amy Krois-Lindner, Matt Firth

and

TransLegal

CAMBRIDGE
UNIVERSITY PRESS

CAMBRIDGE UNIVERSITY PRESS
Cambridge, New York, Melbourne, Madrid, Cape Town, Singapore, São Paolo, Delhi

Cambridge University Press
The Edinburgh Building, Cambridge CB2 8RU, UK

www.cambridge.org
Information on this title: www.cambridge.org/9780521712033

First published 2008

Printed in the United Kingdom at the University Press, Cambridge

A catalogue record for this publication is available from the British Library

ISBN 978-0-521-71203-3 Teacher's Book
ISBN 978-0-521-71899-8 Student's book

Contents

Introduction

Who is the *IILE* Teacher's Book for?

The *Introduction to International Legal English* (*IILE*) Teacher's Book is aimed at all teachers using *IILE* in the classroom. It is designed to make the *IILE* course as flexible as possible, so that it is suitable for a wide range of teaching situations: from individual students to large groups; from prospective law students to experienced lawyers; from single-nationality groups to international classes; and from intermediate to upper-intermediate level. It is aimed at teachers who may have limited teaching experience or little or no knowledge of legal English, or the worlds of law and business. For this reason, more experienced teachers of legal English may find some sections of the book a little obvious, but it is hoped most teachers will appreciate the careful guidance. I myself am a teacher, not a lawyer, and throughout the book I have drawn heavily on my own experience of trying to get to grips with difficult concepts and language, and have provided the sort of guidance that I have found useful in my own teaching of legal English.

How is the *IILE* Teacher's Book organised?

At the beginning of this book, there are sections on Teaching lawyers (providing general advice for new teachers of legal English), Writing (providing ideas for making the writing activities more fun), Games and activities (which can be used to supplement many activities throughout the course), and general advice on case studies, which are an essential feature of this course.

Each unit starts with a **Teacher's brief**, designed to introduce non-lawyers to the legal topic of each unit. Where possible, the Teacher's brief relates the legal concepts to the everyday experiences of non-lawyers. To enable teachers to read the briefs quickly and to scan them for specific information, the most important words and phrases are given in bold. These bold terms include key legal vocabulary (most of which is explained in the glossary in the Student's Book) as well as the language skills developed in each unit. The

briefs also include some useful Internet sources related to the unit. Inevitably, given the constantly changing nature of the Internet, some of these links may change over the years.

The **teaching notes** usually start with an introductory discussion, designed to get students thinking and talking about the topic from a non-technical perspective. The notes for each unit then follow the organisational structure of the Student's Book, with page numbers provided to take you straight to the relevant section of the Student's Book. The answers to each exercise are included immediately after the notes. (They are also listed at the end of the Student's Book.)

There are also many supplementary activities (**Optional lead-in/extension**), usually designed to exploit the grammar and vocabulary from reading and listening texts more fully. Not all of these activities will be appropriate for all teaching contexts: some classes may find a text so easy that they need no further support or analysis, while others may find a text so difficult and time-consuming that you decide to move on to a new section in the book as soon as possible! However, it is hoped that they will make lesson planning easier, as they offer a good way of using five or ten minutes at the beginning or end of a lesson.

There are also **Language notes** throughout the units to explain difficult language (usually vocabulary from reading or listening texts, but also some unusual or difficult grammar structures). IPA pronunciation is often given inside Language notes, or as separate **Pronunciation notes**. **Background notes** provide guidance on complicated areas of law, or explain something about the authentic cases, texts, etc. referred to in the Student's Book. The aim of these notes is to provide teachers with some background before they start a lesson, or to provide answers to difficult questions from students during lessons. For this reason, the notes contain guidance on some non-technical terms which may none the less cause you problems.

For each listening section, there is a reference to both the relevant CD/track number(s) and the page in the Student's Book where the audio transcript can be found.

Each unit in the Student's Book ends with a self-study Language Focus section. This book does not provide guidance for these (other than answers), as they are self-explanatory. These activities are ideal for homework, but can also be used to fill five minutes at the start or end of a lesson. Needless to say, it is important that you, the teacher, try these activities yourself so that you are ready to deal with any problems students may have with them.

At key points throughout each unit, there are references to **Photocopiable worksheets**, which can be found at the back of the book. Instructions and answer keys for these activities are included within the notes.

The Student's Book also contains three case studies, after Units 2, 5 and 8. Notes for these are given at the same positions in this book, but you should also read the section on **Case studies** on page 10 for ideas for exploiting these case studies.

How can the book be used with different levels?

Although *IILE* is aimed at students at intermediate level, this does not mean that it cannot be used with lower or higher levels. For weaker students, you should provide plenty of support, including supplementary activities, with the aim of getting them through the course. With stronger students, on the other hand, your aim should be for them to master most of the language used in the book, with a view to producing it, rather than merely understanding it. The supplementary activities should therefore be used to make the course more challenging.

Even in a mixed-ability group, it is possible for all students to make good progress, whatever their initial level, if you encourage them each to push themselves to use difficult, new or sophisticated language as much as possible in their speaking and writing, and if you provide sensitive feedback and error correction.

How can the book be used with different class sizes?

At many points in both the Student's Book and the Teacher's Book, there are instructions for the students to work with a partner. Obviously, if you have only one student or an odd number, pairwork will be impossible, but for the most part this should not cause problems. With one-to-one classes, you will have to be the partner in discussions and role-plays. With odd numbers of students, most pairwork exercises will work equally well with groups of three. In both cases, specific advice has been provided where necessary (for example, with role-plays).

There is no upper limit to the class size. For time reasons, some activities (such as individual presentations) may have to be modified for very large groups, but again specific instructions have been provided where necessary.

About the author

Jeremy Day is a freelance teacher, trainer and writer based in Warsaw, Poland. He has written international ESP courses for the British Council (*Advanced Legal English*) and International House (*English for Marketing Professionals*), as well as the Teacher's book for *International Legal English* (CUP, 2006). He is Series Editor for CUP's series of ESP short courses, *Cambridge English for ...*

Author acknowledgements

Many thanks to Nick Robinson and Clare Sheridan at CUP for overseeing this project. Special thanks to Catriona Watson-Brown for her help and seemingly endless patience during the copy-editing stages. Thanks of course to Amy Krois-Lindner and Matt Firth for teaching me so much about the law and legal English, and for providing many of the ideas in this book. My legal English students at the British Council Warsaw over the years have helped enormously in clarifying issues, and letting me know what they expect in a legal English course (and what they find boring). I also really appreciate the work done by TransLegal to check and correct my understanding of the legal issues discussed herein. Thanks also to members of the excellent EULETA discussion group for clarifying some legal terms for me, especially Natasha Jovanovich, Margaret Marks, alpha.john and johnkuti.

As always, huge thanks to my wife, Ania, and my kids, Emilka and Tomek, for their support and patience while I was working on this book.

Teaching lawyers as a non-lawyer

Most teachers dread the idea of teaching lawyers. Legal English is so full of strange vocabulary and grammar that it seems like a different language. Lawyers themselves can be quite scary: they tend to be highly intelligent, extremely demanding and focused on tiny details. With most other branches of English teaching, it can be enough to be a good teacher with knowledge of English, but with legal English, this is not enough. This section is aimed at teachers who know very little about law.

My first lesson with lawyers was exhausting and stressful. The vocabulary brainstorm activity I had planned as a warmer ended up taking the whole lesson and left me with a list of over 40 items which either I could not explain or was not sure how to pronounce. I then spent several hours before the next lesson checking all the words on my list and turning them into two simple match-the-words-with-their-definitions worksheets. This hard work convinced my students that a non-lawyer could teach them legal English, and my lessons became increasingly stress-free and even enjoyable. As the course progressed, I noticed more and more that I really did understand what they were talking about, and that my opinions, life experience and ideas were just as valid as those of my students. Through a combination of honesty, hard work and professional confidence, I was able to win their trust and become accepted as an authority.

Be honest

It is essential to manage students' expectations. If you pretend to be a lawyer or an expert before or at the beginning of the course, students are likely to be disappointed. But if you admit that you are still learning about law yourself, they may be pleasantly surprised by how much you know. Similarly, make sure that your colleagues involved in marketing your course do not make promises that you cannot keep.

Be prepared

This is the key to successful teaching of legal English. It means making sure you have read all the relevant sections of the Student's Book and Teacher's Book before you step into the classroom, and really know what all of the words and phrases mean and how they are pronounced. It's a good idea to check the Internet for anything you're unsure of. I usually start my searches on **OneLook** (http://www.onelook.com), which provides links to dozens of online dictionaries, including the excellent **Law.com** (http://dictionary. law.com), and **Cambridge**'s suite of dictionaries (http://dictionary.cambridge.org), which are a good source of guidance on pronunciation and usage. OneLook also provides links to **Wikipedia** (http://en.wikipedia.org/wiki/Main_Page), which is now incredibly useful and much more reliable than even a few years ago.

Be armed

Bring a legal English dictionary with you to every lesson. If you have Internet access in the classroom, use online dictionaries to check anything you're unsure of.

Be confident

Remember that, even if you know nothing about law, you can still help students enormously. You can:

○ motivate them (to come to class, to learn in class, to learn at home);

○ be an expert on plain English (the English they need in order to explain things to clients);

○ be an expert on finding things out (using the Internet and dictionaries to answer students' questions – it can be surprising to see how helpless they are when they encounter language problems);

- be a source of real-life experiences (such as signing employment contracts, buying or renting property, borrowing money, etc.), especially if you come from a different country from your students;
- be knowledgeable on universal language problems such as dependent prepositions, punctuation, spelling, articles, tenses, levels of formality, collocations, paragraphing, etc.

You need to feel positive about why students should be paying for you to teach them.

Learn from students

Ask lots of questions during lessons. Lawyers need to practise the skill of explaining complicated things to non-lawyers, so you should exploit this opportunity to the full. At times, you can 'act stupid' (ask questions you already know the answer to) or 'play devil's advocate' (air controversial opinions, even if these are not your own opinions). This means that when you really need to say something which may be stupid or controversial, you can pretend that you are simply using one of your techniques.

Just as good students should take notes and learn from them, so should you as a teacher. Write down everything you learn about what your students do in their jobs and how the law works in their countries, and try to learn from your notes.

Think about what students need

A common mistake made by teachers of legal English is to assume that lawyers spend their time defending or prosecuting criminals in court. In fact, most lawyers deal with contract and company law, rather than criminal law. Most lawyers also spend very little time (if any) in court. Much of their work involves preparing or analysing documents for business clients, and trying to avoid disputes (or at least to resolve them without the need to go to court).

There is also no reason to think that they are particularly interested in US or UK law. As English is increasingly becoming the international language of business, legal English is rapidly losing its ties with English-speaking countries. The most likely scenario is that your students need legal English to explain aspects of their own legal systems (which they already know about) to international clients (who may well be non-native English speakers). Legal English materials (including those in this book) tend to refer frequently to English-speaking countries for the simple reason that these are more readily available in English than materials related to other countries. This means that you should try as much as possible to relate the country-specific materials in this book to students' own jurisdictions.

If you ask lawyers' bosses and clients what sort of English the lawyers need, they might say 'plain English': the language to communicate difficult ideas clearly to non-experts (such as clients). Many lawyers (including native English speakers) struggle to use 'client-friendly' English, with the result that they frequently fail to communicate with their clients. On the other hand, if you ask the lawyers themselves what they need, they might ask for more 'legalese': the jargon that non-lawyers find so incomprehensible. Lawyers like knowing such language because they need to understand it when they encounter it, and they feel they are expected to use it (rather like their formal dress-code).

The answer is that lawyers need both types of English (as well as other formal and informal registers for writing and speaking). Your job is to raise awareness of these differences, and to provide plenty of opportunity to practise them.

Writing

An essential part of the Student's Book is its emphasis on writing, with one or two tasks per unit. The problem is that writing does not seem to fit in a communicative classroom. Students complain if they have to write for extended periods during their lessons, but they are often too busy to write at home. An obvious question is whether it is reasonable to expect students to produce ten or more pieces of writing during the course, and whether you, as a teacher, have to find the time to mark this many pieces from each student. This section offers a few ideas to get around this dilemma.

Writing is one of the best ways of learning and practising language. It provides the opportunity for individual creative production without the time pressure associated with speaking. It allows students to experiment with new or complicated language structures that they would probably avoid when speaking. In fact, written language is fundamentally different from spoken language in many ways:

○ It includes skills such as spelling and punctuation which are not used in speech;

○ It uses many different grammar and vocabulary structures;

○ Accuracy is far more important than in speech because communication breakdowns cannot be overcome using body language or negotiating the meaning with the listener.

For lawyers, such issues are especially acute. Whether they are drafting contracts, legal opinions, internal memos, case summaries or emails to clients, it is essential to use professional, accurate language. A misspelled word or a misplaced comma may dangerously change the meaning of a legal document, and lawyers need practice before they can get it right.

In-class writing

The advantage of in-class writing over homework is that you can guarantee that all the students produce some work, and that a piece of work is actually written by a given student. Unfortunately, in-class writing is often unpopular with students, who prefer to spend their class time in a more interesting way. With this in mind, in-class writing needs to be quick (e.g. set a time limit of five or ten minutes) and different from the experience of homework writing. The following ideas explore how to achieve this.

Team writing

There is no reason why writing has to be a solitary activity. A simple trick is to hand out a single sheet of paper to each pair or group, and to make them plan and produce their writing together. This means that they have to speak with each other to compare ideas and can correct each other's mistakes. This may even be done with the whole class, where one scribe writes the class's suggestions onto the board.

Chain writing

Team-writing activities can be spiced up by telling the teams to swap their pieces of paper with another team after a certain amount of time (or number of words). This forces them to read each other's work and can produce some very creative (or funny) texts.

Oral writing

'Writing' does not have to involve a pen and paper. Students can work with a partner to decide what they would write, and to speak the text as if they were dictating to a secretary. At the end, ask some groups to 'read' their 'writing' aloud to the class.

Written dialogues

Writing can be more satisfying when it is genuinely communicative, so when students have produced a complete text (e.g. an email request), tell them to pass it on to a different student, who can reply to that email (e.g. a polite refusal). Such dialogues can continue over several turns.

Games and activities

This section outlines some games and activities which can be applied to many of the exercises in the Student's Book. They usually require little or no preparation.

First-use game

When you set up role-plays, it is important to encourage students to use new target language (e.g. the useful functional phrases studied in a particular unit). Award a point for the first student to use each phrase from a list (either on the board or on cards). The phrase must be used naturally and appropriately. After the first good use of a particular phrase, cross it off the list and write the student's initial next to it (or give that student the card). At the end of the role-play, the student who has used the most phrases is the winner.

Matching games

Several of the Photocopiable worksheets at the back of this book are designed to be cut up (for students to match, for example, two halves of a sentence or a word with its definition). It is also very easy to make similar exercises yourself, using vocabulary lists or split collocations. Activities where students physically move pieces of paper (and perhaps stand up to work in a team) are an excellent way of changing the focus/pace of a lesson. Some students actually learn best through physical activities like this (as opposed to simply seeing or hearing information). What could otherwise be a boring and solitary activity can be transformed into a communicative and competitive team game by cutting it up and telling students to race the other teams. Give a complete (i.e. not cut up) copy of the worksheet to early-finishers to complete again (the other students will receive theirs later). This will provide good consolidation (as it is much easier the second time), and give students a permanent record of the answers. Always go through the answers carefully, and encourage students to test themselves at home by folding the worksheet vertically, so they can see only one half of each sentence.

Easy-first procedure

This technique is surprisingly useful for turning any exercise into a game, especially those with a large number of questions. It also works if you join several short exercises together. Tell students to complete an exercise in teams. Write the question numbers on the board. When students have finished answering the questions, ask the first team to choose the number of a question they are sure they know the answer to. If they supply the correct answer, draw a circle around that number in that team's colour, and move on to the next team. If they are wrong, move on to the next team. Keep going until all the questions have been answered correctly. The team with the most numbers at the end is the winner. The procedure is called 'easy first' because the best strategy is to answer the easy questions (which other teams are also likely to know) as early in the game as possible, and to leave tricky ones until the end of the game.

Quiz game

This game can be used with most texts. Divide the class into teams of around three or four and tell each team to write, in their notebooks, a given number of questions based on the text. The questions could be based on the language of the text or the factual content. Allow around five minutes for the teams to come up with their questions, and then tell them to close their books. Ask the first group to ask their first question. The next group (going clockwise round the class) should try to answer. If they answer correctly, give them a point (on the board). If they fail, pass the question to the next group. If no groups can answer the question, the group which asked the question gets a point (provided they can remember the answer with their books closed). Continue with the next group's first question. After all the questions have been asked, count up the points to find out which team has won.

Case studies

The aim of the case studies is to provide free-speaking practice within a realistic context. They are an extremely important part of the course, as they are designed to come as close as possible to the type of speaking that lawyers regularly engage in as part of their jobs. As a secondary aim, students should also be encouraged to take risks with new language and especially to try to use the language they have recently studied.

1   Tell students to read the introduction and instructions to find out who they work for (e.g. a law firm) and what they need to find in the text (e.g. the legal issue).

2   Allow time for students to read the introductory text carefully to answer the question. Be prepared to explain plenty of words from the text, as it is essential that all students understand it fully. There are concept-checking questions provided in the notes for each case study.

3   **Task 1: Speaking:** Divide the class into two groups. Make sure everybody knows who they are representing in the role-play. If you have a large class, you may have more groups (e.g. four or six) with two to six people in each group. If you have fewer than four students, Task 1 will not work as a role-play, but can still be done as an informal discussion, where you analyse the case first from one party's point of view, and then from the other party's.

4   Tell students to go through the preparations (**Exercise 1**) for the main meeting by systematically following the instructions and keeping notes of their answers. The preparation stage is still an important part of the role-play, so insist that students speak English, and encourage them to experiment with new language. This stage includes the reading of the relevant legal documents, and again this should be done in character, as if in a real meeting. They should help each other to understand the meaning and relevance of each document. You may need to assign a chair to manage the group discussions and keep them focused. Also set

a time limit of around ten minutes for this preparation stage.

5   At the end of the time limit, give students a chance to ask you about anything they are unclear of, especially from the relevant legal documents. Note that there are language notes and background notes for these texts provided on pages 37, 82 and 133.

6   Move students around so that each student is paired with a student representing the other party (**Exercise 2**). If you have an odd number of students, there will have to be a group of three. If you have only one student, you will have to be one of the parties. Make sure students realise that their aim is to reach an agreement, and that they should therefore try to be polite and be prepared to make concessions. Again, set a time limit of around ten minutes for the role-play. During the role-play, monitor carefully and make notes of successful language as well as important mistakes.

7   At the end of the time limit, bring the role-plays to a close and get students to report back on their negotiations (**Exercise 3**). Finally, give and elicit feedback on the success of the role-plays from a professional and linguistic point of view.

8   **Task 2: Writing:** The writing tasks all require students to write a letter of advice to one of the parties. As the tasks refer to the 'likely outcome', the letters should be based on the information in the SB, rather than on the outcomes of the role-plays. The writing can be done at home or in class.

1) A career in law

Teacher's brief

The first part of the unit offers a general introduction to studying law. It takes the syllabuses of university law courses as its starting point.

Law students in most countries study at the law department of a regular university. In Britain and most other common-law countries, law students typically study for a **Bachelor of Laws** (**LLB**, or *Legum Baccalaureus* – the double L simply means that *Legum* is plural). After completion of this first degree, law students in the UK must then complete a postgraduate qualification before becoming a qualified lawyer: either the **Legal Practice Course** (**LPC**), for those who want to become solicitors, dealing mainly with clients directly, or the **Bar Vocational Course** (**BVC**), for those who want to become barristers, representing clients in court.

An alternative to this normal route to becoming a lawyer in Britain is commonly known as a **law conversion course**. This course allows a graduate from a subject other than law to convert to a law degree. This course, also called a **Graduate Diploma in Law** (**GDL**) or **Common Professional Examination** (**CPE**), is shorter than a full LLB course, as its students tend to bring with them useful knowledge from their first degrees.

The situation in the USA is different. There, students start law school after completion of a bachelor's degree (in any subject), which usually takes four years. After a further three years at **law school**, they then study for a state's **bar exam**. Only when they have passed the bar exam are they fully qualified lawyers.

Reading 2 provides a sample of a **syllabus** for the first two years at a US law school (in this case, the University of Honolulu). The syllabus lists a wide range of **legal terms and concepts**, and as such offers an excellent introduction to the topics that lawyers need to understand. Although the exercises associated with this text encourage students not to check every unknown word and to develop the skill of guessing meaning from context, there is none the less a danger for teachers here that they may be expected to explain large quantities of terminology. It is therefore essential that you read the text, plus the associated notes in this book,

very carefully before the lesson. Try to pass on to the students the responsibility for finding out what the terms mean, rather than trying to explain them yourself.

Listening 1 encourages students to question their needs and expectations from a legal English course, particularly with regard to the balance between work on **practical skills** and **talking about legal systems** in various countries. An important feature of this book is its emphasis on practical skills and helping students to talk about the legal systems in their own countries, not just English-speaking ones.

The second part of the unit, Law in practice, uses the case study of a **graduate recruitment programme** to introduce useful language skills for **making presentations** and **writing summaries**. Such programmes typically take the most promising graduates and support them financially while they complete their studies. They are attractive to students, as they provide useful work experience as well as financial support, and for employers they are a good way of attracting and training talented employees.

Further information

○ A good starting point for information on **studying law in various countries** is Wikipedia. For example, the articles at http://en.wikipedia.org/wiki/Legal_education_in_the_United_Kingdom; http://en.wikipedia.org/wiki/Bachelor_of_Laws; and http://en.wikipedia.org/wiki/Legal_education

○ **LLB course outlines** can easily be found on the Internet by searching for 'LLB'.

○ Each country has its own system for training lawyers, so it is a good idea to find out about **studying law in your students' countries**. This can be done easily by finding the website of important universities in the countries and checking the syllabuses for their law courses.

○ For more information on **becoming a solicitor** in the UK, see http://www.lawsociety.org.uk/becomingasolicitor/careerinlaw.law. For information on **becoming a barrister**, see http://www.barcouncil.org.uk/trainingandeducation/howtobecomeabarrister/.

THE STUDY OF LAW

SB p8 ## Lead-in

With the whole class, elicit the difference between core subjects in a law degree programme and optional subjects, and then discuss the two questions. Ask students also for some examples of optional subjects. (For a good list of core and optional subjects, see Reading 2.) If your students are all from the same country, you could get them to speculate about other countries, for example:

○ How might the study of law differ from country to country (e.g. length of course, core and optional subjects covered, the balance between theory and practice and between formal study and work experience)?

○ Which subjects would be part of the core course in every country?

SB p8 ## Reading 1: A career in law

1 Tell students to read the text to answer the two questions. Emphasise that the first question concerns core subjects. Tell students to underline the sections of the text which contain the answers to the two questions. Allow around two minutes for students to read. When they have finished, tell them to discuss their answers with a partner without looking back at the text. Finally, check the answers with the class. As you go through the answers, elicit what is meant by each of the course titles.

Answers
1 criminal law, contract law, tort law, land law, equity and trusts, administrative law and constitutional law
2 company law, commercial law, and litigation and arbitration

Language notes
○ *Tort law* is a major branch of law. *Tort* means 'civil wrong', and covers all cases of damage or injury, either through negligence or through wilful misconduct. It is usually taken to exclude criminal wrongs, although the same event may be covered by both branches (e.g. if somebody crashes into someone else's car, a civil wrong has occurred, but if the driver was drunk at the time, a criminal wrong has also occurred). The law of torts excludes breaches of contract, which are covered by contract law.

○ *Equity* has several meanings. One meaning, perhaps the most widely known, is important in business and commercial law: an owner's equity in a company is equivalent to the amount of capital that the owner has invested, after liabilities (debts, etc.) have been accounted for. However, in Reading 1, equity refers to a system in common-law jurisdictions (such as England) for ensuring fairness when normal application of the law would otherwise lead to injustice. One important part of the system of equity concerns *trusts*, which typically involve one person formally placing their trust (confidence) in another person. See http://www.lawbore.net/lawboretopicnew.php?topic=8 for a good introduction to equity and trusts, as well as some useful web links.

○ *Legal research* involves the skill of finding and analysing legal documents in order to support legal decision-making. See http://en.wikipedia.org/wiki/Legal_research for some good starting points.

○ The text mentions both a *law practice* (= a law firm, countable) and *legal practice* (= the activities involved in being a lawyer, uncountable). Confusingly, both terms may be used with both meanings.

○ *Company law* (US corporate law) is mainly concerned with the setting up and running of various types of company, including issues such as ownership and liability, while *commercial law* covers the relationships between companies (e.g. sale of goods). These two areas of law are dealt with fully in Units 5 and 6.

○ For an example of a *law clinic*, see http://www.kent.ac.uk/lawb/clinic/.

2 Tell students to discuss the statements in pairs to decide whether they are true or false. Encourage them to read the relevant parts of the text again to check their answers. As you go through the answers, you could turn some of the statements into short class discussions

(Do you have any experience of law clinics? How good at English should law graduates be?).

Answers
1 F Family law is usually an optional course in the UK.
2 T
3 F Law clinics give law students the opportunity to learn about the day-to-day work of a lawyer.
4 F Today, commercial law firms expect recruits to have a good command of English.

3 Elicit from the class the meaning of the word *collocation* (= a pair or group of words which are commonly used together), and a few everyday examples such as *take a photo*, *interested in* and *fast asleep*. Elicit why it is important for learners of a language to pay attention to collocations [**Suggested answer**: Correct use of collocations not only improves accuracy, sophistication and naturalness, but it also increases fluency, as there is less need to choose each individual word separately. Collocations are also important for understanding, as certain words only make sense in the context of their collocations, e.g. the word *afford* in the collocation *can't afford*]. Tell students to look back at the text to find five collocations beginning with the word *legal* and five beginning with the word *law*. When they have finished, go through the answers with the class.

Answers
legal writing, legal research, legal practice, legal assistance, legal community
law degree programme, law student, law practice, law clinic, law firm

Optional extension
Tell students to work in pairs to identify more useful collocations from Reading 1. Encourage them to find adverb–adjective, verb–preposition, preposition–noun, verb–noun, verb–verb, adjective–noun and noun–noun collocations. After a few minutes, collect the answers on the board. You will need to use your discretion as to whether proposed collocations are genuine word partnerships (i.e. if they commonly go together).

As a follow-up, tell students to work in pairs. One should look at the board and read the first part of a collocation to his/her partner (e.g. *intellectually*). The other student, who may not look at the board, has to complete the collocation (e.g. *stimulating*). After a few minutes, they should swap roles.

Suggested answers

adverb–adjective	intellectually stimulating
verb–preposition	to lead to something; to decide on something; to get involved with something
preposition–noun	in addition
verb–noun	to take a course/subject; to run a partnership; to offer a course; to offer assistance; to hire new recruits
verb–verb	to go on to become something
adjective–noun	future career; local community; day-to-day work; a good command (of English)
noun–noun	work experience

(SB p9) # Speaking 1: Law firms and courses

4 Tell students to discuss the two questions with a partner. If they already know each other well, tell them to imagine they are asking and answering the questions at a job interview. Encourage them to give background information, as in the examples.

(SB p9) # Reading 2: Course descriptions

5 Tell students to discuss the questions briefly in pairs, and then open up the discussion to the whole class. The discussion could include dealing with unfamiliar words in their own language, as well as in English. Encourage students to think of situations where each of the five techniques would be most useful.

Suggested answer
The best way to deal with unfamiliar words of course depends on many factors, including:

○ First or second reading? As a general rule, the first time you read a text, you should read quickly to get a general understanding, and avoid analysing the language. Only when you are sure that the text is useful/important enough to spend time on should you spend time analysing words.

○ Intensive or extensive? Some texts demand intensive reading, where it is essential to understand every word, and even analyse every punctuation mark. An example might be a key document in a legal dispute. If this is the case, every unknown word (as well as some half-known words) should be checked carefully. At other times, extensive reading is required, when large amounts of text have to be searched for specific information. An example of this is the process of *due diligence*, when lawyers analyse huge amounts of a company's paperwork, typically to assess the risks associated with buying that company.

○ Reading to read or reading for language? Most reading takes place for its own sake, i.e. to obtain information (or pleasure) from the text. However, language learners can also use texts as a rich source of useful language, in which case the more analysis the better. It is important to keep these two aims separate and, for example, not to get bogged down in language analysis when the aim is to get information.

With this in mind, each of the five techniques is useful in certain circumstances. At one extreme, looking up every word would be useful for intensive reading, or when reading for language, but would be very distracting in most other situations. At the other extreme, ignoring all unknown words permits very fast and extensive reading, but there is always a danger that something will be missed. The three intermediate techniques are all good compromises.

Language note
The root of a word is what remains when all prefixes and suffixes are removed. For example, the root of the word *entrapment* is *trap*.

Optional extension
Tell students to go back to Reading 1 to identify words whose meanings can be worked out (or guessed) using the first technique (surrounding words) and the fifth (analysis). Discuss the answers with the class.

Suggested answers
sole practitioner
○ Surrounding words: the text says *to work alone as a sole practitioner*.
○ Analysis (Italian *solo*, Latin *solum*; French *practiser*, Latin *practicare*; *−er* = noun suffix indicating person who does something (e.g. teach**er**)

*good **command** of English*
○ Surrounding words: previous sentence mentions *language ability*.
○ Analysis: the text mentions that *law firms increasingly expect* this, so it is a desirable thing to possess. Use of article (*a*) and adjective (*good*) indicate that *command* must be a noun.

6   Elicit from the class what they would expect to find in a university course catalogue, then tell them to read the extract on page 10 to compare it with their suggestions. Tell them to read the text quickly (set a time limit of two minutes) to identify whether the university is in the UK or not. You may ask them to find at least three pieces of evidence.

Answers
The university is not in the UK, since this two-year programme does not include some of the usual compulsory courses in the UK, such as land law, equity and trusts, and administrative law. Other indirect evidence includes:
○ *−ize/−yze* spelling (e.g. *familiarize, analyze*), which is frequently (but not always) written with an *s* in British English (e.g. *familiarise, analyse*);
○ the use of the serial comma (i.e. a comma before the final *and*) in lists;
○ the mention of *homicide*, which is used more frequently (but not exclusively) in American English to refer to murder and other killings of people, including causing accidental death, and *impeachment*;

○ prominent mention of US institutions such as the *Uniform Commercial Code*, *state and federal courts* and *the constitution*.

Language notes

○ *Analysis and synthesis* literally means 'taking something apart (*analysis* /əˈnæləsɪs/) and then putting things together (*synthesis* /ˈsɪnθəsɪs/)'. In the context of this text, it means studying individual legal decisions very thoroughly and then relating them to other legal decisions.

○ For a good list of *crimes against public administration*, see http://www.fsmlaw.org/fsm/code/title11/T11_Ch05.htm.

○ *Impeachment* has two meanings. One meaning concerns the proceedings to remove a government official from office. Two well-known examples of this type of impeachment are US Presidents Richard Nixon (who was forced to resign by the threat of impeachment, but never actually impeached) and Bill Clinton (who was impeached but not forced to resign) (see http://en.wikipedia.org/wiki/Impeachment). The second meaning, and the one intended in the text, involves discrediting a witness by demonstrating that he/she has testified dishonestly or inappropriately, see http://dictionary.law.com.

○ For more on *incriminating statements*, see http://dictionary.law.com.

○ The *contract clause* is an important part of the US Constitution which prohibits individual states from making laws impairing the obligations of contracts. See http://en.wikipedia.org/wiki/Contract_Clause.

○ At the end of the Constitutional Law paragraph, *the amendments thereto* means *amendments to that thing*, i.e. *to the constitution*.

7 Tell students to read the text again to choose the correct title for each description. Tell them also to underline new or difficult words, but discourage them from analysing the words at this stage. When they have finished, tell them to compare their answers with a partner,

and then check with the whole class. Avoid discussing difficult vocabulary, as the aim at this stage is to practise understanding a text without analysing it.

Answers
1 Contract law 2 Tort law 3 Criminal law
4 Constitutional law 5 Legal research and writing

8 Tell students to discuss the questions in pairs, and to identify the sections of the text which provide the answers.

Answers
1 Introduction to Law
2 Legal Research and Writing
3 Evidence

9 Ask students to work in small groups to compare their lists of unknown and difficult words. Tell them to avoid simply providing the translations/explanations for each other, but to focus on the clues in the text which will help them to understand the word (or at least to get a general understanding of its meaning). When they have had a chance to work together for a few minutes, open up the discussion to involve the whole class. As you check the meanings, focus not only on whether the students are correct or not, but also on the techniques they used to work out the meaning. In a way, an incorrect answer which was reached through intelligent analysis is more impressive than an accurate translation/explanation reached by checking in a dictionary. For explanations of many of the words and phrases in the text, see the Optional extension exercise below. Some are also explained in the Glossary on page 155 of the Student's Book. However, with so many technical terms in this text, it is also a good idea to have a good legal dictionary to hand, and to make a note of outstanding vocabulary problems, which you can research before the next lesson.

Pronunciation notes
citation /saɪˈteɪʃən/
liability /laɪəˈbɪlɪtɪ/
negligently /ˈneglɪdʒəntlɪ/
nuisance /ˈnjuːsəns/
precedent /ˈpresədənt/

privacy /ˈprɪvəsɪ/
privileges /ˈprɪvəˌlɪdʒɪz/
rationale /ˌræʃəˈnɑːl/
relevancy /ˈreləvənsɪ/
seizure /ˈsiːʒə(r)/
statutory /ˈstætjʊtərɪ/
surveillance /səˈveɪləns/
vicarious /vɪˈkeərɪəs/

Optional extension
(Photocopiable worksheet 1.1)
This contains brief explanations of 26 of
the most useful and/or difficult terms from
Reading 2. Although the aim of Reading 2 was
to focus on the skill of working out meaning
from context, students may still benefit from
this opportunity to increase their vocabularies.

1 Divide the class into small teams and
  give each team a set of cut-up words and
  definitions (Photocopiable worksheet 1.1).
  They have to race the other teams to match
  the words with the definitions, using the text
  in Reading 2 to provide clues if necessary.
2 When the first team has finished, check
  that their answers are correct.
3 While they are waiting for the other teams
  to finish, give each student in the winning
  team a complete (i.e. not cut-up) copy of
  the worksheet to do the matching exercise
  again. The purpose of this is to provide
  a permanent record of the words and
  definitions, as well as to reinforce the
  students' knowledge of the words.
4 When all of the teams have finished,
  check the answers together and clarify any
  misunderstandings.
5 As a follow-up, tell students to fold the
  worksheet in half vertically. They can then
  test each other (and themselves at home)
  by reading a word to elicit a definition, or
  vice versa.

Answers
1 k 2 o 3 t 4 l 5 d 6 p 7 s 8 q
9 c 10 y 11 f 12 e 13 m 14 n 15 h
16 u 17 v 18 w 19 x 20 i 21 z 22 r
23 j 24 g 25 a 26 b

10 Tell students to discuss the question in
   pairs, including whether the contents of their
   courses were broadly the same as those listed
   in Reading 2.

SB p11 1.1 **Listening 1: Law courses**

Elicit from the class the sorts of things that a
good legal English course should offer. Avoid
getting too deeply into specific details at this
stage, as there will be a chance to do this later.
Then tell students to read the introduction to
compare it with their ideas.

This is, of course, a good opportunity to do some
needs analysis. Although you, as teacher, may
already have firm ideas about the best direction this
course should follow, and this will also be shaped
by this book, there is still room for some flexibility,
and it is important to take an interest in students'
perceived needs. If students have unrealistic or
inappropriate expectations of the course, it is
important to address these as early as possible.

11 Tell students to read through the list of course
   contents quickly, then listen to decide which
   speaker did what. Afterwards, tell them to
   discuss their answers with a partner, including
   whether the speakers found the activities
   useful. Play the recording a second time if
   necessary for them to check. Then go through
   the answers with the class.

Transcript » STUDENT'S BOOK **page 124**

Answers

	Heidi's course	Pavel's course
1		✓
2		✓
3	✓	✓
4	✓	✓
5	✓	✓
6		✓

12 Tell students to listen again to find similarities
   and differences with their own experiences of
   learning legal English. After the recording, they
   should discuss their answers with a partner.
   Discuss with the class which course best
   resembles students' experiences, and which
   they would find most useful. It is important
   that you do this with the whole class, as the
   information will be useful to you as a teacher
   when planning the rest of the course.

(SB p12) Language use: Comparative and superlative forms

13 Elicit from the class the meaning of the terms *comparative* and *superlative*, together with an everyday example such as *big* (base form), *bigger* (comparative), *biggest* (superlative). Then tell them to match the sentences with the rules. Point out that there may be more than one rule for each sentence. As you go through the answers with the class, elicit more examples for each rule (see notes below), especially adjectives that are useful for describing courses and language skills (e.g. *interesting, helpful, memorable, boring, theoretical, up-to-date, hands-on, challenging, tough, nice, complicated*).

Answers
1 b   2 c   3 d, h   4 a   5 d   6 d   7 f
8 g, h   9 e

Three quantifiers also have irregular comparatives and superlatives: *much/many, more, most* and *little, less, least*. The quantifier *few* is regular: *few, fewer, fewest.*

- ○ Most longer adjectives (two syllables or more) take *more/most*. The exceptions are two-syllable adjectives ending in *–y*, such as *easy* and *busy*, and a few others (e.g. *quiet, clever, simple, gentle*), which usually take *–er/–est*. Longer adjectives ending in *–y* take *more/most* (e.g. *necessary, more necessary*).
- ○ Almost all adverbs, including those formed by adding *–ly* to adjectives, take *more/most*. A few short adverbs which are not formed in this way take *–er/–est* (e.g. *fast, hard, early, late*).

14 Ask students to complete the task quickly. Go through the answers with them, writing any incorrect responses on the board. At the end, focus on their mistakes and ask students to refer back to the rules in Exercise 13 to analyse the errors.

Answers
1 more practical   2 best
3 more challenging   4 more time-consuming
5 most useful   6 easier

(SB p12) Speaking 2: Learning approaches

15 Tell students to discuss the two questions in pairs or small groups. Make sure they realise that they should try to use comparatives and superlatives in their conversations. If you feel they need further practice, you could ask them to compare the courses in Reading 2 (e.g. *The course on contracts would be more useful to me than the one on evidence. The one on tort seems to be the most complicated.*).

When they have finished discussing in pairs, discuss the topic with the whole class, focusing this time on the content (i.e. what do the students have the biggest problems with) rather than the grammar. As a class, try to come up with solutions to the students' perceived weaknesses.

This highlights some typical problems that learners have, and some practical solutions.

1 Divide the class into groups of four. If your class does not divide exactly into four, allow groups of three, but ensure that one character card is not omitted all the time.
2 Make enough copies of the worksheet for each group, and cut them up. Give each student one of the character cards (1–4). Tell them to read about their character and then explain their problem to the rest of their group. The group should then think of advice to help each character overcome their problems with English.
3 When they have spent a few minutes discussing each of the characters' problems and solutions, give each group a set of the solution cards (a–k). Tell them to decide which of the characters would benefit from each piece of advice.
4 Finally, discuss the answers with the whole class, paying particular attention to any of the students' solutions which were not on the solution cards. Ask the students if they are going to try some of the techniques.

Possible answers
1 a, b, d, f, g, k
2 a, b, c, d, e, g, h, i, j, k
3 a, b, d, e, g, h, i, j, k
4 a, b, c, f, g, h, k

LAW IN PRACTICE

(SB p13) Lead-in

Elicit from the class the differences between working in a small law firm and a larger one. Then tell students to read the introduction to compare it with their suggestions. Discuss the question quickly with the class.

Reading 3: Graduate recruitment programme

16 Elicit from the class what they know about graduate recruitment programmes (e.g. how they work, who they are suitable for, what the graduate can expect to do, what are the benefits). Avoid providing the answers, as

these are given (for this particular programme) in the text. Then tell students to read the text quickly to answer the two questions. When they have finished reading, tell them to check with a partner and then collect the answers from the class.

Answers
1 You do not need a law degree to enter the graduate recruitment programme, just a 2.1 degree in any subject.
2 Barker Rose will pay the full course fees for both the GDL and LPC plus maintenance of £6,000 during the GDL and £7,000 through the LPC study year.

Language notes
○ In common-law jurisdictions such as England, Canada and New Zealand, there has traditionally been a contrast between *solicitors* (lawyers who advise clients) and *barristers* (lawyers who advocate in a legal hearing). Increasingly, this distinction is breaking down, as solicitors can now represent their clients in court (although, in the UK, they have to qualify to have a right to be heard in Higher Courts).
○ The third paragraph may cause problems, as the word *law* has been omitted from all but the last item in a long list: company *law*, commercial *law* and finance *law*, commercial litigation *law*, ... shipping *law* and property *law*.
○ In Britain, a 2.1 (pronounced *two one*, or *upper second class*) is considered a good university degree. The best grade, a first-class degree, is rare and considered exceptional, so employers often ask for a 2.1 or better. Most university students finish with a 2.2, which is very respectable but often not good enough to attract elite employers. A third-class degree is also a pass.
○ In the fourth paragraph, the word *otherwise* reinforces the concept of flexibility: here it means that even if a candidate doesn't have a 2.1, they may still be recruited if they are exceptionally talented or experienced.

○ GDL (*Graduate Diploma in Law*) is also called the Common Professional Examination (CPE) or simply 'law conversion course'. See http://en.wikipedia.org/wiki/Common_Professional_Examination.

17 Tell students to complete the exercise alone and then check with a partner. As you collect the answers from the class, discuss reasons for the answers.

Answers

1 Andrea wouldn't be suitable for Barker Rose, as they only work in the field of commercial law.
2 Although Sandip only got a 2.2, the advertisement says that Barker Rose *are willing to progress candidates whose application otherwise demonstrates first-rate personal qualities and experience.* He might be considered suitable due to his proven business skills and experience, but we cannot be certain.
3 Meral wouldn't be suitable, as candidates must apply by 31st July, two years before the start of the training contract, and she wants to start next year.
4 Oren would be suitable. Barker Rose accept students of any discipline.

18 Discuss the two questions with the whole class. If the recruitment programme is unsuitable for your students (e.g. because they already work in law, or they are already studying law), discuss the sort of people to whom it would be of interest. For question 2, point out that, according to the advert, there will be a presentation on the recruitment programme at a Law Fair, where asking intelligent questions would be a good way to start talking to representatives of the firm. You may need to suggest one or two suitable questions (e.g. *What is your policy on graduates from outside the UK? What level of English do you require?*).

Optional extension
1 Divide the class into groups of three. Each group will conduct interviews for the Barker Rose Graduate Recruitment Programme. If the class does not divide easily into groups of three, allow groups of different sizes, but

ensure that everyone has the chance to interview and be interviewed.
2 Tell them to prepare four or five interview questions, using the advert in Reading 3 for ideas. They may also ask tricky (or humorous) questions to test their interviewees' knowledge of law and legal English, based on the technical terms in Reading 2. Set a strict time limit for the question writing (e.g. five minutes).
3 One member of each group should change groups to be interviewed. The aim is to get the job, so students can lie as much as necessary, as long as they do it convincingly. Again set a strict time limit (e.g. two minutes).
4 The interviewed students should return to their original groups, while a second member of each group goes for an interview with another group. After three rounds of interviews, the original groups should get back together to decide which was the best candidate they interviewed, and whether to offer that candidate a place on the Graduate Recruitment Programme.

(SB p14) Writing: Short email

19 Tell students to read the task and discuss with a partner how they would structure their writing (i.e. what order to mention the points, how to organise them into paragraphs, etc.). The writing can be done at home or in class. (See section on Writing, page 8.)

(SB p14) (1.2 1.3) Listening 2: Graduate recruitment programme

20 Tell students to read the introduction and the six statements, and then elicit from the class who would attend such a presentation [**Answer**: potential candidates for the Graduate Recruitment Programme]. Then tell them to listen to the recording to decide whether the statements are true (*T*) or false (*F*). Point out that sometimes there is not enough information to decide, in which case they should write *NC* (not clear). After listening, tell them to discuss their answers with a partner, including any other information they remember from the recording. Finally, check the answers with the class.

Answers
1 F (They are approaching their mid-term exams.)
2 NC (We are told that she is a graduate, but not what she studied.)
3 F (They have yet to become partners.)
4 T
5 F (There were seven lawyers in 1979.)
6 T

21 Go through the five questions with the class and invite students to predict sensible answers. Then play the recording for them to check their predictions. After they have checked with a partner, go through the answers with the class.

Answers
1 £36,000
2 Associates receive a year-end bonus depending on the firm's overall profitability, how many hours they have worked during the year and how long they have worked for the firm.
3 A standard medical benefits package, life insurance, a retirement plan and voluntary dental insurance.
4 1,800 to 2,000
5 Seven

22 Tell students to do the exercise quickly alone, then go through the answers with the class. Point out that many words in English have several meanings, which creates dangerous traps for learners (and native speakers), who expect a word to mean one thing when in fact it means something different. You may elicit some more examples for this unit, such as *equity* (from Reading 1) and *impeachment* (from Reading 2 – see notes above). Point out also that it is important not only to know both meanings of such words, but also to be aware that other people can easily misunderstand them, and to take appropriate precautions. For example, a lawyer may introduce his/her partner (= co-owner) to a client, but the client may misunderstand the word *partner* to mean a boyfriend/girlfriend.

Answers
1 a 2 a 3 b 4 b 5 b

Language note
In British English, *practice* is a noun, while *practise* is a verb. Both are pronounced the same. In American English, both noun and verb are spelled *practice*.

SB p15 1.2 1.3 **Text analysis: Structuring a presentation**

Ask the class whether any of them have experience of giving presentations in English or in their own language. Brainstorm some situations when lawyers might have to give a presentation [**Possible answers**: reporting back to colleagues after a complicated case; passing on training of a new law or procedure; presenting your law firm to potential new clients or employees]. Elicit also some techniques for structuring presentations, such as *KISS* (see Student's Book page 15) and the motto *Tell them what you're going to say; say it; then tell them what you've said*. Then tell students to read the introduction on page 15 to compare it with their techniques.

23 Tell students to close their books. On the board, elicit an outline of a typical presentation. You may need to give the first few steps (i.e. Welcome the audience; Introduce yourself). Don't confirm or reject the students' suggestions at this stage. When you have a complete outline on the board, tell students to look at the outline in Exercise 23 to see if it covers the same points. Then tell them to work in pairs to find the lines in the audio transcript on SB pages 124–125 where the speaker covers each point. When they have finished, check the answers quickly with the class. Discuss also the question of jokes in presentations: in what situations would a joke be appropriate/inappropriate in a presentation?

Answers
1.2 1 lines 1–2   2 lines 5–7   3 lines 7–8
    4 lines 8–12   5 lines 13–20
    6 lines 21–29   7 lines 30–41
1.3 8 lines 1–7   9 lines 8–25
    10 lines 26–37   11 lines 38–44
    12 lines 45–53

24 Tell students to listen to the recording again to complete the phrases. Point out that they only need to fill in the gaps, and not to complete sentences which end with three dots (...). After the recording, tell them to check with a partner, then go through the answers with the class, paying particular attention to accuracy (including prepositions and articles), as they will later use these phrases as a model.

Answers

1 Hello, everyone, **and thanks for coming** along.
2 It's great that so many of you were **able to make it** this morning.
3 OK, let me just **start by introducing** myself.
4 I've been asked along **to talk about** the ...
5 ... (a programme) I'm sure will be of **particular interest to you** as ...
6 It's right **now that you need** to ...
7 I **remember** when I ...
8 I know from **my own experience** that ...
9 There are **three main points** I'd like to cover today.
10 First, **I'll start by** giving you a little information about Barker Rose. I'll then go on to **outline** what we have to offer to new associates. **Finally**, I'll also talk a little about what we expect from our potential graduate recruits.
11 So, to **start with**, who are Barker Rose?
12 This brings **me to my next** point: what ...
13 This leads **directly to** what ...
14 Let's now **move on to** what we ...
15 To **summarise**, Barker Rose ...
16 Finally, I'd like to **remind you** of what I said at the beginning of my talk today.

25 Discuss this question with the whole class.

Answers
The presentation is not very formal, although the general tone and subject matter remain serious throughout. The speaker uses friendly, often quite colloquial or informal language, e.g. *It's great that so many of you were able to make it this morning; OK.*

Optional extension
Tell students to work in small groups. Tell them to think of a more formal way of saying each of the phrases from Exercise 24. When they have finished, discuss the answers with the class, and write the best phrases on the board. Note that these formal alternatives are not necessarily better, and may in fact sound slightly pompous in many neutral or informal business situations. The avoidance of contractions (e.g. replacing *let's* by *let us*) is rare in spoken English, even in the most formal situations (although still normal in formal written English).

Suggested answers (changes in italics)

1 *Good morning, ladies and gentlemen*, and *thank you* for coming.
2 *I was delighted to see* so many of you *here* this morning.
3 *I would like to* start by introducing myself.
4 *I have been invited here this morning* to talk about the ...
5 ... (a programme) *which* I *am convinced* will be of particular interest to you as ...
6 *It is* right now that you need to ...
7 I *am reminded of one occasion* when I ...
8 I *am aware* from my own experience that ...
9 There are three main points *which* I *would* like to cover today.
10 First, I *shall* start by giving you a little information about Barker Rose. I *shall* then go on to outline what we have to offer to new associates. Finally, I *shall* talk a little about what we expect from our potential graduate recruits.
11 *Let me begin by asking*, who are Barker Rose?
12 This brings me to my next point ... (NB no change)
13 This leads directly to what ... (NB no change)
14 *Let us* now move on to ...
15 To summarise, ... (NB no change)
16 Finally, I *would* like to remind you of what I said at the beginning of my talk today.

Speaking 3: Presentation

26 Tell students to plan their presentations quickly, either at home or in class. They should not attempt to write out the whole presentation in full, but should improvise using their plans and the useful phrases from SB page 16.

If you have a large class, it may be impractical to ask each student to present to the whole class. If this is the case, get them to present to each other in groups of four or five. They should then choose the best presentation from their group, to be performed in front of the whole class.

Language Focus

Answers

1 Vocabulary: types of law firm

1 c **2** d **3** e **4** a **5** b

2 Vocabulary: law vs legal

1 legal **2** law **3** law; legal **4** legal; legal

3 Prepositions

a by; about **b** of; for **c** on; to **d** by
e about; from **f** for **g** about; at **h** with
i to, to

4 Ordering

1 f **2** d **3** a **4** c **5** e **6** h **7** i **8** b **9** g

2 Contract law

Teacher's brief

Contract law is a huge area, and this unit serves as an introduction to some parts of contract law. It is important to realise that a contract does not have to be a formal document. As long as certain conditions are met, an **informal exchange** of emails or **oral agreement** may be interpreted as a **legally binding** contract. A contract may exist even if no words are spoken (if, for example, I park my car in a private car park, by my actions I agree to pay the car park owner's advertised fees).

An important question is therefore what exactly constitutes an **enforceable** contract (i.e. one which the courts will force the parties to carry out). In common-law jurisdictions like England or the USA, the **essential elements** of a contract are an **offer**, **acceptance** of that offer by the other party, and some sort of **consideration**. *Consideration* means something of value: both parties must give the other consideration (e.g. party A gives a car (= consideration) in exchange for party B's money (= consideration); party C pays a salary (= consideration) in exchange for party D's work (= consideration)). In some other jurisdictions (e.g. most civil-law jurisdictions), consideration may not be necessary in order for a contract to be enforceable (so a one-way promise may, in some situations, constitute a contract).

The first part of this unit introduces many of the theoretical principles behind contract law, including **remedies for breach of contract**. Remedies very often take the form of **damages** (monetary compensation), and can be claimed by a **non-breaching party** to a contract from a **breaching party** (i.e. the party who has failed to fulfil its obligations under the contract). Remedies may serve as **restitution** (i.e. the non-breaching party may recover what it has given), **compensation** (i.e. damages to make up for a loss) or **specific performance** (i.e. the breaching party must perform the action promised in the contract).

The second part of the unit uses a case study of a **contract dispute**. When one of the parties fails to perform its obligations, the issue arises as to whether the non-breaching party may safely **terminate the contract** (without risking being **sued** by the breaching party). This problem centres on the distinction between two types of clause in a contract: **conditions** and **warranties**. A condition is an **essential term**. If one party fails to act in accordance with one of these conditions, the other party may terminate the contract. A warranty, on the other hand, is **non-essential**. If one is broken, the non-breaching party may claim damages, but may not terminate the contract. In this case, the clause in question is interpreted as a condition, because the non-breaching party **relied on** the clause (i.e. he was unable to carry out his obligations as a direct result of the breaching party's failure).

The case study provides practice of some key skills for lawyers: reading and **understanding complex contract clauses** and writing an **email of advice** to a client.

Further reading
○ A good guide to the **basics of contract law** can be found at http://www.lawteacher.net/contract.htm.
○ There is an excellent bank of **authentic contracts** at http://www.onecle.com/. Browsing through these provides an excellent opportunity to learn how to read and write contracts.

THE STUDY OF LAW

SB p18 ## Lead-in

1 Elicit from the class the meaning of the word *contract* [**Answer**: a promise which creates legal rights] and how frequently the students enter into contractual relationships in their private lives. If they see contracts as formal documents to be signed, the answer is likely to be 'not very often', with examples including employment contracts and property rental agreements. If, on the other hand, they see contracts in the broader sense as described in this unit, the answer will be 'all the time', including every time they pay for something or take an action that will have to be paid for. The 'contracts' themselves do not need to be written (and signed) but can be oral or even unspoken.

Tell students to work alone to list some contracts (in this broader sense) that they have entered into in the past 48 hours. Make sure they understand the difference between goods and services by eliciting an example of each.

After a few minutes, tell them to compare their lists in small groups to see if there is any disagreement as to (a) what constitutes a contract, and (b) whether there is any important difference between contracts for goods and for services.

Finally, ask each group to report back on any interesting or borderline cases, which you can then discuss with the whole class. You may give some more examples to help students come up with their own, e.g. sending an SMS (= agreeing to pay the stated amount), logging on to a university's computer network (= agreeing to the university's terms and conditions of use). Encourage the class to come up with some tests which could be used to decide on borderline cases (NB this will be covered in Reading 1 and Listening 2). You could also discuss with the class what disputes could arise with these borderline contracts, how the law might resolve such disputes, and what could be used as proof/evidence that a contract existed and was broken.

Language notes
- The distinction between *goods* and *services* is often useful, but sometimes it is better to think of a continuum between pure goods and pure services. Most contracts involve a portion of both. For example, when you pay for a meal in a restaurant, you are not just paying for the food, but for an experience. When you go to the hairdresser, the cost of the service should include the goods (shampoo, hairspray, etc.) that are used during your visit. Subscribing to a magazine to be delivered (a good) is not radically different from subscribing to an online magazine (a service).
- There are obvious differences of detail between contracts for goods and those for services. In the UK, sales of goods are covered by many laws, including the Sale of Goods Act (1979), which serves as a standard set of terms for exchanges of goods where no explicit contract has been negotiated (e.g. buying something in a shop). See http://en.wikipedia.org/wiki/Sale_of_goods. Services are also covered by many laws, including the Supply of Goods and Services Act, which requires services to be carried out with reasonable care and skill, for a reasonable price, and in reasonable time. See http://www.tradingstandards.gov.uk/cgi-bin/bglitem.cgi?file=badv073-1011.txt for a very clear summary of goods and services contracts in the UK.

(SB p18) Reading 1: Contract law

2 Tell students to read the first paragraph of the text, then elicit from the class what is necessary for a contract to be formed. Then discuss the answer with the class, focusing especially on any differences between the requirements for contract formation as stated in the text and those in the students' own jurisdictions.

Also discuss the concept of one-sided promises, and why, in the students' opinions, they should / should not be legally enforceable.

Answer
An offer must be made and it must be accepted. In some legal systems, the parties must give (or promise to give) each other something of value.

Language notes
- *Consideration* will be discussed more fully in Listening 2.
- Paragraph 1 refers to *most legal systems* requiring only an offer and acceptance. Broadly speaking, this means civil-law jurisdictions, as common-law countries (such as the UK or the USA) have a third requirement: consideration (see above). In civil-law countries such as Mexico (see http://www.mexicolaw.com/LawInof03.htm), there must be an object of the contract (or a cause of the contract), i.e. the thing promised to be given or the act promised to be (not) performed. This is not exactly the same as common-law consideration, which requires that both parties give something of value. Japanese contracts, in contrast, do not even require explicit statements of an offer, acceptance and consideration (see http://www.answers.com/topic/japanese-law).
- Some extreme examples of *one-sided promises* may illustrate the dilemma as to whether they should or should not be legally enforceable. Firstly, a father promises to buy his daughter a rabbit for Christmas, but buys something else instead. It is hard to imagine how such a promise could/should be enforceable. Secondly, party A offers to deliver some goods to party B on behalf of a business acquaintance, C, as a goodwill gesture

(A is going to B's factory anyway and has space in his van), but then forgets, causing a dispute between B and C. In this case, A's one-sided promise has important consequences for the party that was given the promise (C), and therefore it is possible to see why, in some jurisdictions at least, this should be seen as an enforceable contract. This relates to the concept of *reliance*, which will come up in Listening 3.

3 Elicit from the students what is meant by *breach of contract*, including some examples if necessary (e.g. various ways that either party could break (= *breach*), say, a contract of employment). Elicit also that the term *remedies* refers to the range of ways of dealing with a breach of contract in order to achieve justice. Then tell students to read the rest of the text quickly to answer the question. Allow a limited time (one to two minutes) for students to read and check with a partner before going through the answers with the group. Discuss whether there are any further options available in the students' own jurisdictions.

Answers

The two remedies mentioned are damages and specific performance.

Background notes

Other possible remedies are:

Compensatory damages: money to compensate you for loss.

Consequential and incidental damages: money for losses caused by the breach that were foreseeable.

Liquidated damages: damages specified in the contract that would be payable if there is a breach.

Specific performance: a court order requiring performance exactly as specified in the contract.

Rescission: The contract is cancelled, and both sides are excused from further performance and any money advanced is returned.

Reformation: The terms of the contract are changed to reflect what the parties originally intended.

Language notes

○ The *essential terms of a contract* are the items which must be included in the agreement. These obviously include a description of what the two parties have agreed to exchange, typically a product or service (= *the subject matter of the contract*) in exchange for money (= *the price*). Other essential terms include the date of delivery and the country whose laws govern the contract. See http://www.businesslink.gov.uk/bdotg/ action/detail?type=RESOURCES&itemId =1075386902.

○ The text mentions certain types of contract which must be in writing to be valid. In common-law jurisdictions, these are governed by a *Statute of Frauds*, and include sale of property (land, buildings, etc.), high-value transactions and marriage (see http://en.wikipedia. org/wiki/Statute_of_frauds).

○ There is no important difference in meaning between *breach* and *break*. The only difference is in terms of collocations: you break a promise (i.e. in a non-legal sense), but you breach a contract, an agreement or someone's trust (in a formal or legal sense).

○ A *lawsuit* /ˈlɔːsuːt/ (or simply *suit*) is a legal action taken by one party against another, to be decided in court. The term *trial* covers only that part of a lawsuit which takes place in court.

○ *Assignment* typically takes place when one party sells a business, or part of a business, and the buyer takes on the contractual rights and responsibilities of the seller.

Pronunciation notes

assignee /əsaɪˈniː/
assignor /əˈsaɪnə(r)/
damages /ˈdæmədʒɪz/

4 Tell students to work alone to decide whether the statements are true or false. Allow them a few minutes to re-read the whole text, and to compare their answers with a partner, before going through the answers with the class.

Answers

1 F (In *most* legal systems, parties must give … – see Language note above.)
2 F (An offer must be accepted before a contract is agreed.)
3 T
4 F (A court *may* force the party to perform the contract.)
5 T

5 Tell students to work alone or in pairs to insert words in the spaces. Check the answers with the class.

Answers

1 formation   2 counteroffer   3 terms
4 oral contract   5 obligations   6 breach
7 damages

Optional extension
Tell students to work in small groups. They should take turns to read aloud a sentence from Exercise 5, substituting the word *blank* for each gap. Their partners have to try to remember the missing word.

6 Tell students to work alone to underline examples of the words *offer, contract, damages* and *lawsuit* in Reading 1, and then to identify which verb, if any, is used together with each underlined verb. Point out that not all the verbs in the box occur in the text, but some of the verbs occur several times. When students have had a few minutes to work alone, tell them to compare their answers with a partner. Then go through the answers with the class.

Answers

1 accept an offer, make an offer, reject an offer
2 breach a contract, form a contract, negotiate a contract, perform a contract
3 award damages, accept damages
4 file a lawsuit

7 Elicit more possible collocations with each of the four nouns using the verbs in the box. You may also elicit some other collocations for the four nouns (e.g. *draw up/draft/sign a contract*; *claim/win/receive/seek/pay damages*; *bring/launch/pursue/win/lose a lawsuit*; *withdraw/increase/submit/receive/consider an offer*).

Answers

enforce a contract, negotiate an offer

Optional alternative to Exercises 6 and 7
Draw the following grid on the board (without the ticks (✓) and question marks (?)). Divide the class into teams and assign each team a colour. The teams should take turns to give a possible collocation. If they give a good collocation, mark a tick in the appropriate square in the table in that team's colour. If they give a bad collocation, mark a cross in the team's colour. Keep going until the teams have found most of the good collocations. The winning team is the one with the most ticks minus crosses. Note that the grid can easily be expanded (more rows and columns) or shrunk, depending on the level of challenge you want. NB Strong collocations are marked ✓; other possible collocations are marked **?**. Do not write question marks on the grid on the board, but negotiate with the class whether they should be ticks or crosses. There may be other possible collocations: if a team can offer a logical and convincing argument for a claimed collocation, you may decide to give them the benefit of the doubt.

	a contract	damages	a lawsuit	an offer	rights
accept		?		✓	?
assign	✓				✓
award		✓			
breach	✓				
create	✓			?	✓
enforce	✓				?
file			✓		
form	✓				
make	✓			✓	
negotiate	?	?		✓	?
perform	✓				
reject				✓	
transfer	✓				✓
withdraw			?	✓	?

8 Tell students to work in pairs to discuss the question for each of the collocations. This activity can easily be extended to include any other collocations discussed during the lesson. As you go through the answers, pay attention to any that caused disagreement.

1 a party makes an offer
   a party accepts an offer
   a party rejects an offer
   a party breaches a contract
   a party performs a contract
2 the parties negotiate an offer
   the parties negotiate a contract
   the parties form a contract
3 the court enforces a contract
   the court awards damages
4 a lawyer files a lawsuit
   a lawyer negotiates an offer
   a lawyer negotiates a contract

SB p.20 Reading 2: Remedies for breach of contract

9 Tell students to read the text quickly to find the answer to the question. After about half a minute, tell them to close their books and tell their partners what they remember from the text, including the three types of remedy.

⟿ **Answer**
The term *remedy* refers to the means to achieve justice in any matter in which legal rights are involved.

✎ **Language notes**
○ *Restitution* literally means 'returning something to its original state'.
○ The text states that *restitution and specific performance are available only in certain circumstances*. In other words, only when a court decides that payment of damages based on a party's loss would not be sufficient to restore justice. See http://en.wikipedia.org/wiki/Restitution and http://en.wikipedia.org/wiki/Specific_performance for examples of such situations.

10 Discuss this question with the class. You may need to clarify that most English-speaking countries have a common-law system (exceptions include Scotland, Malta, South Africa and the US State of Louisiana). If your students don't know what the most common remedies in their jurisdictions are, discuss how they could find out (e.g. an Internet search using the words for *remedies* and *contract law* in their language(s)).

SB p.20 · 2.1 2.2 Listening 1: Asking for clarification and giving explanations

11 Play the recording and elicit from the class what has confused the first student about the excerpt.

⟿ **Answer**
The student is confused about the meaning of the word *damages*, which refers to money paid in compensation for a loss. He confuses it with the word *damage*.

Transcript » STUDENT'S BOOK page 125

12 Tell students to listen again and to tick the expressions they hear.

⟿ **Answers**
3, 5, 6

When you check the answers with the class, discuss the six expressions by asking these questions:

○ Why is this language important for language learners? [**Possible answer**: to check understanding of difficult words and concepts with their teacher or classmates.]

○ Why is this language important for lawyers? [**Possible answer**: Although lawyers like to be seen to understand everything, it is even more important that they check any information they are unsure of. It is better to admit to language weaknesses than to compromise their knowledge of a case in order to avoid asking for help. The language is also useful for checking difficult or confusing concepts.]

○ Which would you already feel comfortable using?

○ Which would you like to use in future?

13 Tell students to work in pairs to discuss the difference between *damage* and *damages*. Tell them to use the expressions for asking for clarification in order to force their partners to give clear and full explanations.

14 Tell students to listen to the second part of the dialogue to compare it with their explanations.

Transcript » STUDENT'S BOOK page 125

15 Play the recording a second time for the students to tick the expressions they hear. After listening, discuss the answers with the class. You could also ask the same additional questions as for Exercise 12 above.

> **Answers**
> 1, 5, 6

16 Discuss the two questions with the whole class. The most formal expression is *Allow me to clarify*, which would normally be used in formal writing or perhaps when presenting a case in court.

(SB p.21) Speaking 1: Terminology

17 Tell the class to look at the audio transcript from part 2 of Listening 1 (SB page 125) to find more techniques for giving an explanation [**Suggested answers**: *... is quite similar*; *... when you* damage your car; *if you* drive into something; *... is the word for ...*]. Elicit some more phrases for giving explanations (e.g. *This is the person who ...*; *This is what you do when ...*; *This is when ... happens*; *When ... happens, it's called ...*) and write these on the board. Then tell students to take turns to explain one of the words to their partner, without mentioning the word. They should use the expressions for giving an explanation, including those on the board, while their partner should use the expressions for asking for clarification in order to work out which word is being defined. After a few minutes, elicit from the whole class good explanations for each of the terms in the exercise, paying particular attention to the phrasing of the explanations. NB All the words are explained in Readings 1 and 2 and in the Glossary on SB pages 155–160.

(SB p.21) (2.3 2.4) Listening 2: Contract law lecture

18 Tell students that they are going to listen to the beginning of a university lecture. Ask them to look at the list of terms in Exercise 19, then to predict what the topic of the lecture might be. Play the recording and elicit the answer to the question.

> **Answer**
> The general subject of the lecture is contract formation.

Transcript » STUDENT'S BOOK page 125

19 Ask students to read the list of seven terms (if they did not already do so in Exercise 18) and check that they remember each one by eliciting an explanation. Then play the recording for them to tick the terms the speaker mentions. After listening, tell them to compare their answers briefly with a partner, and then check with the whole class. Finish by eliciting the answer to question 2.

> **Answers**
> **1** The speaker mentions the terms *agreement, consideration, negotiation, offer* and *acceptance*.
> **2** The lecturer will talk about consideration in more detail next time.

> **Language notes**
> ○ According to the lecture, *[the intention to create legal relations is] understood to exist automatically in the vast majority of cases*. The requirement is intended to distinguish between business agreements on one hand and agreements between friends and family on the other. In the latter case (say, when a grandparent offers to pay for a family holiday), the intention to create legal rights does not go without saying. See http://www.lawteacher.net/Contract/Agreement/Intention%20Lecture.htm.
> ○ A *settled deal* is an agreement reached at the end of a negotiation or which ends a dispute.
> ○ A *tender* is a process whereby several competing parties make *bids* (offers) to supply a good or perform a service. Typically, the lowest bid will be successful, although obviously other factors (reputation, reliability, quality, punctuality, etc.) will play a part. An auction is similar, although in this case, potential buyers compete, so the highest offer typically wins. Auctions and tenders are different from other transactions in that there are three

steps: an *invitation* (e.g. an advertisement for a tender process or the submission of an item to an auction house), *offers* (bids) and *acceptance* (e.g. when the auctioneer's hammer falls). The invitation is not in itself an offer. See the section on auctions and tenders in http://www.fortunecity.com/victorian/delacroix/81/conform.htm.

○ For a good background to the questions raised in the lecture concerning *advertisements*, *price lists*, etc., see http://www.lawteacher.net/Contract/Agreement/Agreement%20Cases.htm.

○ If a contract is not *binding*, the parties are not obliged to act in accordance with it.

20 Tell students to work alone or in pairs to remember / work out which words should fill each gap in the lecture notes. Then play the recording again for them to check and complete their answers. After listening, go through the answers with the class.

Answers

1 agreement   2 consideration   3 legal
4 negotiations   5 accepted   6 price
7 communicated   8 silence   9 price
10 binding   11 consideration

Optional extension

Tell students to look at the audio transcript on page 125 to identify unanswered questions and other controversial issues (see below). Tell them to discuss these issues and questions in small groups, and then open up the discussion to include the whole class. Remind them of the lists of goods and services they made at the beginning of the unit, which may generate some less obvious situations for these issues. The answers are likely to vary from jurisdiction to jurisdiction, and may be a source of debate and controversy within jurisdictions, so in this discussion it is more important to give logical and convincing arguments one way or the other than to know the actual situation in a particular jurisdiction. Of course, you could also set your students the challenge of finding the 'answers' (if they exist) for their own jurisdictions. NB See Language notes above for more information on these questions.

---

1 According to the lecture, the intention to create legal relations is understood to exist automatically in the vast majority of cases. When might this intention not exist automatically? [In an agreement between friends and family.]

2 Why might it be important to determine the time that the negotiation has ended? [To set a timeframe for other events (e.g. payment must be X number of days after agreement; or party A agrees to stop negotiating with party C as soon as it has reached an agreement with party B).]

3 Could there be an important difference between the moment of acceptance and the moment of communication of acceptance? [It could be important if something changes (e.g. a law, an exchange rate, a price, the quality of the goods) between the moment of acceptance and the moment of communication.]

4 Why is the issue of who makes an offer especially relevant in the context of tenders and auctions? [It is not obvious whether the advertising of a tender or putting one's possessions up for auction constitutes an offer, or whether the offer is made by the bidders. In fact, in the UK, it is the bidder who makes the offer; putting one's possessions up for auction is merely an *invitation to treat*.]

5 Is a price list an offer? [No, because it does not specify a maximum quantity. A supplier cannot sell an infinite quantity of goods, so is not contractually obliged to do so. This is why some price lists and advertisements specify 'while stocks last'.]

6 Is an advertisement an offer? [It depends how much specific information it contains.]

7 Does acceptance have to be communicated? [It depends what is meant by 'communicated'. It doesn't have to be communicated in speech or writing, but can be communicated by actions (e.g. parking a car in a car park) or non-actions (e.g. not returning goods supplied). But if there is no communication whatsoever, by definition the offeror is unaware of the acceptance, so there can be no contract.]

8 Can you accept by silence? [Yes. This typically happens in shops, but is common elsewhere, too. The issue is whether more important contracts (e.g. to buy expensive products or services) can be agreed in this way.

9 Can you accept just by getting on with the commercial task? [Yes, although again this will depend on how important the transaction is.]

10 What sort of rules might be used to determine what can be considered 'good consideration'? [See http://www.lawteacher.net/Contract/Agreement/Consideration%20Lecture.htm.]

^{SB p.22} Speaking 2: Summarising the lecture

21 Tell students to work in pairs or small groups to complete the speaking exercise. Remind them that they should use the expressions for asking for clarification and giving an explanation from Exercises 12 and 15.

LAW IN PRACTICE

^{SB p.22} Lead-in

Discuss the question with the whole class. Try to go deeper than simply ways that a contract can be broken (e.g. a supplier delivers a product late, or damaged, or different from that ordered); also discuss the reasons behind such contract disputes, such as deliberate malevolence, accidents, unforeseen events, forgetfulness, lack of planning, etc.

Possible answers

Typical contract disputes include:
○ Business owners involved in lease disputes
○ A shareholder wishing to end his/her participation in a partnership or limited liability company (LLC)
○ Late delivery of goods, especially where the contract involves a chain of sales
○ Late payment for goods or services
○ Customer not satisfied with the quality of goods or services provided
○ Disputes over the details of an employment contract

^{SB p.22} Reading 3: Contract clause

22 Tell students to read the clause carefully to answer the five questions, and to discuss their answers with a partner. Go through the answers with the class, dealing with any language problems that arise. Check the meaning of the word *shall*, and the phrases *two weeks' notice* and *upon notification*.

Answers

1 vessel
2 The clause deals with the amount of notice needed to be given for the delivery of goods by ship.
3 *buyer* and *seller*
4 *Probable readiness* refers to the first date on which it is most likely that the buyer will make a ship available to the seller for the purposes of loading and transporting the goods that are the subject of the contract.
5 *Shall* means the same as *must*.

Language notes
○ *Shall* is usually equivalent to *must* in the language of contracts.
○ *Two weeks' notice* means advance warning about what is going to happen, given two weeks before it is due to happen.
○ *Upon notification* means *as soon as the seller has received notification*.

23 Tell students to work alone to find the four obligations, and to discuss with a partner how to paraphrase them, as if they were explaining them to a client. Check the answers with the class.

Answers
1 Decide on the date that the goods will be shipped (= transported by ship). Clause 2a reads: *The buyer shall nominate the date of shipment.*
2 Notify (= tell) the seller of this date at least two weeks in advance. Clause 2a reads: *The buyer shall give the seller at least two weeks' notice of probable readiness of vessel(s).*
3 Notify the seller of the approximate quantity of goods to be loaded (= similar

amount but not necessarily the exact final amount). Clause 2a reads: ... *and of the approximate quantity to be loaded.*

4 Arrange a port at which the goods can be loaded onto a ship. Clause 2b reads: *Upon notification of probable readiness of vessel(s), the seller shall nominate a port for the loading of goods.*

Language note
The point of these questions is to highlight a key difference between the language of contracts and everyday English. Everyday English tends to have lots of short sentences, with at least one verb in each sentence, as well as more complicated sentences with indirect questions and relative clauses, again with at least one verb in each. In other words, everyday English has lots of verbs, as well as adverbs to go with those verbs. The language of contracts, on the other hand, puts much more information into long noun phrases, typically turning verbs (e.g. *to load*), adjectives (e.g. *ready*) and question words (*how much*) into nouns (e.g. [*the*] *loading* [*of*], *readiness*, *quantity*). These nouns are often accompanied by adjectives (so *probably ready* becomes *probable readiness*). This is the reason that prepositions like *upon*, which are followed by noun phrases, are preferred in contracts to conjunctions like *as soon as*, which are followed by clauses.

24 Tell students to come up with ideas for the two questions, and then open up the discussion to include the whole class. [**Possible answers**: The most important things that could go wrong relate to the four obligations listed in Exercise 22: the parties could fail to fulfil one or more of these obligations. The consequences include the injured party suing the breaching party, or threatening such legal action. NB The consequences of such breaches are discussed in Listening 3 below.]

Optional extension
(Photocopiable worksheet 2.1)
This offers a fairly simple analysis of the contract extract from Exercise 22. Although it may be unreasonable to expect students

at this level to be able to draft contract clauses in English, there is no harm in introducing them to some useful language and techniques, so that when they are ready to draft contracts in English, they will already have some experience of it. The exercise also provides a contrast between the language of contracts and everyday English. It is important that lawyers master both forms of English, as they need to communicate complicated ideas to clients in everyday English.

1 Tell students to close their books and to work in small groups to reconstruct the sentences from the contract using four sets of clues:
   – the explanations in everyday English
   – the number of words in each sentence
   – the selected words already in their correct positions
   – the box of sets of words to use (in alphabetical order).
   There is even a fifth clue: the first words in each sentence still have their capital letters, and the last words have their full stops.

2 Suggest that they start with the shorter sentences (1 and 4), as these will be easiest, and will allow them to cross out some words from the box.

3 The first team to complete all four sentences is the winner.

4 When they have finished, go through the three analysis questions together with the group. You may need to explain or elicit grammatical words like 'noun' and 'adverb' using examples.

5 Note that question 5b refers to *indirect questions*, but a fuller (but rather complicated) description would be *indirect questions* (e.g. when the goods will be shipped, how much is going to be loaded) and *relative clauses* (e.g. [the port] where the goods will be loaded).

Answers
1–4 See the original extract on page 22 of the SB.

5 a everyday English **b** everyday English
   c contract extract **d** everyday English

6 A clause

7 A noun; because the language of contracts puts most of its information into nouns.

Listening 3: Conditions and warranties

25 Tell students to read the introduction and the five questions, and then to listen to the recording to answer them. Allow them to check with a partner before discussing the answers with the class. Discuss also what the client is going to do next. [**Answer**: He is going to speak to his partners, and if they agree, make it clear to Drexler that they are going to terminate the contract.]

Answers
1 Drexler.
2 Because Drexler breached one of the terms (clause 2a). As a consequence, Export Threads were unable to arrange for a port for the loading of goods.
3 No.
4 Yes.
5 If the term breached by Drexler was a condition, Export Threads could end the contract.

Transcript » STUDENT'S BOOK page 125

Language notes
○ If you *sue* /suː/ somebody, you take legal action against them.
○ A *warranty* /ˈwɒrəntɪ/ is a statement that goods are of good quality, that the seller has the right to sell them, etc. A *guarantee* /ɡærənˈtiː/ is similar, but it is a written promise, for example to replace or repair faulty goods. A warranty is therefore a promise about the present, while a guarantee is about the future.
○ If you *incur* /ɪŋˈkɜː(r)/ losses, you lose money as a result of something. It is the opposite of making a profit.
○ A *chain of sales* is the situation when several transactions are related to each other, and cannot proceed until earlier transactions in the chain have been completed. For example, if party A wants to buy a machine from party B and then sell that on to party C, the second transaction obviously has to wait until the first is completed.

26 Do this with the whole class. You may need to identify one example of each type of phrase as an example.

Answers
I don't understand: *I don't see how ...; I'm sorry, I don't follow you. What exactly are you saying?*
Giving an explanation: *It's like this ...; in other words, ...; I'll try to be a little clearer.*

Optional extension
Tell students to work in small groups. They should take turns to pretend to be lawyers explaining terms to a client. They should explain to their partners the terms *condition*, *warranty* and *reliance*, using the phrases they underlined in the audio transcript. Meanwhile, their partners should be clients, and should use the phrases meaning *I don't understand*.

27 Tell students to read the three definitions to try to match them with their sources. Discuss the answer with the class, including how they worked out the answer. Discuss questions b) and c) (including the advantages and disadvantages of the three dictionaries), and whether the students can recommend any other useful dictionaries.

Answers
a 1 c   2 b   3 a
c Where one party has, based on reasonable reliance upon the promises of another party, *changed its position*, then it may be argued that there is an enforceable contract. In cases involving a chain of sales, several parties must rely on the performance by a third party / third parties of a collateral contract before they can perform their own contracts. The consequences of certain breaches may be so severe as to relieve the non-breaching party / parties of their contractual duties (i.e. the breached term may be found to be a condition, rather than simply a warranty).

Background note
Each dictionary is useful in its own way:
○ The Cambridge dictionary (http://dictionary.cambridge.org) is produced by

professional lexicographers, and includes accurate grammatical information, pronunciation guidance and authentic examples of the word in context. It is especially important to notice from the example sentences that *reliance* collocates strongly with *on*. The language of the explanations is carefully designed to be understandable by language learners. However, as it is designed for all advanced learners of English and not just learners of legal English, its usefulness for very uncommon technical language is rather limited. As the definition for *reliance* shows, however, its definitions of technical language can be a good starting point when researching a word.

○ The dictionary at law.com (http:// dictionary.law.com) is an excellent resource for a wide range of legal terms. It has the advantage of being written by and for lawyers, so its definitions are reliable. It does have many disadvantages, too: it is written for native-speaker lawyers, so its definitions can be tough for non-natives and non-lawyers to understand. It is also not as comprehensive as some online dictionaries, in that it doesn't cover all legal terminology. It is also dominatcd by thc law of English-speaking countries, particularly the USA. It contains no pronunciation or example sentences.

○ The Wiktionary (http://en.wiktionary.org/ wiki) is another useful first step or last resort. It is growing continuously, so its coverage is very impressive and getting better all the time. However, it is not written (exclusively) by professionals (lawyers or lexicographers), so there is a danger that its definitions may be unreliable. However, there are systems in place to report and correct mistakes, so in theory it should also become increasingly reliable over time. It also has a translations section, which could be useful in future (at the time of writing, *reliance* is translated only into Finnish).

SB p.24 # Language use: *can / could / may / might*

Write the following gapped sentences on the board:

They _____ sue you.
I really don't see how they _____ sue us.
They _____n't take any action against us.

Point out that the three sentences all come from Listening 3. Elicit from the class which of the following words could fit logically into each gap: *can, could, may, might*. Write students' suggestions onto the board, but avoid confirming or rejecting them at this stage. Then tell them to check their answers with the information on SB page 24. Elicit from the class why some words are impossible for certain gaps.

Language note

Modal verbs each have several meanings.

○ *Can* and *could* are used to talk about ability (*I couldn't swim when I was young, but now I can*).

○ *May* (or occasionally *might*) is used for permission ('*May I smoke?*' '*No, you may not*'). *Can* is also frequently used for permission (*Can I smoke?*), but this usage is often considered incorrect.

○ *May, might* and *could* are used to talk about medium likelihood (*She may/ might/could be at home*). The likelihood can be increased with the use of *well*: (*She may/might/could well be at home*).

○ For medium negative likelihood, *may not* and *might not* are less ambiguous than *could not*. For zero likelihood, *can't* is used (*She can't be at home*).

The explanation in the SB uses the word *possible* for both ability and likelihood. In general, structures with *possible to* + verb refer to ability, while *possible that* + clause refers to likelihood.

---

28 Tell students to complete the exercise alone and then to compare their answers with a partner. You may need to check they understand some of the phrases in the questions (see Language notes below). Point out that there are sometimes several possibilities. As you go through the answers with the class, elicit whether the sentences are about ability or likelihood.

2 If we offer a generous out-of-court settlement, they might not sue us.

3 They might sue you if you breach the contract.

4 If you can assure us that such a breach will not happen again, then we might not take any further action.

5 I think we can/could work together again in the future.

6 If you raised your prices, we couldn't work together.

✐ **Language notes**

○ An *out-of-court settlement* is a negotiated agreement to resolve a conflict without going to court. Going to court is a costly option for both sides (in terms of time, money and preparation), so both sides are often better off if they can settle out of court.

○ If you are *bound by a contract*, you have legal responsibilities which you must fulfil if you are to avoid legal action.

○ The phrase *to take further action* is often used as a euphemism as part of a threat to take the other party to court. The implied threat in sentence 4 is: *If you **can't** assure us that a breach won't happen again, we may take you to court.*

Optional extension

1 Elicit what the options are for Export Threads (e.g. terminate the contract immediately; threaten to terminate the contract if Drexler doesn't offer compensation; give Drexler another chance, to avoid damaging the business relationship; etc.) and what the lawyer advised (i.e. that it would be fairly safe from a legal perspective to terminate the contract).

2 Tell the class to work in groups of three or four to role-play the meeting between the client, Mr McKendrick, and his partners at Export Threads to discuss what to do next.

3 Tell students that they should try to use the language from this unit as much as possible (i.e. phrases for asking for clarification and giving an explanation; *can/ could/may/might*; etc.).

4 Encourage the partners to discuss the issue from both a legal and business point of view, and to invent any necessary details.

SB p.25 **Text analysis: Email of advice**

29 Tell students to read the email carefully to find the four errors. Point out that the errors are not language mistakes but relate to differences compared to the contract clause on page 22 and the dialogue in Listening 3. When some students have finished, tell them to compare their answers with a partner, and then discuss with the whole class what the correct version should be. Pay attention to the contrast between *rule against you* and *rule in your favour*.

⟼ **Answers**

1 In paragraph 2, *two days' notice* should read *two weeks' notice.*

2 In paragraph 2, *a lorry for the transportation of goods* should read *a port for the loading of goods.*

3 In paragraph 4, *the courts would rule against you* should read *the courts would rule in your favour / for you.*

4 In paragraph 5, *renegotiate* should read *terminate.*

✐ **Language note**

○ If you are *liable* /ˈlaɪəbl/ *for damages*, you have to pay compensation.

30 Do this quickly with the whole class. Point out that such a structure would often be suitable for students' own emails of advice, as would be many of the structures and phrases it includes.

⟼ **Answers**
1 a **2** d **3** e **4** c **5** b

31 Point out that successful writers use many fixed expressions in their writing, and that it is important to highlight such expressions when reading good models of writing. Elicit one or two examples from the class, and then tell students to work alone to find more expressions. Allow them to compare their ideas with a partner before discussing the answers with the class.

⟫ **Suggested answers**

(Universal phrases <u>underlined</u>, other useful collocations and structures boxed)

<u>Thank you for coming to see me on 30 May when we discussed</u> the termination of your contract with Drexler Inc. <u>I am writing to summarise our discussion and to confirm your instructions.</u>

<u>You told me that</u> Drexler Inc. agreed to purchase a large quantity of goods (exact amount unspecified) from your firm, Export Threads. Under the clause 2a of the contract , Drexler were to give you two days' notice of the date of shipment so that you could arrange a lorry for the transportation of the goods. <u>You were unable to</u> arrange this because Drexler failed to let you know by the agreed date . <u>You now wish to</u> terminate the contract.

<u>The legal issue here is whether or not</u> Drexler's breach is enough to allow Export Threads to terminate the contract without being liable for damages . If the contract term in question can be shown to be a *condition,* <u>you will be able to</u> terminate the contract without fear of damages being awarded against you . If the term is simply a *warranty,* <u>you will be able to</u> claim damages to cover any costs you have incurred as a result of this breach , <u>but may not actually</u> terminate the contract.

<u>Recent case law suggests that</u> if you do choose to terminate the contract, and if Drexler subsequently decide to sue you, the courts would rule against you . Your contract involves a chain of sales, and <u>in such cases,</u> the need for certainty is very important. You were unable to arrange the loading of the goods as a direct consequence of Drexler's breach of clause 2a, and this term would be interpreted as a condition.

<u>I will write a letter to</u> Drexler Inc. <u>outlining the above and notifying them of your intention to</u> renegotiate the contract. <u>I will request</u> confirmation from Drexler that they accept our interpretation both of the events and of the relevant law, and that your termination of the contract will not lead to any unnecessary legal action on their part .

<u>I will be in touch again shortly. Please do not hesitate to contact me if you have any questions.</u>

With kind regards

Writing: Email of advice
SB p.26

32 Tell students to read the notes carefully to make sure they understand the case. Check they have understood the task and the notes by asking the following questions:

○ Why did your client buy the satellite system? [To record foreign-language TV programmes.]

○ Why was it cheaper than usual? [Probably because it was faulty, but this was not made clear at the time of purchase.]

○ What was wrong with the system? [The timer function was broken.]

○ What has Mr Burnett offered to do? [Repair the system for £130.]

○ What was Mr Burnett obliged to do at the time of sale? [Explain that the reduction was due to imperfection.]

○ What are your client's options? [A full refund or a replacement system.]

○ How good are her chances of winning in the small claims court? [Excellent.]

○ Who are you going to write to? [Your client, Ms Staines.]

○ How many paragraphs are you going to write? [Five, following the template from Exercise 30.]

○ What useful language are you going to use? [Lots of phrases from the email in Exercise 29.]

The writing can be done at home or in class. (See section on Writing, page 8.)

> **Language note**
> A small claims court is a court which hears small private disputes between individuals. See http://en.wikipedia.org/wiki/Small_claims_court.

➡ **Suggested answer**

To: Joanna Staines
Subject: Burnett TV Supplies

Dear Ms Staines

Thank you for coming to see me this morning to discuss your problems with Burnett TV Supplies. I am writing to summarise our discussion and to confirm your instructions.

You told me that Berlingua recently bought a new satellite system (including built-in hard drive) for educational use at 50% of the normal price from Burnett TV Supplies. This was to be used to record foreign-language TV programmes for use during lessons. When you first set the system up and tried to record, you realised that the timer function was broken. When you contacted Mr Burnett to ask for a replacement, you were told that you couldn't expect it to work perfectly at such a cheap price. They refused to replace the system, but did offer to repair it at a cost of £130.

The law is very clear on problems such as yours. If a reduction is offered due to a defect in the product, this defect must be pointed out at the time of purchase. As Mr Burnett did not do this, you may claim either a full refund (at the price you paid) or a replacement system.

Please could you confirm which of the two options you would prefer? I will then write to Mr Burnett on your behalf. I am quite sure that he will see sense; he would have little or no chance in a small claims court.

I look forward to hearing from you.

Kind regards

Susan Carter

SB p.27 # Language Focus

Answers

1 Word formation

Verb	Abstract noun	Personal noun	Adjective
assign	assignment	assignor/ assignee	assigning
breach	breach		(non-)breaching
negotiate	negotiation	negotiator	negotiating
offer	offer	offeror/ offeree	
rely	reliance		reliable

> **Language note**
> The *assignor* /əˈsaɪnə(r)/ is the party that assigns a contract to an *assignee* /əsaɪˈniː/. The *offeror* /ˈɒfərə(r)/ is the party that makes an offer to the *offeree* /ɒfəˈriː/.

2 Prepositions
2 to; under   **3** against   **4** in   **5** to; for   **6** for

3 Language functions
2 I don't follow you.
3 I don't understand that.
4 I don't know what that word means.
5 That doesn't make sense to me.

4 Verb–noun collocations
2 accepted   **3** created   **4** breached   **5** claim

Case study 1: Contract law

(See page 10 for step-by-step instructions to case studies.)

The facts of the case

The legal issue is: Is Deep Blue Pools liable to Gainsborough Construction for any of the costs of the work needed to rebuild the pools to the depth as specified in the contract?

> **Language notes**
> - A *lucrative contract* is one that generates a lot of income.
> - *Misled* /mɪsˈled/ is the past of the verb *mislead*.
> - If you *effect a cure*, you take steps to remedy (= cure) a defect.
> - A *windfall* is a large amount of money received suddenly, which has required little or no effort by the recipient.

Comprehension questions

1 Who are the parties? [Deep Blue Pools (DBP) and Gainsborough Construction (GC)]

2 What do you know about each of them? [DBP is a new company with a good reputation. GC builds luxury properties for wealthy professionals.]

3 What was the agreement? [A contract to build one swimming pool for each of ten houses.]

4 What went wrong? [The pools were too shallow.]

5 What does each side want? [GC wants money to demolish and rebuild the ten pools. DBP wants to minimise the costs of its mistake.]

Relevant legal documents

- **Text 1** is an authentic extract from the UK Sale of Goods Act 1979. It deals only with *warranties* (i.e. non-fundamental parts of the contract). The buyer (Gainsborough) would logically prefer to interpret the depth of the pools as a *condition*, while DBP will try to claim it is only a *warranty*.

Paragraph 1 gives the buyer two choices: choice (a) means he can refuse to pay the full agreed price; choice (b) means he can sue the seller. *Prima facie* in paragraph 3 means 'as it seems at first sight'. This text would seem to support DBP: if they can prove that the depth of the pools was indeed a warranty, they are liable only for damages calculated in paragraphs 2 and 3. Further, they may be able to argue that the exact depth of the pool has a negligible effect on the overall price of a luxury house.

- **Text 2** is a more detailed explanation of how to calculate damages for a breach of warranty. It describes two means of calculating damages: *diminution* (= reduction in size) *of value* and *cost of cure*. The difference between these two measures is especially important when the market price (of performance of the contract) changes between the time of the contract and the time of the cure. In such cases, courts would try to find a balance, based on the three criteria at the bottom of the text. This requirement of reasonableness suggests that a court would try to find a compromise lower than the full amount demanded by Gainsborough.

- **Text 3** starts with what may be DBP's main argument: that the slight difference in depth has little or no financial impact on the value of the houses. The text suggests that such an argument is unfair (it would *unbalance the bargain*). A simple example illustrates this: if I ask a builder to put white tiles in my kitchen, but he actually lays yellow tiles, my flat may not be worth any less on the market, but it is still not what I want for my kitchen, and (as implied by the text) I may be entitled to have my preferred white tiles laid instead of receiving financial compensation. This would seem to support Gainsborough, but since Gainsborough is planning to sell the houses, its relevance could be questioned.

3 Tort law

Teacher's brief

As Reading 1 points out, most non-lawyers are unfamiliar with the word **tort**, but they are likely to be very familiar with the concepts involved. Whenever one person threatens to **sue** another, there is a good chance their dispute involves a tort. The word *tort*, which derives from a French word meaning an 'injury' or 'injustice', ultimately comes from Latin *torquere* (= *to twist*), which also led to the related words *distort/contort/extort* and *torture*.

A good example of a tort would be a car accident. If a driver accidentally drives into the back of my car, he has probably committed the tort of **negligent damage to private property**. I may attempt to recover money (**damages**) from him (or his insurer) to pay for repairs to my car. He may also have committed a crime, such as speeding, in which case the police may become involved, and the state may prosecute and punish him. But even if he was driving legally, the fact that he drove into my car suggests he wasn't paying attention and was therefore **negligent**. Thus, while the same event may be both a crime and a tort, many torts are less serious than crimes. After a crime, the state may prosecute the offender. If the offender is found guilty, he may be fined or imprisoned. After a tort, it is the victim who **sues** the **tortfeasor** (i.e. the **wrongdoer** who has committed the tort). If the wrongdoer is **found liable**, he may have to **pay damages** to the victim.

Negligent torts, as in the example above, form one of the major branches of tort law. They include a wide range of accidents and incidents which are committed unintentionally, but which nevertheless cause **physical, emotional or financial harm**. Negligence can be defined as conduct which falls short of what a **reasonable person** would be expected to do to avoid harming another person. In order to prove negligence, a plaintiff must prove that the defendant had a **duty of care** (i.e. was performing a potentially harmful activity, and was therefore obliged to be reasonably careful) and that there was a **breach of duty** (i.e. the defendant was careless). The third element which must be proved is **causation** (i.e. whether the defendant's carelessness wholly or partially, directly or indirectly, caused the harm which actually occurred). When a wrongdoer recklessly disregards others' rights to safety, **gross negligence** may have been committed. The motive may not have been to inflict harm, but rather to save or make money by endangering other people's safety. In such cases, the plaintiff may seek **punitive damages** to punish the wrongdoer, in addition to **compensatory damages** to compensate the victim.

The second major branch of tort law is **intentional torts**. As the name suggests, these involve the wrongdoer deliberately performing a **wrongful act**, and could reasonably have foreseen that harm would be done. Examples include **assault and battery** (e.g. physically attacking another person), **libel and slander** (i.e. deliberately damaging a person's reputation by lying, either in writing or orally), **trespass to land** (i.e. deliberately entering another person's real property without permission or authorisation) and **conversion** (i.e. treating another person's property as one's own, usually through theft). As these examples illustrate, intentional torts are very often also crimes, so the same act, such as an assault, may lead to both a criminal prosecution by the state (to punish and deter the offender) and a civil claim by the victim (to recover damages).

The third branch of tort law is **strict liability**, which relates, among other things, to businesses making and selling defective products. In such situations, it is not necessary to prove whether the wrongdoer's actions were negligent, deliberate or simply unlucky. The plaintiff only needs to prove that the tort happened and the defendant was responsible. Under strict-liability rules, if an activity is inherently dangerous to other people (such as working with explosives), if somebody performing that activity accidentally harms others, it doesn't matter what precautions were in place – the person responsible is liable for the harm caused.

The unit deals with several important real-life **case histories**: a negligence claim from 1928, which neatly illustrates the arguments around causation (specifically: what was the **proximate cause** of the accident); and a **gross-negligence claim** involving McDonald's coffee, which illustrates the complex procedural history of some cases as they are appealed and/or settled out of court. The second part of the unit presents a case study of a **defamation claim**, involving alleged libel and slander. In the case study, a law student working as a volunteer in a **law clinic** interviews and advises a man who has been accused of these torts. This section presents useful language and techniques for an **initial lawyer–client interview**, with special focus on types of **questions**.

Further reading

○ Wikipedia (http://en.wikipedia.org/wiki/Tort) has an excellent section on **tort law**, with articles and case studies to illustrate a wide range of torts.

○ Law.com (http://dictionary.law.com/) has also a rich source of information on torts, with many **extended definitions** of the concepts from this unit.

○ For a very accessible guide to the **differences between civil law** (i.e. torts and contract law) **and criminal law**, see http://www.rbs2.com/cc.htm.

THE STUDY OF LAW

Lead-in

Elicit from the class what they think the word *tort* means. Of course, it could be that some students already know the answer, in which case elicit a) as many examples of torts as students can think of, and b) some differences between tort law and other areas of law (such as contract law or criminal law). You could also tell students to discuss these two questions in small groups and then feed back to the class.

If students don't know what *tort* means, use the prompt in Exercise 2 to elicit the answer, and then continue the discussion as above.

Suggested answers

a) Examples of torts: see Photocopiable worksheet 3.1.

b) · Differences between tort law and criminal law: see Reading 1, paragraph 5; also http://www.rbs2.com/cc.htm.
- In contract law, the parties have made a prior agreement, either explicitly (through a written or oral contract) or implicitly (through their actions), while in tort law, no such prior agreement exists.
- In contract law, the drafting of contracts is crucial in order to prevent and/or prepare for breaches. In tort law, on the other hand, lawyers can do little to prepare, and are mostly concerned with the consequences of wrongs.
- In contract law, when a breach occurs, the parties can refer to their contract to establish who is at fault, unlike in tort law, where statutes and case law (precedents) determine who is at fault.

1a Tell students to work alone quickly to match the three case names with the descriptions, and then elicit from the class what students know / can guess about the stories. Then use the background notes below to confirm or reject students' ideas/predictions.

Answers
1 b **2** c **3** a

Background notes

a The case involving spilled McDonald's coffee is discussed fully in Listening 1. Scc http://en.wikipedia.org/wiki/Liebeck_v._McDonald%27s_Restaurants.

b OJ Simpson, a former professional American footballer and actor, was acquitted in a highly publicised murder case in 1995. He was later successfully sued by the families of the alleged victims, Simpson's ex-wife and her friend, in a civil trial for the tort of unlawful killing. This case, as well as being a landmark criminal case because of the extraordinary amount of media interest, neatly illustrates the difference between criminal law and tort law, as one system found him not guilty of the murders, while the other found him liable for the unlawful killings. In the criminal case for murder, the state prosecuted, but was unable to convince the jury of Simpson's guilt beyond reasonable doubt. In the civil case, in which the families sued Simpson, the burden of proof was lower: liability for the tort was established based on the preponderance of evidence (i.e. it was decided that it was more likely that Simpson committed the tort than that he didn't). His punishment was a large fine. See http://en.wikipedia.org/wiki/O._J._Simpson_murder_case.

c The case description refers to the 'dog in the microwave' myth, which says that a woman tried to dry her poodle in a microwave, and then successfully sued the manufacturer, claiming there was nothing in the instruction manual warning her not to put pets inside to dry. The story seems to be completely untrue, but illustrates the stereotype that people can do stupid things and then successfully sue others for not warning them not to do such things. See http://www.everything2.com/index.pl?node=do%20not%20put%20pets%20in%20the%20microwave%20to%20dry%20them.

b Discuss this briefly with the class, and use this to elicit a definition of tort which covers all three cases.

Answers

The cases all have in common that people were harmed (either physically, emotionally or through suffering loss) due to the actions of another.

2 Tell students to complete the definition alone, and then check with the whole class.

Answers

1 act **2** harm **3** party **4** damages

SB p.28 Reading 1: Tort law

3 Go through the questions with the class to elicit answers and check students understand. Avoid explaining *injunction* at this stage. Then tell them to read the text carefully to answer the four questions. Allow plenty of time (three to four minutes), as the text and questions are rather difficult. When most have finished reading, tell them to discuss their answers in pairs, and then go through the answers with the class.

Answers

1 The two main objectives of tort law are to provide relief for the loss or harm suffered and deter others from committing the same civil wrongs.
2 Some of the types of loss mentioned in the text are damage to property, loss of earnings capacity, pain and suffering, and reasonable medical expenses.
3 An injunction is a court order telling someone to stop doing something or compelling him/her to do something.
4 strict liability tort

Background notes

(NB Photocopiable worksheet 3.1 provides examples of many of the torts mentioned in Reading 1. The worksheet should be used by students later (after Exercise 6), but you could use it now to help you understand Reading 1.)

○ If a wrong is *remedied* /remədiːd/, it is put right, typically by compensating the victim.

○ Reading 1 mentions that there is some debate over why some wrongs are considered torts, while others are crimes. For more on the *tort/crime distinction*, see, for example, http://www.pointoflaw. com/feature/archives/003644.php.

○ In the torts of *assault and battery*, *assault* is a threat or attempt to physically harm another, while *battery* is the actual act of beating another. Both can be crimes (so the state may prosecute) as well as torts (so the victim may sue). All battery contains some element of assault. A person may also commit assault through physical contact that does not amount to battery, especially if there was no injury to the victim.

○ There is much more information on *criminal law*, and the differences between it and tort law, in Unit 4.

○ The *standard of proof* is the degree of certainty needed to decide a particular case. In most tort cases, the standard of proof is fairly low: *the preponderance of the evidence* (i.e. which explanation is most likely, given the evidence). In some cases, there is a higher standard of proof: *clear and convincing proof*. The most demanding standard of proof (*proof beyond reasonable doubt*) is required for criminal convictions. See http://dictionary.reference.com/search ?q=standard+of+proof&r=66.

○ A *tortfeasor* /ˈtɔːtfiːzə(r)/ is a party who has committed a tort. It is a more technical name for a wrongdoer.

○ *Tortious conduct* /ˈtɔːʃəs ˌkɒndʌkt/ is behaviour which leads to the commission of a tort.

○ The phrase ... *the position he or she would have been in had the tort not occurred* may cause some problems for students. It means 'the position in which he or she would (hypothetically) have been, if (hypothetically) the tort had not occurred'.

Optional extension

Use this comprehension quiz to check students have understood the text and the complicated concepts it deals with, as well as to check/teach the important vocabulary.

1 Who brings an action in a tort law case? [Para 5: a private individual; para 1: the injured party]

2 Who brings an action in a criminal law case? [Para 5: the state]

3 What three types of harm are listed? [Para 1: physical, emotional and financial]

4 What three general categories of torts are given? [Para 2: intentional torts, negligent torts and strict liability torts]

5 What sort of damages are intended to put the victim in the position he/she would have been in if the tort hadn't occurred? [Para 6: compensatory damages]

6 What sort of damages are intended to punish a wrongdoer? [Para 6: punitive damages]

7 What sort of compensation is most suitable for a victim who, as a result of a tort, can no longer earn so much at work as before? [Para 6: loss of earnings capacity]

8 What sort of compensation is most suitable for a victim who has had to pay for hospital treatment? [Para 6: reasonable medical expenses]

9 What is the name of the business tort which involves tricking another party into signing a contract which causes that party to suffer? [Para 7: fraudulent misrepresentation]

10 What is the name of the business tort which involves disrupting a party's ability to fulfil its contractual obligations to another party? [Para 7: interference in contractual relations]

11 What is the name for a person who commits a tort? [Para 6: a tortfeasor]

12 What is the name of a legal order for a tortfeasor to stop tortious conduct? [Para 6: an injunction]

13 What general category of torts includes unfair competition? [Para 2: intentional torts]

14 What general category of torts includes making and selling defective products? [Para 2: strict liability torts]

15 What general category of torts includes causing a road accident by failing to obey traffic rules? [Para 2: negligent torts]

16 What example is given of an overlap between criminal law and tort law? [Para 4: assault and battery]

17 What are the two primary aims of tort law? [Para 6: to provide relief and deter potential tortfeasors]

18 What are the tort law equivalents of conviction and punishment? [Para 5: liability and damages]

19 In which branch of law is the standard of proof higher, criminal or tort law? [Para 5: criminal law]

20 According to the text, how can a civil wrong be remedied? [Para 1: by awarding damages]

4 Tell students to work alone to complete the matching exercise. Allow them to check with a partner before going through the answers with the class. As a follow-up, students can test each other by reading the first part of a collocation to elicit the second.

Answers

1 b **2** e **3** d **4** c **5** f **6** a

5 Students should work in pairs to complete the exercise. When they have finished, go through the answers with the class.

Answers

1 civil wrong **2** injured party
3 monetary damages **4** medical expenses
5 fraudulent misrepresentation
6 contractual relations

6 Tell students to discuss the three questions about the three terms in small groups. After a few minutes, open up the discussion to include the whole class. If students don't know the answer to the third question (i.e. about their own jurisdictions), elicit how they could check (i.e. websites in their own language, textbooks, etc.).

Suggested answers

Examples of assault include hitting a person with a stick or a fist, drawing a weapon, and throwing something with intent to wound or strike. Examples of negligence include a local authority digging a hole in a public footpath and not taking steps to prevent people from falling into it, or when a building owner leaves dangerous electrical wires exposed. A person who enters another person's property or home without permission may be liable for trespass.

Background notes

○ *Assault* has slightly different meanings in different English-speaking jurisdictions. In Australia and New Zealand, for example, it refers to a crime of violence, while in the USA, it refers to a threat of, or attempt to commit, an act of violence (the tort of *battery* refers to the actual act of violence). In some jurisdictions, it may include any bodily contact without consent. Not all acts of violence constitute assault (and/or battery): obvious exceptions include contact sports such as rugby or boxing (as long as the act is within the rules of the game) and medical surgery (i.e. where the patient has given consent). See http://en.wikipedia.org/wiki/Assault for a much fuller analysis of assault and its defences.

○ *Negligence* occurs when there is a breach of a duty of care. A duty of care is the obligation to be reasonably careful during a potentially dangerous act. The most obvious example is driving: the driver has an obligation to avoid endangering others. Another example involves manufacturers, who are responsible for ensuring that their products do not injure people. In fact, victims of such injuries do not need to prove negligence on the part of the manufacturer, as the separate tort of product liability covers all such injuries, whether or not negligence was involved. See http://dictionary.law.com.

○ *Trespass* is the unlawful entering of another person's real property without permission or authorisation. If the entry is for unlawful purposes (such as burglary) or involves violence or damage, trespass can also be a crime. See http://dictionary.law.com. The term can also be used occasionally in a more general sense: 'trespass to the person' includes torts such as assault and battery and false imprisonment.

Optional extension (Photocopiable worksheet 3.1)

This is intended to present a wide range of torts. It is not intended as a complete list, and there may be some overlap between several items in the list, but it includes all the torts mentioned in Reading 1 as well as other well-known torts. The task involves students matching the torts with people who have committed these torts. Again, these examples are not intended as complete explanations of the torts (for which see http://dictionary.law.com and Wikipedia), and of course there is always room for argument when it comes to deciding whether a particular tort has been committed, even in invented examples. The characters may be able to defend themselves by arguing that their actions did not constitute a tort. Nevertheless, the exercise should provide students with an opportunity to think about and discuss these torts.

1 Make enough copies of the worksheet for students to work in small groups of around three.
2 Cut up the worksheets along the dotted lines, and give each group a set of cut-up slips.
3 They should match the torts with the examples as quickly as they can. Point out that there is room for some argument in some cases (see above).
4 When the first groups have finished, check their answers. You could give out more copies of the worksheet (not cut up) for the early finishers to match again (as this will reinforce the concepts in their memories).
5 Finally, check the answers with the whole class and deal with any problems.

Answers

1 c 2 i 3 t 4 f 5 e 6 s 7 m 8 k 9 a
10 b 11 p 12 r 13 j 14 d 15 g 16 o
17 q 18 l 19 h 20 n

Background notes

○ *Medical negligence* is a type of professional negligence.

○ *Conversion* is the tort of depriving a property owner of some property. Very often, it means 'theft', but other acts, such as vandalising, destroying or hiding the property, can constitute conversion. See http://en.wikipedia.org/wiki/Conversion_%28law%29.

○ *Fraud* is a type of deceit. Fraud specifically involves tricking another person into parting with money.

Reading 2: Case note

Elicit from the class what a case note is, and why lawyers and law students might use one. Then tell them to read the introduction on page 30 to compare it with their ideas.

7 Make sure students realise that they don't have to read the text in detail for this exercise, as this will spoil the later discussions. Tell them to work alone quickly to match the headings to the descriptions, and after about a minute, go through the answers with the class.

Answers
1 b 2 d 3 f 4 a 5 c 6 e

Background note
For a full account of the *Palsgraf v. The Long Island Railroad Company* case, see http://www.courts.state.ny.us/history/cases/palsgraf_lirr.htm. There is also a good analysis of the case and its influence at http://en.wikipedia.org/wiki/Palsgraf_v._Long_Island_Railroad_Co.

8 Make sure students cover sections 3–6 while they are reading the first two sections, as this will help them to resist the temptation to read ahead and spoil the discussion. Allow about a minute for students to read the two paragraphs to answer the four questions. While they are reading, write the following words on the board: *plaintiff, platform, passenger,*

package, balance, employee, rails, fireworks, negligence. At the end of the time limit, tell students to close their books to discuss their answers with a partner. Tell them also to use the words on the board to reconstruct exactly what happened. Open up the discussion to include the whole class, and make sure everyone understands the words on the board, the relationship between the three people in the story and the chain of events. As a follow-up, you could ask students how they think the lower court ruled, but avoiding confirming or rejecting suggestions.

Answers
1 The name of the case is *Palsgraf v. The Long Island Railroad Company*.
2 The defendant is the Long Island Railroad Company.
3 The claimant is Ms Palsgraf.
4 The defendant is alleged to have directly caused the injury suffered by the plaintiff/claimant.

Language note
The word *strike* has several meanings, which may cause some misunderstanding. In this case, it means 'hit'.

9 Tell students to uncover and read the rest of the text to check their predictions, and to answer the three questions. Give them a chance to discuss their answers with a partner before checking with the class.

Answers
1 The lower court found for the plaintiff/claimant.
2 The appellate court affirmed the judgment of the first court.
3 The court determined that the explosion of the fireworks was the proximate cause of claimant's injuries.

Language notes
NB Several of the words are explained in Exercise 11.

○ The *proximate cause* of an event is the thing that makes the event happen. If event X (the proximate cause) hadn't happened, event Y (e.g. the injury) wouldn't have happened. There may also be an *intervening cause* between the proximate cause and the injury, which may reduce or eliminate a defendant's responsibility for causing the injury. See http://dictionary.law.com.

○ The phrase … *the harm was not wilful on the part of defendant* … means that the defendant did not intend to cause harm.

○ The phrase … *an act which could not have been foreseen* may cause some problems. It can be thought of as part of a so-called third conditional, which refers to an imaginary past: *The employee didn't try to foresee what was in the package, but even **if he had tried** to, it **would have been** impossible to foresee that it contained fireworks.*

SB p.31 Key terms 1: Reporting procedural history

10 Elicit from the class what the term *procedural history* means, and then tell them to read the information in Exercise 10 to check. Discuss the answer to the question with the class.

> **Answer**
> Sections 3 (Procedural History), 5 (Ruling) and 6 (Reasoning) all contain information about the decision of the highest court.

11 Students should work with a partner to find words and phrases in the text to match the definitions. When the first groups have finished, go through the answers with the class. As a follow-up, students should test each other in pairs by reading the first part of a definition (i.e. up to the gapped phrase) to elicit the phrase and the rest of the definition.

> **Answers**
> **1** claimant/plaintiff **2** defendant **3** finds for **4** appeal **5** appellate court; court of appeals **6** affirms **7** reverses

---

**Optional extension
(Photocopiable worksheet 3.2)**
The text contains several structures for describing cause and effect. The language of cause and effect is essential for analysing both the facts of a case (i.e. what was the proximate cause of the injury) and the

procedural history (i.e. what did the courts base their judgments on). The first part of Photocopiable worksheet 3.2 highlights these structures from the text.

A related structure, equally essential for analysing a case like this, is the so-called third conditional (i.e. structures for describing the imaginary past: if X hadn't happened, Y would/could/might not have happened). Students at this level may be unfamiliar with this structure; or if they are aware of it, they are likely to find it difficult to use and understand. However, it is impossible to avoid when talking about tort law, as shown by the examples so far in Reading 1 (… *the position he or she would have been in had the tort not occurred*) and Reading 2 (… *an act which could not have been foreseen*). The Speaking exercise (Exercise 13) also depends on this structure (… *what do you think might have happened if this case had been brought* …), so it is worth spending some time introducing/practising the structure before the Speaking task.

A

1 Tell students to close their books. Hand out copies of Photocopiable worksheet 3.2.

2 Point out that the 12 sentences in Exercise A all show cause and effect. Most of the sentences are exactly as they appear in Reading 1, but a few have been adapted slightly to fit the exercise. Point out also that several questions have more than one possible answer.

3 Tell students to work alone for a few minutes to complete the sentences, and then tell them to work with a partner to check their answers and complete the exercise.

4 When you go through the answers with the class, make sure everyone understands the difference between the various ways of describing cause and effect. For example, elicit that *as* and *since* are both alternatives for *because*, and that *therefore* and *consequently* are more formal ways of saying *so*, but are used to show the relationship between two separate sentences. Check the difference between *result from* and *result in*.

5 As a follow-up, you could ask students to retell the story from memory, using only the words in the box to help them remember.

Answers

1 to **2** so **3** caused **4** causing
5 result **6** resulted **7** results **8** Since/As
9 As/Since **10** cause **11** Therefore/
Consequently **12** Consequently/Therefore

B

1 Write this sentence on the board: *If the plaintiff hadn't been standing on the platform at the time, she wouldn't have been injured.*

2 Elicit the following:
- what this sentence means (*Is it about the past, present or future? Is it about the real past or the imaginary past?*)
- what actually happened (*The plaintiff was standing on the platform at the time, so she was injured*), and write this on the board beneath the first sentence
- the changes between the real-past version and the unreal-past version (positives become negatives or vice versa, changes in tense in the two halves of the sentence)
- why a lawyer might want to speculate about the unreal past in a case like this [**Suggested answer**: To identify precise cause-and-effect relationships, it helps to imagine different scenarios. It is like running a computer model of an event, and seeing what happens if you change one of the variables.]
- the difference between *what would have happened* (i.e. 100% sure) and *what might have happened* (i.e. one of several possibilities), and why this difference is important for lawyers [**Suggested answer**: The sentence *If the defendant hadn't done X, the plaintiff wouldn't have been injured* suggests that the plaintiff has a good chance of winning the case. But if we change *wouldn't* to *might not*, the defendant is in a much stronger position.]

3 Tell students to work in pairs to complete the exercise. Point out that:
- the numbers in Exercise B correspond to those in Exercise A, so, for example, they can read sentence 5 in Exercise A to help them work out how to complete sentence 5 in Exercise B
- they should think carefully about positives and negatives, and whether *would* or *might* is most appropriate

- the number of gaps is the same as the number of missing words: contractions like *hadn't* and *wouldn't* count as one word. In this exercise, *might not* has been written as two separate words in order to show that the word *not* is stressed.

4 Monitor carefully, as this is likely to be difficult for students, and provide plenty of support when you check the answers with the class.

5 As a follow-up (with strong classes only), tell students to cover Exercise B and take turns to remember the sentences, using only the sentences in Exercise A to help them remember.

Answers

1 hadn't; wouldn't **2** hadn't; wouldn't have
3 hadn't reached; wouldn't have **4** hadn't exploded; wouldn't have struck/injured
5 hadn't been; wouldn't have sued
6 wouldn't have been; hadn't been
7 had been; might/would have been
8 had been; might not have been
9 had been; might have been **10** hadn't exploded; wouldn't have been **11** hadn't been; might have been **12** had found; would/might not have been

SB p.32 **Speaking 1: Case discussion**

12 Students should discuss the procedural history of the case in small groups. Make sure they focus on the sequence of events (what happened in what order) and the causes and effects of the events in court.

Suggested answer

The claimant was injured when a railroad employee caused a package of fireworks in another passenger's arms to fall on the train track. The resulting explosion caused some equipment to fall, injuring the claimant. The claimant sued the defendant, the railroad, for negligence. The trial court found for the claimant. When the defendants appealed, the appellate court affirmed the judgment of the first court. The defendant appealed once more, and the Court of Appeals reversed the decision of the first two courts.

13 Check all students understand the meaning of the question (i.e. that it refers to the imaginary past) – this will be easier if you have already done Photocopiable worksheet 3.2. Discuss the question with the whole class. It is probably best to concentrate on the legal issues in this discussion, as these are quite difficult, rather than expecting students to produce perfectly formed third conditional structures. If students don't know what would have happened, discuss how they could find out (i.e. by searching the Internet for terms like *proximate cause*, *tort* or *negligence* and the name of their country, preferably in the language of that country). Encourage students to research this question as a homework task, and follow it up with a discussion in a later lesson.

SB p.32 3.1 ## Listening 1: Frivolous lawsuits

14 Tell students to read the introduction and task to find out who Maria and Fabio are, and what they are discussing. Discuss the questions with the whole class, and make sure everyone is clear about the difference between the two types of damages. Elicit also what they think the product liability case might involve, and what they think the term *frivolous lawsuit* might mean, but avoid confirming or rejecting their suggestions, as this would spoil the listening exercise.

Answers
Compensatory damages refers to money awarded to reimburse actual costs incurred by the injured party, such as medical bills and lost wages. Punitive damages is the term for money awarded to an injured person, over and above the measurable value of the injury, in order to punish the tortfeasor. In jurisdictions that allow punitive damages, these awards can often be significantly higher than those for general damages.

15 Students should read the questions to check they understand all the terminology, and then listen to the recording to answer the questions. After listening, allow students to check with a partner before going through the answers with the class.

Answers
1 He thinks the lawsuit is not to be taken seriously, and that the amount of damages awarded is far too high for the injury suffered.
2 The plaintiff received third-degree burns from spilled coffee.
3 McDonald's refused to settle because they most likely thought the plaintiff could not win the case, as in other cases the courts had ruled that coffee burns were an open and obvious danger.
4 At first, Liebeck was awarded $200,000 in compensatory damages, which was then reduced by 20% to $160,000. The judge also awarded her $2.7 million in punitive damages, which was then reduced to $480,000.
5 It is not known how much she finally received in damages, but it is thought that the amount was under $600,000.

Transcript » STUDENT'S BOOK page 126

Background notes
○ For a full account of the case, see http://en.wikipedia.org/wiki/Liebeck_v._McDonald%27s_Restaurants.
○ *Third-degree burns* involve loss of part of the epidermis and damage to the underlying ligaments, tendons and muscles. They may be fatal if they cover large parts of the body. See http://en.wikipedia.org/wiki/Burn.
○ An *open and obvious danger* is assumed to need no warning, as it serves as its own warning. An example would be an open fire, where a warning sign might be pointless.
○ *Gross negligence* is a reckless disregard for others' safety, and may involve, for example, the wrongdoer taking serious risks with other people's safety in order to make or save money.

16 Tell students to work with a partner to read through the case note and try to remember as much information as they can about the case. Play the recording a second time for them to check their ideas and complete any information they missed. Allow them to check together again before going through the answers with the class.

➠ **Answers**
  1 settlement 2 defendant 3 found for
  4 awarded 5 damages 6 punitive
  7 appealed

Optional extension

This case provides another opportunity to practise talking about the unreal past, as a follow-up to Photocopiable worksheet 3.2.

1 While students are listening to Listening 1, write these discussion questions on the board, with the references to the unreal past underlined:

  · How hot do you think the coffee was? How hot <u>should</u> it <u>have been</u>?

  · If the coffee <u>had been</u> slightly cooler, what difference <u>would</u> it <u>have made</u> to the case?

  · If there <u>had been</u> a clearer warning on the cup, what difference <u>would</u> it <u>have made</u> to Ms Liebeck's actions? What difference <u>would</u> it <u>have made</u> to the outcome of the case?

  · What <u>would have happened if</u> McDonald's <u>had accepted</u> Ms Liebeck's original claim for medical expenses? <u>Would</u> it <u>have encouraged</u> others to file similar claims?

  · Ms Liebeck settled out of court for an amount less than she was awarded by the courts. <u>Should</u> she <u>have fought</u> to receive the full amount?

2 Tell students to discuss the questions in small groups. After a few minutes, open up the discussion to include the whole class. Encourage students to use the underlined structures in their discussions, but do not expect 100% accuracy at this level.

(SB p.33) ## Speaking 2: Frivolous lawsuits

17 Students should discuss the three questions in small groups. After a few minutes, open up the discussion to include the whole class. Elicit from the class how they could find frivolous lawsuits on the Internet in English and in their own jurisdictions/languages.

➠ **Suggested answer**
  1 The serious purpose of the Stella Awards might be that they question whether those involved in the cases are using the courts to achieve justice for the injured parties, or whether they are simply trying to take advantage of the so-called 'compensation culture' to get money from anyone they can.

📖 **Background note**
  For more on the Stella Awards, see http://www.stellaawards.com/.

LAW IN PRACTICE

(SB p.33) ## Lead-in

Elicit from the class what they think the term *law clinic* might mean, and how it might be connected with tort law. Then tell them to read the introduction to find out. Point out that they will find out much more about law clinics from Reading 3.

(SB p.33) ## Reading 3: The Kent Law Clinic

18 Students should work alone to read the text and answer the questions. After about two minutes, tell them to discuss their answers with a partner, and then check with the class.

➠ **Answers**
  1 (law) students and qualified lawyers
  2 no
  3 interviewing, negotiating and advocacy

📖 **Background notes**
  ○ The *Kent Law Clinic* is a real service. See http://www.kent.ac.uk/law/undergraduate/lawclinic.html for full information.
  ○ A *litigant in person* is a defendant who represents himself/herself in court proceedings.

19 Students should work in pairs to complete the exercise. When you check the answers with the class, discuss any other difficult or useful vocabulary.

1 tribunal
2 litigant(s)-in-person (US: *pro se*)
3 advocacy

20 Tell students to discuss this in small groups. They could also discuss the advantages and disadvantages of such clinics, from both the law student's and the client's point of view. When you open up the discussion to include the whole class, elicit whether such law clinics exist in the students' own jurisdictions, and if any students have experience of them, or similar services.

Suggested answers
○ Advantages for the law student: good practical experience; looks good on CV.
○ Disadvantages for the law student: unpaid; lots of work; lots of stress.
○ Advantages for the client: free legal advice from an intelligent, informed law student.
○ Disadvantages for the client: advice may be unreliable; student may be unprofessional/nervous/confused; client must still represent himself/ herself in court.

SB p.34 **3.2 3.3** **Listening 2: Student lawyer–client interview**

Tell students to read the introduction to find out who Nick is. Ask students if they have ever bought a faulty product and, if they have, how easy it was to get a refund or a replacement.

21 Tell students to read the four questions to make sure they understand what they mean. Pay particular attention to question 4: elicit that *once* means *when / as soon as*, and that the second part of the question is asking us to think about the imaginary past. Play the recording for students to answer the questions, and then tell students to discuss their answers in pairs. When you go through the answers with the class, elicit exactly what happened a) this morning, b) when Charles got the laptop home, and c) when he went back to the shop. Encourage students to predict what happened next.

Answers
1 a laptop (computer)
2 One of the pixels was burned out (not working).
3 Under the terms of the guarantee, seven pixels had to be burned out before the laptop would be replaced. Charles's laptop had only one burned-out pixel.
4 One option would have been first to threaten and then to seek legal advice. Charles might also have complained to a consumer organisation. In some jurisdictions, media sources carrying advertisements have an obligation to follow up complaints arising from problems with their advertisers, so this might have been a further option.

Transcript » STUDENT'S BOOK page 126

Optional extension
1 If you feel students need to listen a second time, write the following words and numbers on the board: *volunteer, sued, four, English, pixel, seven, working, first, mailing lists, furious.*
2 Students should listen a second time to identify in what context each word occurred. They should discuss their answers with a partner before checking with you.

Answers
○ The students are *volunteers*, and also have *volunteer* lawyers to support them.
○ Charles received a letter this morning saying that he was going to be *sued*.
○ He bought the laptop *four* months ago.
○ He studies *English*.
○ A *pixel* was burnt out in the middle of the screen.
○ Under the guarantee, at least *seven* pixels had to be burnt out.
○ Charles didn't see the laptop *working* in the shop.
○ The *first* time he used the computer, it was faulty.
○ He threatened to write to *mailing lists*.
○ He was *furious* when he left the shop.

22 Tell students to read the questions and then listen to the recording. After listening, tell them to discuss their answers with a partner and then go through the answers with the class.

Answers
1 Charles threatened to write to as many mailing lists as possible to tell people not to buy computers from Carmecom.
2 Charles stood outside and told potential customers about his experience with Carmecom. He also told them not to buy anything from the store, as their computers were 'rubbish' (poor quality).
3 Charles has to sign a retraction or he will be sued for defamation.

Transcript » | STUDENT'S BOOK page 127 |

Background note
A *retraction* is a clear and complete statement made by a defendant after an alleged defamation, which has the effect of reversing the original defamatory statements.

Optional extension
1 Again, for a second listening task, write words on the board and tell students to listen again to establish what was said about each: *Christmas*, *get them back*, *replacement*, *rubbish*, *address*, *defamation*, *retraction*, *reputation*, *campaign*.
Point out that this information about the case will be useful when they read and write about it later.

Answers
○ At the time, many people were buying computer stuff for *Christmas*.
○ Charles wanted to *get* Carmecom *back* (= get revenge by hurting them).
○ He didn't just want a *replacement* because he was so angry.
○ He told potential customers that Carmecom's computers were *rubbish*.
○ He was tricked into giving his *address*.
○ Carmecom are threatening to sue Charles for *defamation*.
○ They want him to sign a *retraction*.
○ They say he is trying to damage their *reputation*.
○ Nick describes Charles's actions and threat as a *campaign*.

2 Finally, discuss the case and the lawyer–client interview with the class, using these prompts:
○ What do you think of Charles's behaviour? Did he commit a tort?
○ What do you think of Carmecom's behaviour?
○ What should Charles do next? What would you advise him to do?

(SB p.34) Language use: Asking for information

23 Students should do this alone. Check the answers with the class.

Answers
Nick's questions
1 … could you first tell me what happened?
2 And there was a problem with it?
3 So you took it back to the shop?
4 What did they say?
5 And you didn't accept this?
6 Did you see the laptop working in the shop before buying it?
7 So what did you do when they refused to replace it?
8 Unless they replaced the laptop?
9 Did you leave the shop *without* the laptop?
10 What do you mean?
11 To hurt Carmecom?
12 You *didn't* just want a replacement?
13 Anyway, what happened next?
14 How did they react to this?
15 So they asked for your address – is that right?
16 What did the letter say exactly?

Charles's questions
17 … are you one of the lawyers?
18 Could I see a lawyer, please?
19 Can't I just speak to a lawyer directly?

24 Students should work in pairs to complete the matching exercise. You may need to check they understand some of the grammar terminology: auxiliary verb (e.g. *do/be/have* or a modal verb, such as *can/could, will/would*, etc.) and subject (check by giving a sentence like *Tom sued Joe* and asking who is the subject and who is the object).

Answers
1 c 2 a 3 b

Optional extension
Ask students to identify examples of each question type in the recordings (students can refer to their answers to Exercise 23). When you check the answers with the class, point out that not all the questions from the audioscripts fall neatly into the three groups, mainly because not all are direct requests for information.

Answers (numbers refer to key for Exercise 23)

1 Normal open questions
   4, 7, 10, 13, 14, 16

2 Negative questions
   5, 12, 19
   (NB Questions 5 and 12 are marked only by intonation, not word order.)

3 Closed questions
   2, 3, 6, 9, 15, 17, 18
   (NB The three words at the end of Question 15 have the function of turning a statement into a closed question to check an assumption. Question 18 is a request rather than an information question, but is still closed in the sense that it requires a yes/no answer.)

Other questions
Question 1 (*… could you first tell me what happened?*) has the form of a closed question, in that it seems to require a yes/no answer, but it functions as an open question, in that it is a polite way of asking 'What happened?'.

---

25 Students should work in pairs to complete the exercise. When they have finished, or if they are struggling, go through the answers with the class.

Answers
1 If I don't sign the retraction, will I have to go to court?
2 How long do you think a trial would last?
3 What would be my chances of winning?
4 Would I have to pay anything for my defence?

5 What are the consequences if I lose the case?
6 Do you think there is a chance of me getting a new computer?

Language note
Question 3 may cause problems, as it is structured like a subject question. Questions with *be* as the main verb often have two possible forms, as it is often difficult to say what the subject is. The alternative (*What would my chances of winning be?*) is more logical (since *my chances of winning* is the subject), but less natural (since *be* is stranded at the end of the question).

SB p.35

Text analysis: Initial lawyer–client interview

Elicit from the class what a lawyer must do in an initial lawyer–client interview, and what the four main steps might be. Then tell students to read the introduction on page 35 to check their ideas. You may need to check that students understand the verb *to part* (= to separate from somebody, to say goodbye).

26 Tell students to work with a partner to complete the table. Point out that the table already contains an example piece of advice for each interview stage. When students have finished, discuss the answers with the class. There may be some disagreement over the function of some of the points. As you check, deal with any vocabulary problems (e.g. *sympathetic, encourage, go on, periodically*).

Answers
This is the suggested most likely grouping. In some cases (e.g. *k*), an argument may be made for having one point in more than one section.
1 i
2 b, d, g, j
3 a, e, h, k
4 c, f, k, l

○ The *merits of the case* means the aspects of the case that support the action.

○ A *non-legal solution* does not mean an illegal solution. It simply means one which does not require a lawyer's formal action. An example might be a face-to-face meeting with or without lawyers, or a simple apology.

27 Students should discuss this in pairs, and then feed back to the class.

Suggested answers

Other factors include:

Before the interview

- Prepare yourself in advance as far as possible. Has the client used the firm before? If so, you may be able to get some useful information on the client from colleagues.
- Use checklists with caution. Some people find it useful to prepare a checklist before an interview, but be careful not to base the list on too many assumptions before the client has had the chance to explain his/her problem in detail. Checklists can impose an agenda on an interview which may prevent you from actively listening to the client. However, they can be useful. Many lawyers find that checklists provide something to fall back on if they lose concentration or want to make sure an important point isn't forgotten. The key is to remember that the interview is principally a listening, not a questioning activity.

During the interview

- Consider the impact of non-verbal communication on the interaction. Appear confident, sympathetic and friendly.
- Give information on the service levels your firm provides, such as how often the client will be updated on the progress of his/her case.
- Don't make your introductory comments too long; allow the client the chance to speak early on in the interview.

- Invite your client to talk using questions such as *Tell me about …*
- Don't be afraid of silence. Sometimes clients need time to think through an answer or to find the right words.
- Pay attention to your note-taking skills. As soon as possible after the interview, write up your notes clearly and accurately.
- Make sure that the client knows how to contact you or the appropriate colleague.
- Confirm that the client is aware of any action he/she has to take and by when it has to be taken.

28 Discuss this with the whole class, in terms of the WASP structure and any further ideas that came out of Exercise 27. Encourage students to use structures like *He could have done X, He should have done Y* or *It would have been better if he'd done Z*.

Suggested answer

Generally speaking, Nick did well, especially considering the fact that he is a student volunteer and not a trained lawyer. Nick may have got more information earlier on from Charles had he used more open questions, e.g. when Nick asked *So you took it back to the shop?* Charles's response was fairly brief, and Nick then had to ask a second, open, question in order to find out exactly what happened. Open questions allow the client to tell the story in their own words; the less this flow is broken, the more information the client is likely to give.

Nick could have used active listening techniques to periodically summarise what had been said. Although he didn't do this, he did seek confirmation where necessary.

Towards the end of the interview, Nick seemed to make a subjective judgment on Charles's behaviour, which caused Charles to become defensive:

Nick: Well, they're probably just trying to stop you from taking your campaign any further.

Charles: It's hardly a campaign!

At the start of the interview, it seemed that Charles might be a difficult client; Nick handled this well, and gained Charles's confidence early on.

Reading 4: Letter threatening legal action

29 Allow about two minutes for students to read the text and answer the two questions. When they have finished, allow them to discuss their answers with a partner and then go through the answers with the class.

⏩ **Answers**
1 *Defamatory* describes a statement or action that injures a person's or a company's reputation.
2 He must sign a retraction by a given date.

✏ **Language notes**
○ A *posting* is a contribution to an online forum / discussion group.
○ A comment/action/posting is *defamatory* /dɪˈfæmətri/ if it is untrue and damages another's reputation. It is *slanderous* /ˈslɑːndərəs/ if the defamation takes place orally and *libellous* /ˈlaɪbələs/ if it is done in writing. (See Exercise 32.)
○ If you *harass* /həˈræs/ somebody, you continually contact them (which may include threats, verbal abuse, lewd comments, etc.), in a way which they clearly find annoying. In the letter, the lawyers use *harass* in a looser sense of *speak to and irritate*.

30 Students should read the letter again and discuss this question with a partner, and then feed back to the class.

⏩ **Answers**
○ Charles went straight to the front of a queue of shoppers.
○ Charles demanded a refund immediately (and not a replacement).
○ Charles dropped a bag containing the computer onto the cash desk.
○ Charles shouted (*allegedly* defamatory) statements as he left the shop.
○ Charles was carrying a second bag from one of Carmecom's competitors. NB: The implication here is that Charles bought the same laptop at a different shop for less money – which is the real reason that he wanted his money back for the computer he bought at Carmecom.

○ Carmecom have lost business due to Charles's actions (during the interview, this is what Charles said he wanted).

Optional extension
The letter in Reading 4 is a good model which students could use if they ever have to threaten legal action. Therefore it is worth spending a few minutes analysing it for useful language.

1 First, tell students to work in pairs to work out the function of each of the six paragraphs, and then feed back to the class. (**Suggested answer**: Paragraph 1: introduction to client and incident; Paragraph 2: background events leading up to alleged tort; Paragraphs 3 and 4: alleged tort; Paragraph 5: evidence of alleged tort; Paragraph 6: consequences of alleged tort, threat of legal action, presentation of alternative to legal action; Paragraph 7: polite close.)
2 Then elicit from the class what techniques the lawyer uses in the second, third and fourth paragraphs to suggest that Charles was solely responsible for the dispute. (**Suggested answers**: Almost all sentences in these paragraphs have *you* as the subject. The verbs connected with *you* tend to refer to excessively dramatic actions: *demanded, dropped, shouting, harassed*. In contrast, the verbs which have the client as subject have much 'calmer' verbs: *asked, noticed*.)
3 Finally, tell students to identify useful phrases which they could use in their own letters threatening legal action, especially phrases for distancing the lawyer from the allegations. (**Suggested answers**: *According to our client, ...; Based on what our client has learnt from ...; ... it is our understanding that ...; ... our client noticed that ...; ... we have learnt ...; Our client believes ...*)

31 Students should work with a partner to come up with a list of around five to eight questions that Nick should ask Charles. You may elicit one from the class in order to give students an idea of what you expect. Encourage students to use a range of question types, and to follow the guidelines in Exercise 26.

After a few minutes, collect questions from each group, and write them up on the board, as they will be useful for the role-play in Exercise 33. Pay particular attention to the correct formation of questions.

SB p.37 Key terms 2: Defamation

32 Students should work alone to complete the exercise. Allow them to check with a partner before going through the answers with the class. As a follow-up, elicit whether there is a similar distinction in their jurisdictions between oral and written defamation.

Answers
1 tort 2 statement 3 Libel 4 Slander

SB p.37 Speaking 3: Lawyer–client interview

33 Tell students to read the information. Make sure they realise that the lawyer is now a fully qualified lawyer, who has taken over from the law student who conducted the first interview. Therefore, the interview should follow the procedure of an initial lawyer–client interview, as described in Exercise 26, and can cover some of the same ground as Listening 2, but also making use of the additional information from Reading 4. Point out that the client (Charles) should invent any details that are not already given, and that the lawyer could use the questions from Exercise 31.

If you have an odd number of students, the extra student in one group can be Nick, the law student. Allow at least five minutes for the interviews, as there is a lot of ground to cover. Monitor carefully, paying attention to the language and techniques from this unit. At the end, give feedback on both the strengths and weaknesses of the lawyer's performance. If there is time, students should swap roles and role-play the interview again, so that everybody has a chance to be the lawyer.

34 Students should discuss this in groups of at least four, or as a whole class, so they can compare the advice given in each of their role-plays. After a few minutes, open up the discussion to include the whole class. Focus especially on the letter that Charles's lawyer should send to Carmecom's lawyers, as this will serve as a lead-in to the writing tasks below. Elicit possible defences (i.e. arguments that Charles could use to defend himself against the allegations), and if possible, relate these to the typical defences which are available in students' jurisdictions.

Answer
As the advice given will be dependent on the true facts of the case, it is important that the lawyer finds out exactly what happened. Depending on the facts, the lawyer may advise Charles to sign the retraction to avoid further legal action. However, assuming that Charles' version of events was accurate, Charles could raise a 'justification by truth' defence to the allegations of defamation (should the case proceed to trial). Charles could then make a counter-claim in order to pursue his demands for compensation for the faulty laptop. Alternatively, Charles could simply deny the facts. However, should the case then go to court, this might be a difficult defence to prove, as he has already admitted some of the allegations.

SB p.37 Writing: Reply to a demand letter defending or denying the allegations made

35 Tell students to work in pairs to put the elements in order. You may need to check some of the words (*alleged/allegations*, *deny*). Afterwards, check the answers with the class.

Answers

d, c, a, e, b

Language notes

○ *Failing which* means 'and if you fail to do this'. For example, *You should provide a replacement computer and full apology within ten days, failing which we will commence legal proceedings immediately.*

○ If you *contend* that something is true, you argue or claim that it is true.

36 Students may write the letter in class or at home. (See section on Writing, page 8.)

Suggested answer

Dear Sirs

Re: George Hardy, Carmecom Ltd.

Alleged defamatory statements made by Mr Charles Tholthorpe

We write to advise that this matter has been referred to us. All further correspondence should be sent to the above address.

Our client denies completely the version of events presented in your letter of 5 December 2008.

We can confirm that our client requires a full refund for the price paid for the faulty laptop computer.

We look forward to receiving payment of £899 within 14 days, failing which we will take steps to issue proceedings.

Yours faithfully

The Kent Law Clinic

Optional extension

Ask students how they think Carmecom's solicitors will react to the letter, and how the case will end.

SB p.38 Language Focus

Answers

1 Word formation

verb	noun
misrepresent	misrepresentation
interfere	interference
settle	settlement
injure	injury
sue	suit
award	award
rule	rule, ruling

noun	adjective
negligence	negligent
liability	liable
intention	intentional
compensation	compensatory
procedure	procedural
reason	reasonable
appeal	appellate

2 Legal verbs

2 found for   **3** awarded   **4** appealed
5 reversed   **6** affirmed   **7** found that

3 Interview questions

Suggested answers

1 What are the facts of the case? / Could you tell me the facts of the case?

2 Did you know the trunk was broken when you received the car?

3 You couldn't close the trunk? / The trunk could not be closed? / When did you find out that the trunk was broken?

4 Where were you standing? / How did you try to close the trunk? / What did your friend do?

5 Did you see the car coming? / What happened next?

4) Criminal law

Teacher's brief

Most lawyers and law students who need English use it to deal with corporate clients, which is why legal English tends to focus on company and contract law rather than criminal law. Criminals and their victims tend to use the language of the country where the crime took place, and so don't need a lingua franca such as English. However, criminal lawyers also increasingly need a good command of English, either to deal with international clients accused of crimes, or simply to communicate with international colleagues. They may also need to deal with international treaties in criminal law and procedure, as well as international terrorism and other cross-border organised crime.

Reading 1 deals with some of the differences in concepts and terminology between criminal law and civil law. For example, in civil-law cases, a **claimant** brings a **suit** against a **defendant**, who may be found **liable** on the **balance of probabilities**. In criminal law, a **prosecutor**, acting on behalf of a government, brings an **action** against the **accused**, who may be found **guilty** if the crime is **proved beyond reasonable doubt**.

There is a further important contrast between **crimes** (**criminal wrongs**) and **torts** (**civil wrongs**), as explained in Exercise 6. One key difference is that most crimes require **criminal intent** (mens rea – a desire by the criminal to do harm), but this is not essential for a tort to be committed.

The unit starts by listing a wide range of **crimes**, some extremely well known (such as theft and murder) and others less well known (such as larceny and embezzlement). This is not a definitive list, but provides a good range. Crimes can be categorised in many ways (e.g. **serious crimes**, known in the USA as **felonies**, contrast with **minor** or **petty crimes**, known in the USA as **misdemeanors**).

Another important contrast is between **street crimes** and **white-collar crimes**. Street crime refers to the most visible and common crimes which occur in public places, such as mugging, vandalism, pick-pocketing, etc. White-collar crime, on the other hand, is much less visible in terms of the damage caused. This loose term covers crimes committed by people of high status (e.g. senior businesspeople) in the course of their work, and includes many types of fraud, bribery, computer crime, embezzlement, etc. This unit focuses especially on white-collar crime, as this tends to be more relevant to international business (and therefore English-speaking lawyers). Listening 1 is an extract from an authentic interview with an expert in white-collar crime, who claims that white-collar is in some ways more serious than violent crime.

Reading 2 focuses on one type of white-collar crime: **insider dealing**. This is when an employee or other person who has inside knowledge of a company's financial situation and plans uses that knowledge to give himself/herself an unfair advantage when trading in that company's shares. For example, an accountant knows that his company is about to make a takeover bid for another company, and that this will push up the target company's share price. He buys shares in that company (or instructs or advises someone else to buy the shares) before the takeover is announced, when the price is still low, and then sells those shares after the announcement, when the price has risen. Such a crime may appear victimless, but it damages the whole financial system by undermining trust.

The second half of the unit focuses on another type of white-collar crime: **identity theft**. This typically involves a criminal using another person's personal data to obtain a loan. When the loan is not repaid, the victim of the identity theft may be held responsible for repaying the loan. Other types of identity theft examined in Listenings 2 and 3 include: **changing addresses** (in order for bank statements, etc. to be sent to a false address, to prevent a victim from noticing problems with his/her account); **phishing** (sending false letters and emails claiming to be from the victim's bank, in order to trick the victim into providing confidential information); **theft** (e.g. stealing laptops containing personal data); and **bin raiding** (when a criminal hunts for useful data which the victim has thrown away).

The unit includes language work on a range of grammar and functional areas which are useful for discussing crime: **passive voice** (e.g. *he was acquitted*), talking about **cause and effect** (e.g. *White-collar crimes affect millions of people*), giving **advice** (e.g. *You should review your credit reports carefully*) and expressing **obligation** (e.g. *You must be vigilant*).

Further information

○ For a long and useful **list of crimes**, see http://criminal.findlaw.com/crimes/a-z/.

○ There are many excellent sites with information on **white-collar crimes**, such as http://www.whitecollarcrimefyi.com/index.html, http://www.whitecollarcrimeinfocenter.com/index.php and http://www.fbi.gov/libref/factsfigure/wcc.htm.

○ See http://en.wikipedia.org/wiki/Insider_trading for a good introduction to **insider trading**.

○ The Identity Theft Resource Center (http://www.idtheftcenter.org/) has lots of good information on **ID theft**, as does Wikipedia (http://en.wikipedia.org/wiki/Identity_theft).

THE STUDY OF LAW

Discuss these questions with the group.

○ Do lawyers in your country need English more for civil law or criminal law? Why? [**Suggested answer**: In most cases, it is likely that English is needed more for civil law than criminal law. Globalisation has meant that many civil lawyers have to deal with multinational clients in English, or advise local clients which are doing business internationally. But criminals and their victims tend to be in their own country, so are less likely to need to speak English to communicate with their lawyers or in court.]

○ Why might a lawyer in your country need English for criminal law? Think of examples. [**Suggested answer**: Most obviously to represent a foreigner (e.g. a victim of a crime or someone accused of a crime). They may also need to support a person from their own country who is involved in a criminal case abroad (as victim, defendant, witness, etc.). Corporate lawyers in multinational companies may also work on cases involving white-collar crime.]

○ What sorts of crimes and criminals do lawyers in your country deal with in English? [**Suggested answer**: They may well deal in English mostly with white-collar crimes involving businesses, rather than street crimes involving individuals.]

(SB p.39) Lead-in

1 Elicit from the class a definition of the terms *crime* and *offence*, then tell students to compare their definitions with the one in the SB. Point out that *offence* (US: *offense*) is often used as a synonym for crime, but also has a second meaning (= irritation caused by rudeness: *Sorry if that sounded rude. I hope I didn't cause any offence*). Check that students understand the difference between *acts* (= things done) and *omissions* (= things not done, but which should be done) and elicit examples of possible crimes involving omission (e.g. omitting to tell the police a vital piece of information, failing to reveal important evidence, or failing to exercise care when doing something dangerous).

Tell students to look through the list of crimes, choose four that they know, and define each one for a partner to identify. Encourage students to correct their partners if they think a definition is wrong.

Students should then discuss with their partner any crimes that they don't know, or aren't sure of. When they have finished, go through the list with the class, paying attention to less well-known crimes such as *larceny*, *embezzlement* and *stalking*.

✎ Language notes

All the crimes are defined briefly in Photocopiable worksheet 4.1 (see answers below), although inevitably the definitions have been simplified to fit on the worksheet. For full definitions and excellent explanations of most of the crimes listed, see http://dictionary.law.com/.

○ *Theft* and *larceny* are often treated as synonyms, but there are differences in usage. *Theft* is the more general word and is an element of a range of crimes such as shoplifting, burglary, robbery and pick-pocketing. For instance, robbery requires some violence against a person plus theft; burglary requires housebreaking plus the intent to commit some other crime, but not necessarily theft. *Larceny* is mostly used in the USA, and is often used with a more restricted meaning which excludes these additional aspects. See http://en.wikipedia.org/wiki/Larceny.

○ *Homicide* is a general term for causing a person's death by the act or omission of another person. It includes crimes such as murder, manslaughter (killing without intent) and suicide, as well as acts which are not crimes, such as causing death by misadventure (accidents) and execution by a state.

○ *Extortion* involves threats to a person's property, reputation, loved ones, etc., and may take place over a long period of time (e.g. an extortioner may extract regular payments every week for years), whereas *robbery* involves more immediate threats of physical violence, and takes place as a single event. *Blackmail* is a type of extortion involving threats to reveal information. The crime of *kidnapping* often includes an element of extortion.

○ *Assault* (attempting to harm somebody) and *battery* (actually harming a person) are often treated together as a single crime (called *assault and battery*). Both can be criminal wrongs (crimes) as well as civil wrongs (torts). See http:// dictionary.law.com/.

Pronunciation notes
embezzlement /emˈbezlmənt/
fraud /frɔːd/
homicide /ˈhɒmɪsaɪd/
larceny /ˈlɑːsəni/
manslaughter /ˈmænslɔːtə(r)/
money laundering /ˈmʌni ˌlɔːndrɪŋ/
stalking /ˈstɔːkɪŋ/

**Optional extension
(Photocopiable worksheet 4.1)**
This contains definitions for all the crimes listed in Exercise 1.

1 Photocopy and cut up enough copies of the worksheet for students to work in groups of three to five. You could also make more copies, not cut up, for students to keep as a permanent record.
2 Give each group a set of cut-up slips and tell them to race the other groups to match all the crimes with the definitions.
3 Encourage them to match the easy ones first and then try to work out the difficult ones by a process of elimination.
4 The first team to finish is the winner. When you check the answers with the class, pay attention to any problems, including difficult words in the definitions.
5 As a follow-up, get students to test each other by reading a definition to elicit a crime (or vice versa).

Answers
1 w **2** m **3** b **4** u **5** j **6** h **7** aa **8** c
9 p **10** s **11** o **12** e **13** f **14** n **15** y
16 r **17** v **18** a **19** x **20** d **21** g **22** z
23 t **24** q **25** k **26** i **27** l

2 Check if any students know what the term *white-collar crime* means, and then tell students to read the exercise to check. Go through the list with the class to identify the white-collar crimes.

Answers
embezzlement, fraud, insider dealing, money laundering, tax evasion

Language note
Traditionally, a company's or country's workforce is divided into *blue-collar workers* (who typically do manual work such as operating or repairing machines, are paid weekly wages, and wear a uniform, often blue) and *white-collar workers* (who typically do administrative or managerial work in an office, are paid monthly salaries, and wear a suit, often with a white shirt). Crimes committed by these salaried professionals during their work are therefore called *white-collar crimes*.

SB p.39
Reading 1: Criminal law

3 Tell students to discuss the four questions quickly with a partner to predict the answers. Then tell them to scan the text to answer the questions. Allow them to check their answers with a partner before checking with the whole class.

Answers
1 The state initiates a criminal case, while the victim brings the suit in a civil case.
2 Offences against the person, offences against property, public-order crimes, and business (or corporate) crimes.
3 In criminal cases, the burden of proof is often on the prosecutor to persuade the trier that the accused is guilty beyond a reasonable doubt of every fact of the crime charged. If the prosecutor fails to prove this, a verdict of 'not guilty' is rendered. In civil cases, the claimant generally needs to show a defendant is liable on the balance of probabilities.
4 A felony is a more serious offence, and a misdemeanour is a less serious offence.

Language notes
○ For most purposes, *criminal law* and *penal law* /ˈpiːnəl ˌlɔː/ can be treated as synonymous, but there are subtle differences. *Penal* refers to any action

which punishes wrongdoing, so could include punitive damages, for example. An important collocation is *penal code*, which details laws on crime and punishment in civil-law jurisdictions. For this reason, the term *penal law* is more likely to be used in civil-law jurisdictions; in common-law jurisdictions, the term *criminal law* is far more widely used.

○ If you *bring a suit*, you initiate a lawsuit against another party in a civil case.

○ *Corporal punishment* involves inflicting bodily pain or suffering as a deterrent.

○ *Imprisonment* and *incarceration* are near synonyms, but while imprisonment refers only to serving a sentence in prison after conviction, incarceration is used more generally for loss of liberty (e.g. being held in police custody while awaiting trial, or involuntary hospitalisation for mental health reasons).

○ A *suspended sentence* is one which only has to be served if certain conditions, as decided by the judge, are met (e.g. if the offender commits a further crime or fails to make restitution to the person harmed).

○ *Parole*, *probation* and *community service order* are explained in Exercise 12.

○ A *trier* /ˈtraɪə(r)/ is simply the person (judge) or group of people (e.g. a panel of judges or a jury) who *try* a defendant (i.e. to decide if the defendant is guilty or not).

Pronunciation notes
actus reus /ˈæktʌs ˌreɪʌs/
felony /ˈfeləni/
mens rea /ˈmenz ˌreɪə/
misdemeanour /ˌmɪsdəˈmiːnə(r)/

4 Tell students to work alone to match the verbs with the nouns, and then check the answers with the class.

Answers
1 d **2** f **3** a **4** c **5** b **6** e

5 Get students to work in pairs to discuss which of the people listed carries out the six actions. Go through the answers with the class.

Answers
An offender commits a crime.
A victim brings a suit.
A lawyer resolves a dispute, brings a suit, (commits a crime).
The court resolves a dispute, renders a verdict, sentences an offender, suspends a sentence.
A judge resolves a dispute, renders a verdict, sentences an offender, suspends a sentence.

Optional extension
Check students have fully understood Reading 1 by having a comprehension quiz (see section on Games and activities, page 9).

1 Which form of punishment involves inflicting bodily pain or suffering on the offender? [corporal punishment: paragraph 2]

2 What sort of crime is prostitution? [a public-order crime: paragraph 3]

3 Which form of punishment involves killing the offender? [execution, also called capital punishment: paragraph 2]

4 What example is given of an incident which led to both a criminal prosecution and a tort? [the OJ Simpson case: paragraph 6]

5 What are the two elements which characterise most crimes? [a criminal act (actus reus) and criminal intent (mens rea): paragraph 4]

6 What word in the text means 'prohibit'? [proscribe: paragraph 3]

7 What is another name for criminal law? [penal law: paragraph 1]

8 What is the name for less serious crimes, such as petty theft? [misdemeanours: paragraph 6]

9 What two types of trier are given in the text? [judge and jury: paragraph 5]

10 What example is given in the text of an offence against property? [burglary: paragraph 3]

11 What is the name for more serious crimes, such as rape? [felonies: paragraph 6]

12 Who brings a suit in a civil case? [the victim: paragraph 1]

13 What, in percentage terms, does 'the balance of probabilities' mean? [more than 50% probable: paragraph 5]

14 What sort of crime is insider dealing? [a business/corporate crime, also known as a white-collar crime: paragraph 3]

15 Who brings a prosecution in a criminal case? [the state / a prosecutor: paragraph 1]

16 What is the balance of probabilities called in the USA? [preponderance of the evidence: paragraph 5]

17 What two examples are given of strict liability crimes? [statutory rape and some traffic offences: paragraph 4]

18 What two terms are used to refer to the need for the prosecutor to prove guilt beyond reasonable doubt? [burden of proof and standard of proof: paragraph 5]

19 What are two names for loss of liberty? [imprisonment and incarceration: paragraph 2]

20 What example is given in the text of an offence against the person? [assault: paragraph 3]

6 With the class, discuss the difference between a crime and a tort. Note that the question is answered fully in the text in Exercise 7. Discuss what students know about the OJ Simpson case, but avoid discussing it at length, as this will be the focus of Exercise 11.

Answer
A crime is a wrong committed against society and requires criminal intent; a tort is a wrong committed against an individual and does not require criminal intent.

7 Before you ask students to complete the extract, check that they understand all the words in the box. Point out that several (*is brought*, *is committed*) were used in the collocations exercise (Exercise 4). Check that students understand that *try* has a special meaning in criminal law, connected with *trials* (i.e. attempting to establish whether a defendant is guilty or not). Then tell students to work alone to put the verbs into the gaps. When you check the answers with the class, discuss whether the definitions of crime and tort are similar to the ideas they came up with in Exercise 6.

Answers
1 is committed   **2** is punished   **3** is put
4 is fined   **5** is committed   **6** was caused
7 are tried   **8** is brought   **9** is resolved

Language notes
- The answers to gaps 3 and 4 are *he or she **is put** in prison* or ***is fined***, but it would be more natural to avoid repeating the second *is*: *he or she **is put** in prison or **fined***. This elision of repeated words is very common (and also explains why *he or she* is also not repeated), but is only possible after co-ordinating conjunctions (*and*, *or* and *but*). There is another example of this in Exercise 11: *Simpson **was found** liable … and **sentenced** to pay …*, where *was* does not need to be repeated.
- A *wrongdoer* /ˈrɒŋduːə(r)/ is a person who does wrong, in this case by committing a crime or a tort.
- The phrase *without intent to do harm on the wrongdoer's part* means that the wrongdoer does not intend to do harm. The construction *on somebody's part* (or *on the part of somebody*) is a useful alternative to passive constructions with *by*.

8 Tell students to work in small groups to discuss how the crime/tort distinction works in their jurisdiction(s). Encourage them to consider all the points in Exercise 7. Afterwards, get one student from each group to present the results of their discussions to the class.

Optional extension
Before the discussion, tell students to find in the text (Exercise 7) three ways of talking about contrasts:

- *A tort, **on the other hand**, is a wrong which is …*
- ***A key difference between the two is that** a crime …, **whereas** a tort …*
- *A tort, **conversely**, is resolved in the …*

Elicit more ways of making contrasts (e.g. ***While** a crime is X, a tort is Y; **Unlike** a crime, a tort involves Z*) and write these on the board. Point out that the easiest way of making contrasts (*Crime involves X*, **but** *tort involves Y*) is not wrong, but also not very professional, especially if this structure is overused. Then encourage students to use the phrases in their discussion.

SB p.41 Language use 1: Passive constructions

9 Discuss the questions together with the class.

> **Answer**
> The passive voice is used to focus on the action, not on the person doing it. The agent is named in ... *the harm which is caused* **by the wrongdoer** and *An action is brought* **by a governmental body** ...

> **Language note**
> There are two contrasting reasons for using the passive:
>
> **1** To avoid mentioning the agent (the doer of the action) because the agent is unknown, unimportant, etc. (e.g. *The victim was assaulted* [the agent is unknown]; *Crimes are tried in criminal courts* [the agent is less important than the place]; *A tort is a wrong which was committed against an individual* [the agent is unimportant]). The passive is used for this reason in many languages.
>
> **2** To put special emphasis on the agent by placing it towards the end of the sentence (e.g. *The money was stolen by the company's CEO* [more emphatic than *The company's CEO stole the money*]). Similarly, the passive is used to maintain cohesion through a text, with old information (the topic) placed at the beginning of sentences and new information towards the end. This reason is less commonly used in some other languages, especially in those which have a flexible word order (i.e. languages which allow a subject to be placed at the end of a sentence with no change to the verb), and presents more problems for learners of English who speak such languages.

Both of these reasons for using passive constructions are connected with more formal language, where we tend to talk about more abstract concepts, so non-human subjects can be used as sentence topics (e.g. **Considerable harm** *was caused by the wrongdoer*) and impersonal, general statements can be made by avoiding human agents altogether.

The most problematic features of the passive in English are its use with indirect objects and prepositional objects:

- ○ *She killed* **him**. (*him* = direct object) → **He** *was killed*.
- ○ *The judge gave* **her** *a suspended sentence*. (*her* = indirect object) → **She** *was given a suspended sentence*.
- ○ *She broke into* **the shop**. (*the shop* = prepositional object) → **The shop** *was broken into*.

Many languages make the passive from direct objects (as in the first example), but very few do so with indirect or prepositional objects, so many students find such sentences difficult to understand.

10 Tell students to complete the rules alone and then check in pairs. Go through the answers with the class, and write the two parts of passive constructions on the board: *be* (in whatever tense is necessary) + V3 (the past participle).

> **Answers**
> **1** *(to) be*   **2** past participle (also known as the third form of a verb, or V3)   **3** *by*

11 Tell students to complete the exercise alone. Check that students can form the past simple passive (*was/were* + V3). When they have finished, check the answers with the class, paying attention to the meaning of the verbs. Note that there is further practice of the passive in the Language Focus on page 49 of the SB, and in Photocopiable worksheet 4.2, which should be used after Listening 3.

> **Answers**
> **1** was charged   **2** was tried; was acquitted
> **3** was found; was sentenced

Language notes

- If somebody is *charged with* a crime, they are formally accused of it.
- If somebody is *acquitted of* a crime, they are found not guilty.
- Note the contrast between being found *guilty* in criminal cases and being found *liable* in civil cases.

Optional extension

Write the five verbs from the exercise on the board (in the infinitive). Tell students to close their books and then retell the OJ Simpson story to a partner, using the verbs to help them remember, but making sure to use passive.

Key terms 1: Punishments
SB p.42

12 Elicit from the class as many types of punishment as they can think of, perhaps using the list of crimes from the lead-in on page 39 as inspiration. Then students should work alone to try to match the punishments with the explanations. Allow them to check with a partner before discussing the answers with the class. As you go through the answers, elicit some examples of crimes for which these punishments might be suitable. This could provoke some good discussion, although a discussion on capital punishment (execution) could get too heated, so should be treated with caution. Finally, elicit from the class why the passive is used in the examples.

Answers

1 d **2** f **3** a **4** e **5** b **6** c

The passive is used in these examples because the action which can be taken in each case – the punishment given to an offender – is the focal point of the sentence, rather than the agent (in this case, the courts) who takes the action.

13 Students should discuss the questions with a partner, focusing on advantages and disadvantages of each type of punishment. After a few minutes, open up the discussion to include the whole class.

Listening 1: White-collar crime in the 21st century
SB p.42 · 4.1

Tell students to read the introduction to find out who they are going to be listening to. Then discuss briefly with the class what a university course in white-collar crime might involve.

14 Discuss the question with the class, and elicit ways in which white-collar crime might be more serious and less serious than violent street crime. Avoid providing the answers, as these will come out of the listening. Then play the recording. Allow students to discuss the answer in pairs before checking with the class.

Answer

He thinks it is as serious as violent street crime.

Transcript » STUDENT'S BOOK **page 127**

Background notes

- Professor Poulos mentions that *more white-collar crime is being committed within corporations*. Not all white-collar crime involves corporations (e.g. much computer crime is committed by individuals or gangs), and often individuals commit white-collar crimes without their corporations' knowledge (e.g. insider trading by an individual employee). But Professor Poulos's point is that it is becoming more common for large corporations to engage in (or tacitly approve of) illegal activity (e.g. the Enron scandal – see below).
- Professor Poulos mentions that the (US) *federal government changed the sentencing of white-collar criminals*. This followed various high-profile cases of white-collar crime (e.g. the Enron scandal) and were granted by Congress by the Sarbanes-Oxley Act 2002. For example, see http://www.ussc.gov/PRESS/rel010803.htm.
- A *savings and loan scandal* is a scandal involving a savings and loan association (S&L) (a type of US financial institution similar to UK building societies). In the 1980s and 1990s, many of these S&Ls failed, resulting in huge financial losses for those who had savings with them.

See http://en.wikipedia.org/wiki/ Savings_and_Loan_crisis.

○ The *Enron scandal* was revealed in 2001. Enron, one of America's most successful companies, had been involved in accounting irregularities, and the case highlighted the need for more regulation in the financial markets, especially as the scandal also brought down Arthur Andersen, Enron's accountant. See http://en.wikipedia. org/wiki/Enron_scandal.

Language notes

○ *Corporate malfeasance* /ˈkɔːpərət mælˈfiːzəns/ means 'corporate crime'. *Malfeasance* is a term in legal English for deliberately doing something which is legally or morally wrong. It contrasts with *misfeasance* /ˈmɪsfiːzəns/, which involves doing a lawful act improperly (e.g. by mistake or accident). See http://dictionary.law.com.

○ A *heinous* /ˈhiːnəs/ crime is one that is shockingly brutal or cruel.

○ A *scam* is a plan to make money illegally or by tricking people.

15 Tell students to read the five true/false questions to check they understand. You may need to check some vocabulary (*harshly* = severely; *employees high up in the corporate hierarchy* /ˈhaɪərɑːkɪ/ = senior managers; *significant* = big, important). Then play the recording again for them to answer the questions. Allow them to discuss their ideas with a partner before going through the answers with the class.

Answers

1 F (Professor Poulos says 'I do think that with the growth of technology ... the opportunities for white-collar crime have increased greatly'.)

2 F (Professor Poulos says 'Before the federal government changed the sentencing of white-collar criminals, the very strict punishments [...] for [...] street crime drove many people [...] to white-collar crime because it gave them more rewards for less risk.' [i.e. the situation is now different]

3 T
4 T
5 F (Professor Poulos says 'Part of the slow recovery of the economy is the effect of white-collar crime on the investment environment'.)

Language use 2: Talking about cause and effect
SB p.43

16 Elicit from the class the causes of the increase in white-collar crime, according to Professor Poulos [**Answer**: the growth of technology, the internationalisation of the economy and perceived light sentencing] and the effects [**Answer**: suffering by the many victims who have lost money and the slow growth of the economy]. Then tell students to read through the six sentences and see if they can remember/predict what the missing words are. Point out to students that each gap needs between one and five words. Finally, play the recording for students to check their predictions. Go through the answers with the class by asking them to read out the complete sentences.

Answers
1 has led to **2** has a big impact on
3 affect **4** impacted **5** adversely affect
6 is the effect of

Language notes

The phrases for cause and effect are simple but may still cause a few problems.

○ Students often make mistakes with the spelling of the irregular verb *lead–led–led*.

○ Students often confuse *effect* (noun) with *affect* (verb), which are pronounced identically (/əˈfekt/) in many accents. To add to the confusion, there is a verb *to effect* (as in the collocation *to effect changes* = to make changes happen), but this is much less common than the normal uses of *effect* and *affect*.

○ *Impact* is normally used as a noun (an *impact*), but as the example shows, it can also be used as a verb, with identical pronunciation to the noun (/ˈɪmpækt/).

17 Students should match the two halves of the sentences alone, and then check with a partner before you check with the whole class. You may need to check the phrase *adversely affects* (= has a negative effect on).

Answers
1 e   2 c   3 d   4 a   5 b

(SB p.43) Speaking 1: White-collar crime

18 Have students discuss the three questions in small groups and then open up the discussion to include the whole class. Encourage students to use as many of the expressions for cause and effect as possible.

(SB p.43) Reading 2: White-collar crime: insider dealing and market abuse

Ask the class:

a what they understand by the term *insider trading* (or *insider dealing*), and if there are any famous cases they are aware of;

b what has been done to prevent it.

Answers
a The act of trading in securities by people who have confidential information about a company's finances or operations.
b The introduction mentions one preventative measure (the adoption of the Financial Services and Markets Act), but there have been many similar efforts.

Then tell students to read the introduction on page 43 to compare it with their ideas. Elicit also why it is important to prevent insider dealing [**Suggested answer**: to prevent abuse and increase confidence in the financial system].

19 Tell students to read the questions first to check they understand all the words, and then to read the text quickly to find the answers. Set a short time limit (about two minutes), after which get students to discuss the questions with a partner. Go through the answers with the class. Avoid explaining vocabulary at this stage.

Answers
1 audit manager   2 market abuse
3 He knew that the company was planning to sell its electrical division.
4 He made a profit of £3,750.

Background notes
○ The *Financial Services Authority* (FSA) is the independent regulator of the UK's financial services industry. See http://www.fsa.gov.uk/pages/About/What/index.shtml.
○ The *Financial Services and Markets Tribunal* is an independent tribunal which reviews decisions made by the FSA. See http://www.fsa.gov.uk/pages/doing/regulated/law/focus/tribunal.shtml.
○ The *Financial Services and Markets Act 2000* (FSMA) transferred many new powers from other bodies to the FSA. See http://www.fsa.gov.uk/Pages/About/Who/History/index.shtml.

20 Tell students to complete the exercise in pairs, then discuss the answers with the class.

Answers
1 F The case was heard before the Financial Services and Markets Tribunal.
2 F Mr Mohammed was sentenced to pay a fine for his crime.
3 F The defendant was partially responsible for the audit of the company.
4 T

21 Students should complete the exercise alone. When you check the answers with the class, discuss any further problems with vocabulary and interesting/useful words.

Answers
1 confidential   2 purchase   3 proposed
4 held   5 provisions

22 Discuss this with the whole class. Of course, this question has engaged lawmakers (and criminals) for years, so your students are unlikely to come up with a fool-proof system, but it could be an interesting exercise to try to come up with solutions and then try to find ways criminals could find to beat the system.

LAW IN PRACTICE

Lead-in
(SB p.45)

Elicit from the class what they understand by the term *identity theft*, and what can be done to help victims. Then tell them to read the introduction on page 45 to compare it with their ideas.

23 Students should discuss the questions in small groups and then report back to the class. Then tell them to compare their ideas with those in the definition. Check that students have understood all the words in the text (e.g. *impostor*, *scam*), but avoid explaining those that come up in Exercise 24.

Suggested answers
1 Identity theft occurs when someone uses someone else's personally identifying information, such as their name, social security number or credit-card number, without their permission, to commit fraud or other crimes.
2 Possible answers include: credit-card fraud, services (utilities) fraud, banking and financial fraud, government documents fraud (e.g. getting an official ID in the name of another person).

Background note

The *Identity Theft Resource Center* provides support to victims of ID theft and advice to governments and businesses about preventing ID theft. See http://www.idtheftcenter.org/.

Pronunciation notes

impostor /ɪmˈpɒstə(r)/   phishing /ˈfɪʃɪŋ/

Key terms 2: Identity theft
(SB p.45)

24 Tell students to work in pairs to do the matching activity. Tell them to start with the easier examples and then try to guess the more difficult examples. When they have finished, check the answers with the class.

Answers
1 f   2 a   3 d   4 e   5 c   6 b

25 Discuss the questions with the whole class.

Listening 2: Podcasts
(SB p.46)(4.2–4.9)

Elicit from the class how lawyers can learn from podcasts, and then tell students to read the introduction on page 46 to check.

26 Tell students to listen to the four podcasts to identify which type of identity theft is described in each. After listening, tell students to compare their answers in pairs, and also to discuss what they remember from each extract. Then go through the answers with the class.

Answers
1 Changing addresses   2 Phishing
3 Stealing   4 Bin raiding

Transcript » STUDENT'S BOOK page 128

27 Tell students to read the five questions to check that they understand, and to try to remember some of the answers from the extracts that they heard in Exercise 26. You may need to check the meanings of some words (e.g. *compensate*, *contributing*). Point out that as these are now longer extracts, not all the questions were answered in the extracts they heard earlier. Play the recordings for them to complete the exercise. Students should discuss their answers with a partner before feeding back to the class.

1 Criminals may ensure that bills and bank statements are sent to an address other than the victim's.
2 They must verify your identity before issuing credit to you.
3 Creating look-alike websites, often of banks and other financial institutions, and duping people into visiting them and giving out personal information.
4 On the grounds that the customer's negligence was a contributory factor.
5 Although banks generally claim they will never send emails to their customers asking for, or quoting, any confidential information about the customer, they often do just that.

Transcript » STUDENT'S BOOK page 128

✎ **Language notes**
○ If you are *vigilant*, you are very careful and alert to potential problems occurring.
○ A *fraudster* is a person who commits fraud.
○ A *credit report* is a document produced by a bank or credit rating agency summarising a person's or business's credit history (e.g. their reliability when repaying debts) and financial situation.
○ If you *dupe* somebody *into* doing something, you trick them in a way that makes them look stupid.
○ If you *con* somebody *out of* money, you use tricks to get them to give you the money.

28 Repeat the procedure used for Exercise 27. You may need to check that students understand *former*, *targeted*, *extract* (verb, /eks'trækt/), *encryption key*, *reveal*, *sort code*.

⇒ **Answers**
1 a 2 c 3 a 4 c

Transcript » STUDENT'S BOOK page 128

✎ **Language notes**
○ Your *social security number* is a unique number which identifies you when you pay social security (a type of tax) and claim social security benefits.
○ In the context of the listening, *compensation* means *earnings*.
○ A *credit reference agency* provides information on an individual's or business's credit-worthiness (i.e. the level of confidence that lenders should have that they will repay any loans). See http://en.wikipedia.org/wiki/Credit_reference_agency.
○ If you *commission* a company to do something for you, you pay them to do it on your behalf.
○ A *sort code* is a number identifying the bank and branch where your account is held, which, together with your bank account number, uniquely identifies your account. In many countries, the sort code is included in a much longer account number.

**Optional extension
(Photocopiable worksheet 4.2)**
Listening 2 contained many examples of passive voice. Photocopiable worksheet 4.2 highlights a range of these examples to illustrate the passive in context, and to test students' ability to use passive with a range of tenses. It also introduces an important use of passive in reduced relative clauses (participle clauses).

1 Hand out a copy of the worksheet to each student. Remind students of the form of passive, and to use the verb *to be* in the same tense as the paraphrase in brackets.
2 Do the first question together with the class as an example. The exercise could prove quite challenging for students who are unfamiliar with passive voice, so you will need to offer plenty of support.
3 When they have finished, play the recordings again for students to check their answers. Point out that two of the examples in the recordings are slightly different from those on the worksheet, and that you will discuss the differences after listening.
4 After listening, check the answers quickly, and elicit which four examples were different.

5 Elicit the rule: when passive voice is used in a relative clause, it is possible to omit a relative pronoun (*that/which/who*) together with a form of the verb *to be* (e.g. *Police have found the laptop ~~which was~~ stolen last week*).

Answers
1 are being told   **2** might be denied
3 must be made; are caused*   **4** being fooled   **5** is also used   **6** were told   **7** are being targeted   **8** have been affected*
9 was (*or* were) encrypted   **10** could be linked   **11** has been recognised

* In the recordings, the relative pronoun and verb *to be* are omitted in sentences 3 (*… losses ~~which are~~ caused by …*) and 8 (*… for those ~~who have been~~ affected*).

Speaking 2: Short presentation
SB p.47

29 Tell students to read the introduction and task carefully to find out what they have to do and for whom. Ask the class if they can remember the format of presentations that was outlined in Unit 1, and then allow them to check on page 15.

You could ask students to prepare their presentations at home or in class, in which case allow them to work in small groups to prepare. It may be impossible to allow every student to give a full presentation on all four types of identity theft from Listening 2, in which case they should each present one of the four types. For larger classes, get students to present to each other in groups of around four.

Give feedback on the presentations (and elicit such feedback from other students) in terms of their format and content, not just their grammatical accuracy.

Language use 3: Giving advice and expressing obligation
SB p.47

30 Elicit from the class at least one way of giving advice and one of expressing obligation, in order to make sure students understand the sort of language you would like them to find in the audio transcripts. Then tell them to work in pairs to find as many examples of the two functions as possible. When they have finished, check the answers with the class.

Answers

Advice
If you think you may be the victim of identity theft, you should place a fraud alert on your credit report as soon as possible.
You should then review your credit reports carefully.

Obligation
… members of the public are … being told that they must be more vigilant about discarding personal records.
… potential creditors must use what the law refers to as 'reasonable policies and procedures' …

31 Elicit from the class the difference between *must* and *have to*, and between *mustn't* and *don't have to*. Then tell them to read the information in the box to compare it with their ideas.

Do the exercise with the whole class. Make sure all students understand the difference before moving on to Exercise 32.

Answers
1 don't have to   **2** mustn't

Language notes
The information in the SB is inevitably simplified for students at this level.

○ The difference between *must* and *have to* is very subtle, and is connected with the source of the obligation. If the obligation comes from the speaker, *must* is more suitable (e.g. a company policy on data protection might state: *You must report any data losses immediately*). If the speaker is talking about an obligation imposed by another person, *have to* is more suitable (e.g. *We've got a new policy on data protection. Apparently we have to report any data losses immediately*).

○ Note that *must* is very commonly used to express probability (e.g. *You must be joking = I'm sure you're joking*). Usually the meaning of *must* is clear from context, but occasionally, a sentence could be ambiguous (e.g. *You must be very careful = I'm sure you're a careful person* OR *It's necessary to be careful*). In such cases, *have to* is preferred.

○ The difference between *mustn't* and *don't have to* is much less problematic: *mustn't* expresses an obligation not to do something (e.g. *You mustn't take sensitive data out of the building*), while *don't have to* expresses a lack of obligation (e.g. *Banks don't have to compensate victims of phishing, but they usually do because it is good for public relations*). Note that, like *must*, *mustn't* expresses an obligation from the speaker. When an obligation not to do something is expressed by a speaker other than the obligor, *be + not allowed to* is often used (e.g. *According to our new policy, we're not allowed to take sensitive data out of the building*).

○ A similar distinction exists between *should/ shouldn't* (speaker = adviser) and *(not) be + supposed to* (speaker ≠ adviser). This is summarised below:

	From speaker	**Not from speaker**
Obligation to do	must	have to
Obligation not to do	mustn't	be + not allowed to
Lack of obligation	don't have to	
Advice to do	should	be + supposed to
Advice not to do	shouldn't	be + not supposed to

32 Tell students to try the exercise alone, and then check with a partner. You may need to check that students understand the beginning of sentences 1 (*If you want to register ...*) and 2 (*People who are convicted ...*).

▶ **Answers**
Note: these are the most likely answers, although others may be possible, depending on the context.
1 must / have to (obligation)
2 must / have to (obligation)

3 should (advice)
4 must / have to (obligation)
5 should (advice)
6 have to (obligation)

(SB p.48) Speaking 3: Role-play: advising a client

33 Tell students to read the instructions but not the four situations yet. Elicit what the WASP technique is for and how it works, and then refer them back to page 35 to check. Make sure students realise that when they play the role of the client, they should avoid giving all their information at the beginning, to give their partner a chance to use the WASP technique.

Divide the class into pairs. If you have an odd number of students, the extra student in a group of three should be a senior lawyer supporting the less-experienced lawyer who is dealing with the client. If you have only one student, you should play the client in all four situations.

Tell students to read the four situations to make sure they understand all the words (e.g. *forwarded, threatening, outstanding, personnel, comprehensive*). It is important to check understanding before the role-plays start in order to avoid having to stop and start the role-plays later.

Tell students to start the role-plays, and to move to the second when they finish the first, and so on, without waiting for you to tell them. They should spend a few minutes on each. Make sure they know to use language for advice and obligation during their role-plays. After about ten minutes, or when the first pairs have finished, bring the exercise to a close. Give feedback on successful and unsuccessful language you heard, paying particular attention to the language of advice and obligation. Feed back also on the success of the client interviews in terms of the WASP technique. Finally, discuss with the whole class the four situations, and ask whether any of the students has experience of similar situations.

(SB p.48) Writing: Letter of advice

34 The writing can be done at home or in class. (See section on Writing, page 8.)

Language Focus

Answers

1 Prepositions

1 for **2** of **3** against **4** of **5** to **6** on
7 on **8** on

2 Words easily confused

1 **a** prove **b** proof (prove)
2 **a** prosecution **b** persecution (prosecution)
3 **a** prescribe **b** proscribe (prescribe)

3 Passive constructions

1 The co-conspirators were found guilty on several counts, most notably fraud and conspiracy.

2 Employees, consumers and citizens alike are affected by white-collar crime.

3 The former CEO was sentenced to 87 months in federal prison for his role in arranging fraudulent loans that led to the company's forced bankruptcy.

4 If the prosecutor fails to prove that the accused is guilty beyond a reasonable doubt, a verdict of 'not guilty' is rendered.

5 The company founder was prosecuted for tax evasion, and he is now serving a three-year sentence.

6 The prisoner was put on parole after four years of good conduct in prison.

7 The defendant was given a suspended sentence for the theft of his sister's car while intoxicated.

5 Company law

Types of company vary in their specific details from one jurisdiction to another, which can create problems for lawyers and their foreign clients in terms of mutual understanding of business concepts. However, the general breakdown of businesses into **companies**, **partnerships** and **sole proprietorships** is very widely used. In simple terms, a **sole proprietor** is a person who works by himself, for himself (or herself). The person is the same as the business, so any successes or crises for the business will directly affect the person. A classic example of a sole proprietor is a plumber. If the plumber's business grows, he has two main options: he could join up with another plumber to form a **partnership** (in order, for example, to share marketing, accountancy or raw-materials costs). In such a partnership, the partners are still essentially the same as the company. If one of the partners dies or retires, the partnership will cease to exist. In many countries, **law firms** are required to be sole proprietorships or partnerships. The logic behind this requirement is that a lawyer should be personally responsible for representing a client, and might not give such impartial advice if he/she were protected within a company.

The second option available to the plumber, initially more bureaucratic, would be to **incorporate as a company**. In this case, the business would take on a life of its own (indeed, it is known as a **legal person** – a person in the eyes of the law). The plumber is now simply the owner of the business, and not the business itself, so he can sell all or part of it. Crucially, he is no longer personally **liable** for the company's problems. Liability means an obligation to make restitution or pay debts. If something goes wrong, the person liable may be sued. In a sole proprietorship or partnership, it is the people who are sued; in a company, it is the legal person (i.e. the company itself) which is sued. The owners can lose no more than their investments. In other words, they have **limited liability**.

Within the sphere of companies, many jurisdictions distinguish between those whose shares are **traded publicly** (i.e. on a stock market) and those which are **traded privately**, if at all (as in the example of the plumber's small company). In the UK, the abbreviation **plc** is used for a public limited company, and **Ltd** is used for private limited companies. In the USA, the main distinction is between **C corporations** (which pay corporate taxes and tend to be larger) and **S corporations** (which are taxed through their owners and tend to be smaller).

The second part of the unit deals with a new area of company law in the UK, arising out of the **Companies Act 2006**. According to this Act, companies are explicitly required to **act in the best interests of their owners** (and not, for example, in the interests of individual directors), and to consider, when doing so, the impact of their actions on the local community, the environment, their employees, etc. Information on how they have complied with these requirements must be included in a **report to shareholders**. This Act has made it more difficult for companies to conceal their less attractive business practices, as such disclosures could damage their reputation and lead to a reduction in the value of the company (and may lead shareholders to try to change things). Inevitably, some people have complained that the Act imposes unreasonable restrictions on their ability to do business, while others complain that the Act doesn't go far enough to ensure **corporate responsibility**.

Reading 3 illustrates one example of a company coming to terms with the requirements of the Act, and focuses on the interaction between **lawyers and public relations**: the need not just to act within the law, but to use the law to manage customers' perceptions of the company.

Further information
- There is a useful text in this course's sister book *International Legal English*, page 223, which deals with the origins of **law partnerships** and some issues connected with their recent growth.
- For descriptions of **types of company** in many countries, see http://www.corporateinformation.com/defext.asp.
- For full, authentic samples of a wide range of **legal documents**, including the constitutional documents mentioned in this unit, see http://contracts.onecle.com/type/index.shtml.
- For more information on the **Companies Act 2006**, follow the links provided on page 76 of this book.

THE STUDY OF LAW

Lead-in
SB p.50

Elicit from the class what they understand by the terms *company law* and *commercial law*, and some examples of essential knowledge for commercial lawyers. Elicit also what additional knowledge commercial lawyers might need in English. Then tell them to read the introduction on page 50 to see if it mentions anything they missed. Check everyone understands the term *business entity* /ˈentɪtɪ/ (= a general name for a business, i.e. a company or a partnership or a sole proprietorship, etc.).

➤ **Suggested answers**
- ○ Company law is a branch of the much wider area of commercial law. Company law deals with the formation, operation and closing of companies. For a list of commercial law topics, see Unit 6, Reading 1.
- ○ Essential knowledge for commercial lawyers: see Reading 2 for examples.
- ○ Additional knowledge in English: awareness of types of business entity in English-speaking jurisdictions (especially the USA and UK), as well as in their international clients' jurisdictions.

1 Tell students to discuss the three questions in small groups. Make sure they realise that 'types of business entity' in the first question relates to the ways business entities may be created and organised, and to focus on the differences in terms of the different legal requirements for different types of entity. After a few minutes, open up the discussion to include the whole class. Elicit and write on the board a list of types of business entity in your students' jurisdictions. If they don't know the English translation for some, elicit how they could find out.

📖 **Background notes**
- ○ A good source of information on the English translations of different types of business entity in different countries is http://www.corporateinformation.com/defext.asp.
- ○ In the UK, the most important types of business entity are: sole proprietorship, general partnership, limited partnership, private limited company (Ltd) and public limited company (plc).
- ○ In the USA, the most important types of business entity are: sole proprietorship, general partnership, limited partnership, C corporation and S corporation. Note that C and S do not stand for anything: they simply refer to the alphabetical subchapters of the US Internal Revenue Code which deal with these types of entity.

Reading 1: Company law
SB p.50

2a Tell students to discuss the questions to predict the answers, and then read the text to find the answers. Allow enough time for students to read carefully (about three minutes) and then tell them to discuss their answers with a partner before going through them with the class.

➤ **Answers**
1 T **2** T **3** T **4** F (The memorandum of association states the principal object of a company.)

✎ **Language notes**
- ○ The term *company member* is used throughout this unit to refer to owners (shareholders) of a company.
- ○ The term *legal person* contrasts with *natural person*. A natural person is a real human being. A legal person is not a human being, but a company; however, it shares several legal characteristics with natural persons (especially the ability to sue and be sued). This relates to the term *personality* from the text: the treatment of a business entity as a legal person. A company has personality; a partnership doesn't.
- ○ The number of *shareholders* (= joint owners of the company) can vary enormously. *Private limited companies* typically have a small number of shareholders, who typically have a long-term personal relationship with the company. In *publicly traded companies*, there can be thousands of shareholders, including many who own only a tiny fraction of the company, and who may see their relationship with the company

only in terms of how much money they can get by keeping or selling their shares.

○ A company's *creditors* typically include lenders such as banks and other financial institutions, as well as suppliers who deliver first and receive payment later.

○ The text mentions that companies may be formed by *individuals, agents, attorneys or accountants*. There is no legal reason why all companies shouldn't be formed by individuals, but agents, attorneys (lawyers) and accountants often have more experience and specialised knowledge, and form companies on their clients' behalf.

○ The *objects* of a company are its purpose: what it was created in order to do.

b Students should work with a partner to come up with explanations of the differences, and then feed back to the class.

Answers

A sole proprietorship is a business that is owned by a single individual who earns all the profits and assumes all the liabilities. In the case of a partnership, these profits and liabilities are shared between the partners, who between them own the business. A publicly listed company is one which is able to sell its shares to the public and whose directors and shareholders are not personally liable for the company's losses beyond their own investments in the form of shares.

Key terms 1: Who does what in company law
(SB p.51)

3 Tell students to work in pairs to complete the exercise. When they have finished, go through the answers with the class. As a follow-up, students can test each other in pairs: one student should ask questions based on the definitions (e.g. *Who or what has rights and duties under the law just like a natural person?*) in order to elicit the key terms.

Answers
1 has   2 manages; makes   3 own; enter into; sue   4 invests   5 serves on   6 owes   7 monitor   8 owns; is

Reading 2: Course in company law
(SB p.52)

4 Elicit from the class the types of topic that they would expect to be included in a university course in company law. Then tell them to read the seven topics listed, to check a) if they are similar to the topics they mentioned, and b) that they understand all the words (e.g. *dealings, dissolving*). Then tell them to read the text carefully to identify which of the topics are mentioned in the course outline. Allow them to discuss their answers with a partner before you check with the class.

Answers
1, 3, 4, 7

Language notes
NB Many of the terms from the text are explained in Exercise 5.

○ *Incorporation* is the term for the process of forming a company (corporation).

○ *Corporate governance* refers to the processes and procedures for managing the way a company is directed, particularly in connection with its objectives and responsibility for its impact on other affected parties (stakeholders such as employees, customers, suppliers, creditors, neighbours, etc.).

○ *Corporate insolvency* is the state of being unable to pay one's debts. *Winding up* is the process of closing down a company: distributing its assets among creditors, shareholders, etc. It may occur as a result of insolvency, or may be simply the result of a desire to close the company.

○ The terms *corporate personality* and *business vehicle* should not be confused. Corporate personality refers to the existence of a company as a legal person. Business vehicle refers to the types of business entity (e.g. sole proprietorship, company, partnership). In this text, the business vehicle it refers to is the company.

○ *Corporate rights* are simply the rights that a corporation has, e.g. as a result of its contracts with other parties. The term also refers to the protections offered to corporations, similar to those offered to natural persons, justified on the basis of corporate personhood. It also includes the rights and privileges offered to corporations by the law or the state.

○ For more on the *Companies Act 2006*, see page 76.

○ A stakeholder is someone with a direct interest, investment or involvement in a business, such as a shareholder, employee, supplier or customer. A *non-affiliated stakeholder* is not directly controlled by nor joined to the business in question, so is limited to customers, suppliers and other independent people affected by the activities of the business, such as neighbours.

5 Students should work alone to complete the matching exercise, and then check with a partner before feeding back to the class. As a follow-up, students can test each other in pairs, by reading a definition to elicit the terms.

Answers
1 c 2 a 3 e 4 d 5 b 6 f

6 Write the word *corporate* in the middle of the board, and elicit from the class any collocations with it that they know/remember. Write these on the board, to create a mindmap, and encourage students to copy the mindmap into their notebooks. Point out that mindmaps can be an effective way of organising and learning vocabulary, and that they should add more collocations to the mindmap as they come across them later. Then tell them to work in small groups to read the two texts to find more examples. You may make it easier by telling them to find two collocations from Reading 1 (including the footnotes) and five collocations from Reading 2. After a few minutes, go through the answers with the class, and write the collocations on the board.

Answers
corporate law, corporate contracts, corporate personality, corporate governance, corporate rights, corporate finance, corporate insolvency

7 Tell students to discuss this question with a partner. After a few minutes, open up the discussion to include the whole class. Elicit how students could find more examples of such course outlines, and point out that such outlines are an excellent way of identifying useful vocabulary and concepts to learn.

Background note
There are thousands of such course outlines available online. Simply search for 'company law' + 'course outline'.

SB p.53 5.1 5.2 **Listening 1: Lecture on company law**

8a Elicit from the class one or two possible advantages and disadvantages of corporations, in comparison with other business vehicles such as sole proprietorships and partnerships, but avoid confirming or rejecting students' suggestions. Then tell students to listen to the recording to answer the question. Afterwards, tell students to discuss the question in pairs, and to discuss what they remember from the listening about the points the professor made. When you go through the answers with the class, be careful not to undermine Exercise 8b by giving away the answers.

Answers
The professor discusses both advantages and disadvantages of corporations.

Language notes
○ The terms *shareholder* and *stockholder* are the same, and can be used interchangeably. Both refer to people or institutions which own (hold) *shares* (pieces) of a company's *stock* (ownership).

○ If a creditor *goes after* the stockholders, he/she takes legal action to recover debts from those stockholders.

○ A *shortfall* in this context is the difference between what is owed and what can be repaid.

○ An *officer* is a senior official in a company, who is hired by the directors, and who is authorised to make contracts on behalf of the company. Examples include the Chief Executive Officer (CEO) and Chief Financial Officer (CFO).

○ A *pass-through entity* is a US business, such as a sole proprietorship, partnership or limited liability company (LLC), which pays no tax itself, but rather the owners pay tax on the company's profits as part of their personal tax. See http://www.residual-rewards.com/llcvsscorp.html.

○ A *tax election* is a formal decision by the owners of a US LLC (see above) to become an S corporation.

b Tell students to listen again to answer the three questions. If you think this will be too easy (i.e. if students have already mentioned the answers to these questions in the feedback to Exercise 8a), write the following words and phrases on the board, and tell students to listen to identify what was said about each of them: *bank account*, *debts and liabilities*, *go after*, *shortfall*, *board of directors*, *officers*, *C corporation*, *dividends*, *pass-through entity*, *S corporation*.

Answers
1 According to the speaker, the primary advantage of a corporation is that its owners (stockholders or shareholders) are not personally liable for the debts and liabilities of the corporation.
2 The significant disadvantage she mentions is double taxation, which means that in some cases a corporation pays a corporate tax on its corporate income, and the stockholders pay income tax on the dividends they receive.
3 One way to avoid double taxation is to make a special election to be taxed as a pass-through entity, like a partnership or a sole proprietorship; the corporate profits 'pass through' to the owners, who pay taxes on the profits at their individual tax rates.

Transcript » STUDENT'S BOOK page 129

9a Tell students to listen to the second part of the lecture to answer the question. After listening, students should discuss their answers with a partner, including what else they understood/remember from the lecture. You could tell them to discuss the questions in Exercise 9b before you go through the answers with the class.

Answers
The speaker mentions five advantages and three disadvantages.

Language notes
○ For more on *self-employment tax* in the USA, see http://en.wikipedia.org/wiki/Self_employment_tax#Taxation_in_the_US.

○ *Avenues to raise capital* include debt (borrowing money) and equity (selling shares in the company).

○ The listening refers to *types of stock with different voting or profit characteristics*. There are two main types: preference shares (US: preferred shares) and ordinary shares (US: common shares). Preference shareholders are often entitled to a fixed dividend (= payment of part of the company's profits) even when ordinary shareholders are not. Ordinary shareholders, on the other hand, are allowed to vote at general meetings, while preferential shareholders may not. See http://www.bized.ac.uk.

○ *Transfer* refers to the process when ownership passes from one party to another, typically through sale.

○ A company's *assets* are everything it owns. Its *licences* are formal rights to use somebody else's property, including intellectual property. Its *permits* are licences issued by government bodies, allowing the company to do something (such as produce a dangerous product in a particular location).

○ In the USA, *unemployment tax* is paid by employers to cover the cost of unemployment benefits. See http://en.wikipedia.org/wiki/Federal_Unemployment_Tax_Act.

○ A *shareholder-employee* is both a shareholder and an employee of a corporation.

b Tell students to complete the table in pairs. It should be possible to do this without listening a second time, but if students are struggling, avoid confirming or rejecting answers and check the answers when you check Exercise 9c below, after the second listening. Note that question 2 may cause problems: the answer is sole proprietor because it has only one owner; a partnership has owners (plural).

Answers
1 corporation 2 sole proprietorship
3 corporation 4 partnership;
sole proprietorship 5 corporation

c Tell students to work with a partner to predict/ remember what might go in each space, but not to write the answers until they have checked in the listening. Then play the recording a second time for them to complete the notes. Afterwards, allow them to check with a partner before going through the answers with the class.

Answers
1 debts 2 savings 3 life 4 money
5 transfer 6 cost 7 formalities 8 tax

Transcript » STUDENT'S BOOK **page 129**

Language use: Discussing advantages and disadvantages
(SB p.54)

10a Tell students to work alone to underline the phrases. You could elicit the first phrase from the whole class as an example to get them started. Allow students to check with a partner before feeding back to the class. Point out that these phrases will be useful for the role-play in Exercise 11.

Answers
The main advantage of a corporation is that its owners, known as stockholders or shareholders, are not personally liable for its debts and liabilities.
One major disadvantage of a traditional corporation is double taxation.
Corporations enjoy many advantages over partnerships and sole proprietorships.

But there are also disadvantages.
So what is the main advantage?
The second benefit of corporations is self-employment tax savings.
The third advantage of a corporation is its continuous life.
The fourth advantage is the fact that it is easier for a corporation to raise money.
The fifth and last advantage is the ease of transfer.
The first of these drawbacks is the higher cost.
The second disadvantage is the formal organisation and the corporate formalities.
The third and final disadvantage is unemployment tax.

Optional extension
Part 2 of the recording (audio 5.2) also contains several good examples of structures for contrasting one type of organisation with another. While students are hunting for advantages and disadvantages for Exercise 10a, they could also find examples of structures for contrasting in Part 2.

Suggested answers
In contrast, in the case of sole proprietorships and partnerships, …
With a corporation, **only** salaries (**and not** profits) …
The life of a corporation, **unlike that of** a partnership, does not …
The business of a sole proprietorship or partnership, **on the other hand**, cannot be sold whole; **instead**, …
While observing corporate formalities is not difficult, it can be time-consuming.
This is not the case with either a sole proprietorship or a partnership, …
A stockholder-employee … is required to pay unemployment taxes …, **whereas** a sole proprietor or partner is not.

b Make sure students complete the exercise from memory, and don't simply copy from the audio transcript. Check answers with the whole class.

Answers
1 main 2 major 3 enjoy; over 4 benefit
5 drawbacks

Optional extension 1

Students will have a chance to practise the language of advantages and disadvantages in the role-play in Exercise 11, but if you feel they need some controlled practice first, tell them to work with a partner to come up with similar sentences to describe the advantages and disadvantages of sole proprietorships. They should use the phrases they underlined in Exercise 10a (as well as those for contrasting information from the extension activity above) as templates, substituting the words *sole proprietorship* for *corporation*, and using their knowledge (and the information in the listening) to complete the sentences in a logical way. As a follow-up, they could repeat the exercise for partnerships, but this time without looking at the underlined phrases.

Optional extension 2
(Photocopiable worksheet 5.1)

This focuses on some useful collocations connected with company law, from Listening 1.

1 Distribute the worksheets and tell students to work in pairs to match the two halves of each sentence. Note that some extracts have been edited slightly for the exercise.

2 When the first pairs have completed the exercise, go through the answers with the class.

3 As a follow-up, tell students to fold their worksheets and test their partners: one should read the beginning of a sentence to elicit the end from their partner. Point out that students can also test themselves this way after the lesson.

Answers

1 b 2 k 3 l 4 j 5 h 6 c 7 e 8 i
9 d 10 f 11 g 12 a 13 x 14 r 15 w
16 s 17 p 18 m 19 q 20 n 21 v 22 o
23 t 24 u

(SB p.54) Speaking 1: Role-play: lawyer–client interview

11 Assign roles, and tell students to read their role cards. If you have an odd number of students, the extra student in one group should be a second lawyer. Make sure everyone understands what a *plumber* is, as

well as other key terms from the role cards (*apprentice*, *retirement community*). Point out that the lawyers should invent any information which they have not been given (such as the tax rates for the various taxes mentioned in the listening). Elicit how the WASP approach works, and encourage students to use the techniques from Unit 3 as well as the useful language from this unit.

During the role-play, monitor carefully for the lawyers' techniques as much as the language they use, and at the end of the role-plays, give and elicit feedback on the strengths and weaknesses of their performances. If there is time, repeat the role-play with the roles reversed, and allow the client to choose a different line of business.

Background note

The advice given will depend largely on what information the client gives the lawyer. Generally speaking, the plumber may benefit from incorporation, especially if her business involves significant risk. For example, if she were to flood the retirement home during the course of her business, she would be afforded more legal protection from creditors as a company. However, one of the disadvantages may be double taxation.

LAW IN PRACTICE

(SB p.55) Lead-in

On the board, write *The UK Companies Act 2006* and elicit from the class what it might include. Use the date of the Act to elicit recent trends in company law that might be included (e.g. corporate responsibility scandals, concern about environmental issues and globalisation, etc.). Then tell students to read the introduction to check. Discuss the lead-in question with the whole class.

Background notes

○ Much of the Act serves to bring together and update existing legislation. Despite its size, there is relatively little in it that is completely new or radical.

○ Wikipedia has a straightforward summary of the changes introduced by the Companies Act: http://en.wikipedia. org/wiki/Companies_Act_2006.

○ For much more detailed information on the Act, see http://www.companiesact. org.uk/. This site links to a very clear explanation of the two sections mentioned in Reading 3: http://www. opsi.gov.uk/acts/acts2006/en/ ukpgaen_20060046_en.pdf.

○ The BBC news website has an analysis of the background to and political arguments surrounding the Act: http:// news.bbc.co.uk/2/hi/uk_news/ politics/6125316.stm

12 Tell students to read the task and to discuss the three questions in small groups. Encourage them to think laterally when thinking of interested parties (so not just obvious business partners such as customers and employees, but also neighbours, victims of a company's pollution, struggling competitors, the employees' families, etc.). It may help to think in terms of specific companies (a supermarket, a factory, a travel agency, etc.). After a few minutes, open up the discussion to include the whole class.

Reading 3: Breach of Companies Act 2006
SB p.55

13 Elicit from the class how a supermarket might breach the Companies Act, bearing in mind the information given in the lead-in and Exercise 12. Then tell students to read the letter to check their predictions and to try to work out who wrote the letter. After they have finished reading, discuss the answer with the class.

Answer
Although it is not explicit in the letter, Pippa is definitely a person concerned by green issues. She is possibly also involved in campaigning.

Background notes
○ *Palm oil* is used to make a very wide range of products, from soaps and washing powder to margarine and many processed foods. See http://en.wikipedia. org/wiki/Palm_oil for a good introduction

and links to many environmental campaigns connected with palm oil.

○ *Section 172* of the Companies Act 2006 stipulates that directors must act in a way that promotes the success of the company, while considering matters such as the impact of the company's business on the environment (see extract on page 57 of the SB). *Section 417* requires directors to report how they have performed their obligations under section 172, in a *business review* for shareholders. See http://www.opsi. gov.uk/acts/acts2006/en/ukpgaen_ 20060046_en.pdf.

○ The *Secretary of State for Business, Enterprise and Regulatory Reform* is a senior member of the UK government. Before 2007, this post was called *Secretary of State for Trade and Industry.*

14 Tell students to read the letter again and discuss the questions with a partner. When you discuss the answers with the class, elicit whether any students know about palm oil and the environmental issues connected with it. Check also the meaning of the word *respectively* in the second paragraph.

Answers
1 The sourcing of palm oil
2 Sections 172 and 417
3 The Secretary of State for Business, Enterprise and Regulatory Reform

Language note
The word *respectively* is used to show that the first item in a list relates to the first item in a different list, the second item relates to the second item, and so on. In the letter, the writer means that section 172 imposes a duty to take environmental issues into consideration, and section 417 imposes a duty to report on them to shareholders.

15 Tell students to discuss the phrases with a partner to try to come up with a definition. Then open up the discussion to include the whole class.

1 The process of identifying, conducting negotiations with and forming supply agreements with vendors of goods and services
2 A legal obligation to consider certain matters when deciding on policy
3 Causing little or no damage to the environment and therefore able to continue for a long time
4 Duty to compel obedience to a law

16 Tell students to discuss this question in small groups. Tell them to consider not just legal issues, but also issues connected with business ethics and marketing/PR. After a few minutes, open up the discussion to include the whole class.

Optional extension
The letter in Reading 3 has been sent to many companies (as shown by the very general greeting *Dear Directors/Chief Executive*) and is therefore careful to avoid explicitly accusing companies of specific failures. Elicit from the class some of the phrases the writer uses to make her accusations less direct.

Suggested answers
○ *As you may or may not be aware, …*
○ *I do not believe that your company is doing enough … [less direct than I believe that your company is not doing enough …]*
○ *I am therefore concerned about whether this may consequently be a breach …*

SB p.56 **5.3 5.4** **Listening 2: Directors' meeting**

17 Tell students to read the introduction and the questions. Elicit some ideas as to what Simon might send to Pippa Solloway. Then play the recording for students to check. Allow them to discuss with a partner, including anything else they understood/remember from the listening, before going through the answers with the class.

⟫ **Answers**
A copy of the press release of March 2005 and the (environmental) policy statement. He hopes this will stop Pippa Solloway going to the press and saying that Baggers don't care about green issues (the environment and associated issues of concern).

Transcript » [STUDENT'S BOOK **page 129**]

Language notes
○ A supermarket's *own-brand* products are those sold under the same brand as the supermarket itself. They are usually cheaper than well-known brands.
○ *Goodwill* means trust and respect that customers have for a company in terms of quality, reliability and corporate responsibility, typically built up over a long period of time.
○ If a company is *carbon-neutral*, it balances the carbon dioxide produced when it burns fossil fuels by, for example, planting trees (or paying others to pollute less).

18 Tell students to read the question, and elicit what they think a *business review* might be (see Background notes to Exercise 13 above), and how often they would expect it to be published. Then play the recording for them to answer the question. Allow them to discuss with a partner, including anything else they understood/remember from the listening, before going through the answers with the class.

⟫ **Answer**
Not for at least another 12 months

Transcript » [STUDENT'S BOOK **page 130**]

Language notes
○ If you are *covered*, you are protected from a potential danger.
○ The phrase *a cut-and-paste job* refers to the idea that the letter writer has copied the same letter to many recipients, having made only superficial changes for each recipient.

○ If you *gauge* /geɪdʒ/ something, you attempt to measure it by using a small sample as a test.

○ If you *pre-empt* /priːˈemt/ something, you act before another party acts, in order to make any attacks from that party ineffective.

19 Students should discuss the statements with a partner to try to remember whether they are true or false, and then listen to the recording (parts 1 and 2) to check. Allow them to check again with a partner before going though the answers with the class.

Answers
1 T   2 F   3 F   4 T   5 T

Key terms 2: Public relations
<small>SB p.56</small>

Elicit from the class what they understand by the term *public relations* (PR) and why a lawyer might need to understand and be involved in PR.

Suggested answer
PR professionals need to be aware of the legal implications of their actions, and the laws they must comply with. Lawyers must be aware of the bad publicity that can arise out of following the letter of the law rather than paying attention to public opinion and the effects of negative publicity.

20 Tell students to complete the matching exercise with a partner, and then go through the answers with the class.

Answers
1 e   2 g   3 c   4 a   5 b   6 f   7 d

Optional extension
The directors' meeting in Listening 2 contained many phrasal verbs and idioms. It is often said that phrasal verbs are only used in informal English, but this listening demonstrates that there are many which may be used in formal situations.

1 Tell students to work with a partner to read the audio transcripts to audio 5.3 and 5.4 on pages 129–130 to find 19 examples of phrasal verbs and 17 idioms.

2 You might want to find one example of each with the class to get them started. Point out that there may be some disagreement as to exactly what constitutes a phrasal verb or an idiom; the point is to find useful vocabulary, rather than to worry about precise definitions.

3 When you go through the answers, elicit the meanings of the phrasal verbs and idioms, and encourage students to learn and use some of them.

Suggested answers

Phrasal verbs
… the press release we **put out** in March …
… goodwill we've **built up** from …
… the message isn't **getting across**.
… we've **given in** under pressure.
Sara, you've **come up with** a few ideas.
… you can **talk** us **through** …
… has just **picked on** one issue …
So, if we **go with** Simon's suggestion …
… we … **put out** our policy …
… we need to **find out** what …
And if it **turns out** that …
If it does **turn out** that …
… we're prepared to **stand by** …
… **call on** our competitors to …
… outline the law before I **go on**?
Section 172 **deals with** directors' duties.
… our position on this one is **set out** in our …
… we can **turn** the situation **round** to …
… and maybe **catch up on** …

Idioms
… during **the run-up to** the Act.
… **the bottom line** is that …
But **all it'll take is** one letter to the press, …
… some **room for flexibility** …
… we need to **get our facts straight** on …
… a well-organised campaigner **who means business**.
I want people to see us as **setting the agenda**.
OK, let's **look at this step by step**.
… to **gauge our reaction**.
… but it will **buy us time**.
It's one thing being seen to comply …
… for **drawing this to our attention**.
… **we'll do everything in our power to** …
… **spinning the issue** to our favour.
… call on our competitors to **follow our lead**.
We're **on track** …
… **as far as** the rest of the Act **is concerned**, …

Text analysis: Reading a statute

21 Elicit from the class what they remember about the two sections of the Companies Act 2006 mentioned in Reading 3, but avoid giving away details that will spoil the exercise. Then tell students to read the section of the Act to choose the best title. After a short time (around a minute), discuss the question with the class. Avoid explaining the subsections in detail at this stage, as this will spoil later exercises.

➠ **Answer**
b

✎ **Language notes**
NB Many of the difficult sentences from the text are explained on Photocopiable worksheet 5.2 (see page 80).

○ If you do something in *good faith*, you honestly intend to act in a way which does not take an unfair advantage of another person.

○ If you *have regard to* something, you bear it in mind.

○ If you *foster* relationships, you take care of those relationships to encourage them to grow.

○ In 1(f), *the need to act fairly **as between** members of the company* means you must not unfairly treat some shareholders differently from others. The word *as* is essential, because the expression *act fairly between members* would suggest that shareholders should be fair with each other, but in fact it is the director who must be fair to all shareholders.

○ Paragraph 2 refers to *subsection 1*. The terms *paragraph* and *subsection* are synonyms, although *paragraph* is much more commonly used by lawyers (and is the term used elsewhere in this book and the SB). The term *subsection* is still used by some legislators (which is why it appears in this Act).

○ If a subsection *has effect*, it applies; it is legally binding.

○ In subsection 3, the effect of the phrase *subject to* is that laws requiring directors to act in the interests of creditors (i.e. when a company goes into liquidation, and its creditors must be protected) must take precedence over the duty to act to promote the success of the company.

22 Tell students to discuss these questions with a partner, and then open up the discussion to include the whole class. Try to identify some of the techniques used to make some sections easier to understand, and any implications for students' own writing.

➠ **Suggested answer**
Subsection 1 is probably clearest, because the information is set out as a list, although the words *as between* in 1f are very difficult to understand.

Subsection 2 is difficult to understand, because it takes a long time to get to the subject and main verb of the sentence (*subsection (1) has effect*). The sentence also relies on omitting repeated words (as in the parts with *or* and the phrase *were to achieving*, which need to be read several times before they can be understood.

Subsection 3 is fairly clear, although it would be much clearer if the *certain circumstances* were spelled out, rather than hinted at.

See Photocopiable worksheet 5.2 below for a much deeper analysis of these issues.

23a Tell students to read the question and discuss it briefly with a partner, and then open up the discussion to include the whole class. Note that the answers are given in Exercise 23b.

b Tell students to read the list of ideas to compare it with the ideas they came up with, and to identify which of the bullet points could be useful when interpreting the extract on page 57.

➠ **Suggested answer**
○ The first bullet point is useful for all reading.
○ The second bullet point is relevant, as the extract contains several lists with *and* as well as four pairs of alternatives with *or* (*where or to the extent that*; *consist of or include*; *enactment or rule of law*; *consider or act in*).

○ The third bullet is especially important: it is worth spending some time thinking about the use of *as* in 1f and *to* at the end of subsection 2, as well as several pairs of commas which mark off certain groups of words as additional information.

○ The remaining three points are general points, which are less relevant in this case, as we have only one extract, with no references to other extracts.

24 Discuss this with the class.

➠ **Suggested answer**
Provision (d); possibly also (e), depending on how this provision is interpreted.

25 Tell students to discuss this with a partner, and to come up with a plain-English version of the subsection, as if they were explaining to a client. Point out that they should try to use an example to make the rewriting easier to understand. When they have finished, elicit some rewritings from the class.

➠ **Suggested answer**
In the case of charitable companies, a director must act in the way he or she thinks would be most likely to achieve the goals of the charity.

**Optional extension
(Photocopiable worksheet 5.2)**
This illustrates four more techniques for understanding statutes and other complex legal writing. Even if students completely understand the statute by now, it is still worth going through the exercises, as the techniques will help them next time they have to read something complex.

Distribute copies of the worksheet, and tell students to work through the first three exercises in pairs. You may need to monitor closely, as some of the answers require some lateral thinking.

Afterwards, go through the answers with the class. As you discuss each technique, elicit whether a) it is useful for this particular extract of the text, and b) whether it would be useful with other extracts. The expected answer is that for this particular extract, the techniques are over-the-top, as it was already

mostly understandable. In fact, some of the 'improvements' seem more complex than the originals. It is important to get a balance between clarity (being understandable) and brevity (being concise). But the techniques should be useful when dealing with more complex texts.

Suggested answers
1 b You should try to respect your employees' rights and expectations.
   c You need to build up good relationships with your suppliers, customers and others.
   d You should consider how your operations affect the community and the environment.
   e You need to consider whether you want your company to maintain a good reputation for the way it behaves.
   f You must not unfairly treat shareholders differently from one another.
2 a where or to the extent that; consist of or include
   b *Where* relates to *consists of* (i.e. the purposes of the company are 100% for this other objective) and *to the extent that* relates to *include* (i.e. the purposes of the company are partly for this other objective).
   c Where the purposes of the company consist of purposes other than the benefit of its members, or to the extent that the purposes of the company include purposes other than the benefit of its members, subsection (1) has …
   d … were a reference to achieving those purposes.
3 a It refers to the whole section, which consists of three subsections. The duty is the duty to promote the success of the company.
   b The rules of Y apply first, and then, within the limits of Y, the rules of X apply.
   c An enactment is a law from statute. A rule of law is a legal principle of general application used by courts to guide their decision-making.
   d Because it comes after the word *directors*, it refers to *to consider or act*, but in this case the circumstances are the same, so it makes no difference.
   e The creditors include unpaid suppliers (who have supplied goods but are

awaiting payment) and other lenders (such as banks). You might consider creditors' interests when the company is approaching bankruptcy, but be required to act in their interests after declaring bankruptcy.

f Yes, there is a difference. If you consider somebody's interests, it is one of several factors which you take into consideration. If you act in somebody's interests, it is the only or main factor which you take into consideration.

Set question 4 as a homework research task. Point out to students that if they have problems following the link, the explanatory text can be found by searching Google, Wikipedia, etc., for 'Companies Act 2006'.

Answer
4 According to the explanatory notes, subsection 2 is relevant to altruistic or partly altruistic companies, such as charities or community interest companies. Subsection 3 is intended to apply to insolvent companies, and may apply to companies approaching insolvency.

As a follow-up, you could encourage students to find section 417, which is also important for this case study, and to use the four techniques to understand and analyse it.

26 Discuss this with the class.

➡ Answer
The duty to promote the success of the company may be qualified by (*subject to*) any future regulations concerning creditors (i.e. under certain circumstances, the creditors' interests may come before those of the company).

Ⓢ Speaking 2: Role-play: lawyer–client interview
SB p.58

Elicit from the class what options are available to Baggers' Executive Committee for dealing with the letter from Pippa Solloway, and then tell students to read the list of four options on page 58 to compare it with their ideas. You may need to check the meanings of some words (*immaterial* = not relevant/important; *to mitigate the issue* = to minimise the damage caused). You could also check

why option 2 refers to a report to shareholders [**Answer**: Because this report to shareholders is required under section 417 of the Companies Act].

27 Assign roles for the role-play. If you have an odd number of students, the extra student in one group should be a second lawyer. Allow several minutes for students to prepare for the role-play, and then at least five minutes for the role-play itself. Point out that students should use the language from this unit on advantages and disadvantages, as well as the techniques from Unit 3, during the role-play. While they are doing the role-play, monitor for good techniques as well as language problems, and give and elicit feedback at the end.

Optional extension
Students should write the response to Pippa Solloway, based on their discussion in the role-play. Note that no model answer has been provided for this writing, but it could still be useful as a freer practice of the writing techniques that have been studied so far in this book.

Ⓢ Language Focus
SB p.59

Answers
1   **Word formation**

verb	noun
form	formation
register	registration
incorporate	incorporation
regulate	regulation
enforce	enforcement
wind up	winding-up
dissolve	dissolution
fund	funding

2   **Collocations with *company***

The verb which does not collocate with *company* is *enforce*. You can enforce rights or enforce a law, for example.

3   **Adjective collocations**
a   **2** f   **3** a   **4** b   **5** d   **6** e
b   **2** constitutional documents   **3** sole proprietor   **4** corporate funding   **5** third party   **6** publicly listed/owned company

Case study 2: Company law

(See page 10 for step-by-step instructions to case studies.)

The facts of the case

The legal issues are: Is Cordeaux Gabelle entitled to the remedy of recission under section(a)(2) of the US Securities Act of 1933? Is an alternative remedy available under section 11?

> **Language notes**
> ○ A *public offering* is the process of selling securities (shares) to the general public. Typically in the USA, sales of securities to more than 35 people are considered public offerings, and therefore require more formal procedures (e.g. registration with the Securities and Exchanges Commission (SEC)) than private sales. See http://www.investopedia.com/terms/p/publicoffering.asp. In private sales, the buyer is responsible for checking whether the sale is properly researched and documented.
> ○ A *prospectus* is a formal written offer to sell securities (shares), which provides all the relevant details prospective buyers need to make an investment decision. The SEC requires a prospectus for public offerings, but other types of sales of securities do not need a formal prospectus. See http://en.wikipedia.org/wiki/Prospectus_%28finance%29#United_States: the US meaning of *prospectus* is relevant to this US-based case study.
> ○ There is a good introduction to the *Securities Act 1933* at http://en.wikipedia.org/wiki/Securities_Act_of_1933, which includes a link to the full text.
> ○ A *material* misstatement or omission one that is relevant or significant.

Comprehension questions

1 Who are the parties? [Alex and Leslie Ballentine, former owners of Solaris Energy, and Cordeaux Gabelle, the company which bought Solaris Energy.]

2 Why was a prospectus prepared? [Because the initial plan was to sell the company by public offering. It was not actually necessary for the private sale that took place.]

3 What did the parties expect to happen to the value of the company? [That it would increase.]

4 What actually happened? [The company turned out to be worth much less than CG paid for it.]

5 What would be the simplest way to resolve the problem? [The Ballentines could pay the difference ($1.2 million) to CG, as stated in the contract.]

6 What does Cordeaux Gabelle want to do? [It wants to rescind the contract (i.e. undo the earlier sale by exchanging its shares for the money it originally paid, $14.6 million).]

7 What is the difference between sections 11 and 12(a)(2) of the Securities Act 1933? [Section 11 concerns sellers who use a prospectus; section 12(a)(2) concerns registration statements. Both sections deal with material misstatements or omissions.]

Relevant legal documents

○ **Text 1** is a summary of the relevant sections of the US Securities Act of 1933. Note the phrase *liability flows from the requirements for filing a registration statement*. A key question in this case is whether, as a private sale, there was any such requirement, even though a prospectus was actually filed (and was presumably a key factor in Cordeaux Gabelle's decision to purchase Solaris Energy). Even if it can be established that there was such a requirement, the Ballentines may still be able to defend themselves by claiming that they took reasonable care when preparing the documents.

○ **Text 2**, part of a Supreme Court judgment that clarified the law in such cases, also seems to support the Ballentines. On the other hand, the documents prepared by the Ballentines when they were planning a public offering can hardly be described as 'casual communication'. The judgment limited the reach of the statute to such cases of casual communication, but the facts in the Ballentines' case are much less clear-cut.

○ **Text 3** is an extract from an article in a law journal. In this text, *standing* means the right to sue under this statute. It refers to Gustafson, which is a shorthand name for the case that Text 2 comes from. Although the Gustafson decision clarified the issue to some extent, it also created new questions, particularly whether the decision covered section 11 as well as section 12(a)(2). This document may suggest a line of argument for Cordeaux Gabelle's lawyers: even if they cannot sue under section 12(a)(2), they could argue that they may still sue under section 11. Of course, they might still have to show that they can trace their securities to those sold in the public offering, which could be problematic, since the public offering never actually led to a sale.

6 Commercial law

THE STUDY OF LAW

(SB p.60) Lead-in

Elicit from the class what they understand by the term *commercial law*, and how it might differ from company law. Elicit also some of the areas that are covered by commercial law.

> **Answer**
> Commercial law is much broader than company law. According to the list in Reading 1 (paragraph 1), company law is just one of many branches of commercial law.

1 Tell students to discuss the three questions in small groups. You may need to check students understand the difference between *trade* and *commerce*, and the two meanings of the word *bodies* as used in the questions (see Language notes below). After a few minutes, open up the discussion to include the class.

> **Language notes**
> ○ *Trade* and *commerce* are usually used as synonyms, although *trade* literally means 'the exchange of goods', while *commerce* means 'buying and selling for money'.

○ The term *bodies of law* is rather vague. It describes sets of laws, such as all the laws of one jurisdiction in contrast to another, or a particular part of one jurisdiction's laws, such as criminal law, constitutional law or commercial law.
○ *International bodies* which set guidelines for commercial transactions include the World Trade Organisation and the European Union.

Reading 1: Commercial law

SB p.60

2   Tell students to read the four statements to predict whether they are true or false, and then to read the text carefully to check their predictions. After about three minutes, tell them to discuss the answers with a partner, and then go through the answers with the class.

Answers
1 T   **2** F (Non-contentious work includes these things.)   **3** F (The UCC applies to the USA, not the EU.)   **4** T

Language notes
○ *Private law* deals with the legal relationships between private individuals, and includes family law, commercial law and labour law. *Public law*, in contrast, always involves the government, in its dealings with its citizens, with other governments, etc. (Source: http://www.duhaime.org/LegalDictionary.aspx.)
○ *Jurisprudence* /ˈdʒʊrɪsˌpruːdəns/ is the branch of philosophy concerned with the theories of law.
○ The 18 *areas of commercial law* are explained in the Glossary (see SB pages 155–160). Nine of them are also explained in Exercises 3 and 4. Note that this is not a complete list: each area has many sub-areas, and new areas are developing all the time.
○ Generally speaking, most areas of law can be either prefixed *the law of* or suffixed with the word *law*. For example, some lawyers talk of *the law of contract*, others call it *contract law* and others

call it simply *contract*. The first two are probably equally common, with the first being more common in academic circles. *Contract* alone would be favoured by lawyers, probably resulting from their familiarity with the subject.
○ Similarly, the word *agency* alone is commonly used to refer to this area of law, but it is often followed by *law*.
○ Similarly, the term *mercantile agency* /ˈmɜːkənˌtaɪl ˈeɪdʒənsɪ/ is used here to refer to an area of law (mercantile agency law), rather than mercantile agencies themselves. A mercantile agency is an agency which supplies reports on the creditworthiness and financial strength of other firms. The best-known mercantile agency is Dun and Bradstreet. Mercantile agencies should not be confused with credit-rating agencies, such as Moody's, and Standard and Poor's.
○ *Negotiable instruments* are documents which are used in place of money. A simplistic example might be an IOU (i.e. if I borrow money from X, I could write a note promising to repay X a certain amount of money). Negotiable instruments are obviously much more formal than this simplistic example, and are negotiable in the sense that ownership may be transferred from one party to another. In the example, X might use the IOU to buy something of equal value from Y, in which case I now owe the money to Y. For a very good introduction to negotiable instruments, see this course's sister book, *International Legal English*, Unit 12.
○ *Secured transactions* are a way of guaranteeing that a borrower will repay a loan. A well-known example is a pawning: I can borrow money from a pawnbroker by leaving my television in his shop as security (called the *pledge*). If I fail to repay my debt, he may keep or sell the television. Most secured transactions in business are non-possessory (i.e. the creditor does not take possession of the pledge, but instead creates a *charge*: a right to claim some property in the event

Unit 6 Commercial law   85

of a default). For a very good introduction to secured transactions, see *International Legal English*, Unit 13.

○ *Substantive law* contrasts with *procedural law*. Procedural law deals with the way the legal system works, while substantive law deals with the principles, rights and limitations used to govern society. (Source: http://dictionary.law.com.)

○ The full text of the *Uniform Commercial Code* is available at http://www.law.cornell.edu/ucc/. Its list of topics is a good source of fields of corporate law.

○ For more information on the European Union's attempts to unify their commercial codes, see http://en.wikipedia.org/wiki/European_civil_code. At the time of writing, such a unified code is still being planned.

○ *Treaties* and *conventions* can be treated as synonyms, although technically a treaty is a type of convention. Both involve formal agreements between two or more states, or between states and an international body.

○ *Adherence* /ədˈhɪərəns/ comes from the verb *adhere*, meaning 'stick to something', either literally (using an adhesive = glue) or metaphorically (to act in compliance with agreements).

Pronunciation notes
carriage /ˈkærɪdʒ/
contentious /kənˈtenʃəs/
debtor /ˈdetə(r)/
mortgages /ˈmɔːɡədʒɪz/

(SB p.61) Key terms: Fields, institutions and concepts in commercial law

Optional lead-in
Tell students to work in small groups to look at the list of 18 commercial law areas mentioned in paragraph 1 to try to guess / work out what they each mean, and what each might involve. Most of them should be fairly easy to work out, and the most difficult ones are all explained in Exercises 3 and 4. Discuss the answers briefly with the class, but avoid explaining the nine areas mentioned in Exercises 3 and 4.

3 Tell students to work with a partner to answer the questions. They may need to guess one or two answers. When you go through the answers with the class, make sure all students understand what the five areas of law mean. Refer them to the Glossary if they struggle.

Answers
1 intellectual property   2 competition
3 mercantile agency   4 carriage of goods
5 tax

Language note
Note that in the law of carriage of goods, the *shipper* (= owner) is not the same as the *carrier* (= party which transports the goods). The terms *receiver* and *consignee* /kɒnsaɪˈniː/ are synonyms; *consignee* is the preferred term in the shipping industry.

4 Students should work in pairs to complete the exercise. Some of the sentences may present problems, but the purpose of the exercise is to teach new vocabulary rather than to test existing knowledge. When you go through the answers with the class, make sure all students understand what the four areas of law mean. Refer them to the Glossary if they struggle.

Answers
1 on behalf of   2 owe; creditors
3 transaction; lender   4 payment

Optional extension
1 In pairs or small groups, students should test each other on the areas of law mentioned in Exercises 3 and 4. One student should ask one of the questions in Exercise 3, or create a question based on the statements in Exercise 4 (e.g. *What is the term for …?*).
2 The other student must try to remember the answer without looking at his/her book.
3 You could expand this activity to include all the terms in bold from Reading 1, with students taking definitions from the Glossary.

Listening 1: Profile of a commercial lawyer

5 Tell students to read the introduction on page 62 to find out who Michael Grant is. Then elicit some areas of commercial activity (e.g. manufacturing, distribution, marketing, banking) and what an alumni association /əˈlʌmnaɪ əˌsəʊsɪˈeɪʃən/ might be [**Answer:** A 'club' for ex-students of a particular university to stay in touch with their university and each other].

Then tell students to listen to the podcast to answer the two questions. Allow them to discuss their answers with a partner, including anything else they understood/remember from the recording, before checking the answers with the class.

Answers
1 To get a Master's degree in e-law.
2 He advises students to try out as many different areas of the law as they can and then to choose one they are genuinely interested in.

Transcript » STUDENT'S BOOK **page 130**

Language notes
○ *Privacy law* is connected with individuals' right to privacy, particularly when it comes to the protection of personal data.
○ *Spam law* is intended to place legal restrictions on what may and may not be sent as unsolicited email. See http://www.spamlaws.com/spam-laws.html.
○ The terms *dry work* and *wet work* are used among some shipping lawyers (see http://www.lawgazette.com.sg/2000-3/focus4.htm). As mentioned in the listening, *dry work* is concerned with day-to-day events such as resolving charter party disputes and handling cargo claims. *Wet work* is connected with rarer but more complicated events such as *groundings* (= when a ship runs aground), *collisions* (= crashes between ships), *salvage* (= saving goods from danger) and *torts*.

○ A *charter party* is a contract between a ship's owners and a cargo company, where a ship is hired for a voyage or for a period of time. (Source: http://www.trans-inst.org/seawords.htm#c.)
○ A *cargo claim* is a claim for compensation for goods lost or damaged by a shipping company.
○ A *bill of lading* is a receipt issued by a carrier to the shipper in exchange for the goods to be shipped, containing all the details of the goods. The shipper sends the bill of lading to the consignee, who exchanges it back for the goods when they arrive.
○ *Incoterms* are International Commercial Terms, a set of universally used codes used in international sales. They are concerned with issues like who pays for what (e.g. insurance) and who is responsible for the goods during shipment. (See http://en.wikipedia.org/wiki/Incoterm.) In the listening, Michael mentioned the following Incoterms: FOB (free on board), CFR (cost and freight), CIF (cost, insurance and freight) and EXW (ex works).

6 Tell students to discuss the list with a partner to try to remember which of the types of work Michael did before he joined his current firm. You may need to check they understand some of the words and phrases (see Language notes above). Then play the recording again for them to check and complete the exercise. Allow them to discuss their answers with a partner before going through the answers with the class.

Answers
3, 4, 5, 7, 8

Language use: Adverb functions

SB p.62

Elicit from the class what adverbs are and how they are used in English. Then tell them to read the information in the box to check. Make sure they realise that adverbs do not always end in *–ly*, and do not always answer the question 'how' (see Language note on next page).

Language note

Many adverbs end in *–ly* (e.g. *quickly*), but not all words ending in *–ly* are adverbs (e.g. *friendly* is an adjective); there are also many adverbs that do not end in *–ly* (e.g. *fast, often, yesterday*).

In the sentence *Apparently, the lawyer usually goes home late*, all the words apart from the subject (*the lawyer*) and the verb (*goes*) are adverbs. They describe when something happens (*late*), where (*home*) and how often (*usually*), as well as commenting on the speaker's attitude to the statement (*Apparently*).

The same functions can also be achieved with phrases rather than single words, in which case they are called adverbials: *According to my sources* [speaker's attitude], *from time to time* [how often] **the lawyer goes** *to his flat* [where] *after spending hours drafting contracts* [when].

Adverbs and adverbials can also answer questions such as why something happens (*because he is ambitious*) and how (*feeling exhausted*), as well as showing contrasts (*although he is only an unpaid intern*), etc. Adverbs can also modify adjectives (**completely** *exhausted*) and other adverbs (**extremely** *late*).

7a Tell students to work with a partner to find the adverbs in the sentences and to decide what their function is. Then go through the answers with the class.

Answers

1 a He's <u>currently</u> undertaking a Master's of e-Law at Monash University.

2 b There's something about the challenge of taking a complex commercial transaction and expressing it <u>clearly</u> and <u>concisely</u> that <u>really</u> appeals to me.

3 c I <u>also</u> had to write patent drafts, which are <u>incredibly</u> detailed descriptions of the inventions in precise legal terms.

4 c It was interesting, although at times <u>extremely</u> difficult and demanding.

5 b But I <u>quickly</u> realised that what I liked best was working <u>closely</u> with the other lawyers on litigation, defending or enforcing patents.

6 a I <u>usually</u> spend most of the day reviewing documents, drafting agreements, meeting with clients and, of course, answering emails.

Language note

Students may find more adverbs in the sentences which do not fit into the categories in Exercise 7a: *really* (an intensifying adverb) and *also* (a linking adverb).

Optional extension

The audio transcript on pages 130–131 contains many more examples of adverbs. Tell students to underline all the adverbs in the audio transcript, and to decide which, if any, of the three functions each adverb has. When you go through the answers with the class, elicit what other typical functions there are for adverbs (see below).

Suggested answers

… and **now** advises a wide range of clients … [time]

It's an **extremely** wide range of work, … [qualifying an adjective]

There isn't **really** a standard day, … [comment]

I also **particularly** liked advising clients. [comment]

I **finally** made the difficult decision … [time]

But it was **definitely** the right decision! [comment]

And **strangely** enough, I also enjoy … [comment]

… the work we do is **usually** based around … [time]

… the high-stress periods **typically** only last … [time]

I realised **pretty early** in my studies … [qualifying an adverb; time]

I **also** learned all the incoterms … [linking]

… but **ultimately** maritime law wasn't for me. [comment / time]

… before I **finally** discovered IT law. [time]

… the Master's is **really** the first chance … [comment]

b Discuss this with the class. Try to find rules which account for all the adverbs in Exercise 7a.

Language notes

There are three common positions for adverbs when they describe verbs:

○ Initial position (i.e. before the subject) is common for comment adverbs (e.g. *unfortunately*) and linking adverbs (e.g. *firstly*, *however*).

○ Final position (i.e. after the object) is common for adverbs and adverbials consisting of several words (e.g. *expressing it* **clearly and concisely**; *working* **closely with the other lawyers**) and often when adverbs are stressed as the most important piece of new information (e.g. *She speaks English fluently*).

○ Mid-position (i.e. after the first auxiliary verb, or, in sentences with no auxiliary verbs, before the verb) is the preferred/ only position for many common adverbs (e.g. *often*, *just*, *already*, *never*). With less common adverbs, mid-position can be used when the verb is stressed more than the adverb (e.g. *I quickly* **realised** vs. *I realised* **quickly**).

8 Students should complete the exercise in pairs, applying the rules they generated in Exercise 7b. Make sure they understand that they are looking for the adverbs that *don't* fit. When you discuss the answers with the class, elicit whether you need to modify any of your rules to account for the uses of adverbs in the exercise.

Answers
1 carefully; remarkably **2** closely
3 quickly; mainly **4** extremely; regularly

Optional extension
(Photocopiable worksheet 6.1)
This highlights some useful collocations for legal English and business English from the listening.

1 Distribute the worksheet and tell students to work with a partner to complete the

---

sentences from the listening by using the words from the boxes below each set of sentences. Point out that there may be more than one possible answer.

2 When they have finished, either go through the answers with the class, or play the recording again before checking with the class. As a follow-up, elicit some useful collocations from the exercise, e.g. *which verbs collocate with 'patent'* or *which nouns collocate with 'draft'*.

Answers
1 joined; advises; representing
2 undertaking
3 advise on; negotiate; draft; litigate
4 drafting; advising on; resolving
5 reviewing; drafting; meeting with; answering
6 Supervising
7 reading and analysing; determine
8 drafted; submitted; secure
9 write; form; granted
10 defending; enforcing
11 advising
12 Working with; doing
13 litigating; bringing
14 drafting
15 require; meet
16 had
17 completed; specialises
18 resolving; handling; concerning
19 navigating; apply to

(SB p.63) Speaking 1: Internships

Elicit from the class what an internship is and where they can be done. Then tell students to read the introduction on page 63 to compare it with their ideas.

9 Students should discuss the three questions with a partner, and then feed back to the whole class.

(SB p.63) Text analysis: Letter of application for an internship

Elicit from the class how students can apply for an internship, and then tell them to read the introduction to compare it with their ideas.

10 Tell students to read the letter quickly to find out which of the two types it is, a prospecting letter or a letter of application in response to a specific advertisement. When they have finished reading, check the answer with the class. Elicit whether it is a successful letter of application (which of course it is intended to be).

Answer
It is a letter of application replying to a specific advertisement.

Language notes
○ An *elective course* is one that students choose to attend from a list of options.
○ A *résumé* /ˈrezʊmeɪ/ is the same as a CV (*curriculum vitae*). The former tends to be used more in US English, while the latter is more common in British English, but both terms are recognised internationally. *Résumé* is often written with no accents (or only one), but this may lead to confusion with the verb *resume* (= *start again*).

11 Students should read the letter again more carefully to answer the four questions, and then discuss their answers with a partner. When you check the answers with the class, check everyone understands all the words and concepts in the letter.

Answers
1 She is applying to a commercial law firm in the UK.
2 She is interested in commercial law in general, but also in debtor–creditor and negotiable instruments.
3 She worked at a small tax law firm for the summer.
4 She has enclosed a résumé (CV) and writing samples (letters).

12 Tell students to work alone to underline all the adverbs, and then to compare their answers and discuss the function of each adverb with a partner before feeding back to the class. NB For the purposes of this exercise, concentrate only on adverbs derived from adjectives, i.e. those ending in –*ly*.

Answers
successfully, particularly, frequently, especially, extremely, sincerely, confidently, particularly

The writer uses the adverbs to intensify her statements and convince the reader that she would be suitable for the internship.

13 Students should work with a partner to complete the matching exercise. Make sure they realise that there is not a one-to-one relationship between the sections a–m and the sentences 1–18: some letters are used more than once, as are some numbers. When they have finished, discuss the answers with the class.

Answers
1 b   **2** h   **3** d   **4** k   **5** g   **6** g   **7** a, l
8 i   **9** i   **10** f   **11** f   **12** c   **13** e   **14** m
15 m   **16** c   **17** j   **18** j

Optional extension
1 Elicit from the class whether letters in their own countries are structured in the same way (i.e. position of addresses, date, etc.). Point out that there is no single official format for business letters in English (see http://owl.english.purdue.edu/owl/resource/653/02/ for some alternative formats), although the format presented in Exercise 10 is very widely used.
2 As well as analysing the letter sentence by sentence, you could ask students to analyse the paragraphs: what is the main function of each paragraph and what sort of information does each paragraph contain? When you check with the class, elicit whether this paragraph structure could be used in their own writing.

Suggested answers
○ 1st paragraph: **Introduction** to writer, reason for writing, reference to where you found out about the internship
○ 2nd paragraph: **Factual information** about writer's studies and work experience
○ 3rd paragraph: **More subjective information** about writer's character, aims, strengths, etc.
○ 4th paragraph: **Addressing a key requirement** of the internship, in this case good English skills

○ 5th paragraph: **Polite close**, including call for action

3 Finally, tell students to work in pairs to do some 'oral writing' (i.e. saying orally what they would write, but not actually writing anything down). They should take turns to read Julia's letter to their partner, substituting details specific to Julia for their own personal details. Do the first one with the class as an example (e.g. *I am a student of … at the University of …*). When you feed back with the class, elicit the benefits and dangers of this technique for writing.

Suggested answers
The benefit is that it is possible to write a very high-quality letter very quickly, using another letter as a template. Templates such as this are easily available online (see for example http://www.4hb.com/letters/index.html). The danger is that letters written using templates may feel unnatural, and if many people use the same template (for example, if every user of this book uses the letter on page 64 as a template), the recipient will realise that it is simply copied and may be offended.

Reading 2: Commercial law internship
SB p.65

14 Tell students to read the text quickly to answer the question. After about one minute, check the answer with the class.

Answer
The ad appeared on the website of a university's internship programme.

Language notes
○ *Antitrust law* is the US term for *competition law*.
○ *World trade law* is mainly concerned with the international treaties surrounding the World Trade Organisation (WTO).
○ The advert states that *the internship takes place from May to July **inclusive**.* This means it includes the whole of the three months of May, June and July.

15 Tell students to read the text again to find the answers to the four questions, and to discuss their answers with a partner before feeding back to the class.

Answers
1 Students taking International Commercial Law courses in Mergers, Comparative Antitrust Law and World Trade Law who get top marks on the essays they submit in these courses can apply for the internship.
2 Students will be selected on the basis of the essays they write for those courses plus an interview.
3 The internship will take place from May to July in the Powderhouse Sommerville Frankfurt Office.
4 A student can apply using the online application located on the page of the announcement.

Writing 1: Letter of application
SB p.65

16 This writing can be set as homework or done in class (see section on Writing, page 8). Encourage students to use some of the useful phrases from Julia's letter (see Optional extension after Exercise 13 above), but not to overuse it as a template. If students do not have anything like the experience required for this internship, you may allow them to invent facts (i.e. lie), or to change the advertisement slightly so it is more appropriate to their backgrounds and career plans.

LAW IN PRACTICE

Lead-in
SB p.66

Elicit from the class a possible relationship between internships and globalisation, and then tell them to read the introduction to check.

17 Tell students to discuss the questions in pairs. After a few minutes, open up the discussion to include the whole class.

Suggested answers
1 The term *globalisation* often refers to the increase of trade around the world, especially by large companies producing and trading goods in many different countries.
2 There are many factors, including government policies and trade

agreements aimed at facilitating the free flow of goods, services, capital and people across national frontiers (e.g. the EU, NAFTA), the growth in power of institutions such as the World Bank and the IMF, the rise in power of corporations and the development of the Internet.

3 a Globalisation has led to a rapid increase in the levels of international trade and capital mobility; information, goods and services emanating from one part of the world are increasingly in demand globally. This creates challenges and opportunities for businesses.

  b As capital moves away from fixed legal structures within nations, there is an ever-growing interdependency of transportation, distribution, communication and economic networks across international borders. This raises the need for commercial lawyers to develop increasingly complex legal frameworks within which companies can operate.

Reading 3: Role of commercial agents

SB p.66

Elicit from the class what commercial agents are (NB agency law was mentioned in Reading 1), and why they might need protection. Then tell them to read the introduction on page 66 to check. Note that the introduction doesn't explicitly state that agents need protection from their principals, so when you discuss the answer with the class, avoid giving away information from Reading 3.

18 Tell students to discuss the three statements with a partner to predict whether they are true or false, and then read the text to check their predictions. Allow about two minutes for them to read, after which allow them to discuss with a partner before feeding back to the class.

Answers
1 F (only goods)
2 F (they are paid a commission)
3 T

Language notes

○ If agents were paid a *flat rate*, they might receive the same amount every month, regardless of how much business they generated for their principal, or perhaps a fixed amount for every new deal they complete, regardless of how big the deals are. In fact, most agents are paid *on a commission basis*, i.e. they get a percentage share of the sales they generate.

○ An *intermediary* /ˌɪntəˈmiːdjərɪ/ is a negotiator who serves as a link between two parties.

○ The definition of a commercial agent in paragraph 1 is rather difficult to understand, as the two parts separated by *or* are very similar. The definition allows for two different types of agent. The first type is authorised only to **negotiate transactions** on behalf of his principal. The second type is permitted both to *negotiate transactions on behalf of his principal* and to **conclude such transactions** in the name of his principal. If you *conclude a transaction*, you reach an agreement and sign a contract. The difference between doing something **on behalf of** someone and **in the name of** someone is that in the former, you act as a substitute for another party; in the latter case, you act as that party.

○ In the first paragraph, the word *provision* is used not in its normal legal English meaning of a legal clause or requirement, but simply the act of providing something.

○ If you *penetrate a market*, you gain access to it, typically by overcoming some difficulties/barriers.

○ A *branch* is a part of a company, typically in a different geographical area from other branches, usually with its own office. A *subsidiary* /ˌsʌbˈsɪdjərɪ/ can be like a branch, but it is a separate company, owned by the parent company.

○ The expression *no cure, no pay* is of course used metaphorically in this text. It originates from medical English, but has a surprisingly long history in legal

English (see http://www.answers.com/ topic/no-cure-no-pay).

○ If an agent *procures* knowledge, he/she obtains it as a result of his/her efforts.

○ If you *circumvent* /ˌsɜːkəmˈvent/ something, you go around it in order to avoid it.

○ If a feeling or temptation is *overwhelming*, it is too strong to resist.

19 Students should read the text again to answer the two questions, and then discuss their answers with a partner. When you discuss the answers with the class, discuss also whether any students have experience of such situations, and what, if anything, can be done to protect agents.

Answers

1 It enables a foreign supplier to penetrate an overseas market by benefiting from local knowledge with limited expenditure.

2 As sales build, principals often enter into direct relationships with customers (avoiding the agent altogether).

20 Tell students to complete the matching exercise quickly alone, and then check with a partner. Then go through the answers with the class.

Answers
1 d   **2** c   **3** a   **4** b

Reading 4: Commercial agency contract
(SB p.67)

Elicit from the class what they understand by the term *standard form contract*, and where lawyers might get them. Then tell them to read the introduction to check.

Background notes

○ For more on the International Chamber of Commerce, see http://www.iccwbo. org/id93/index.html.

○ The full agency contract, including the missing paragraphs, is available at http:// www.jurisint.org/doc/orig/con/en/2001/ 2001jiconen2/2001jiconen2.pdf.

21 Tell students to discuss this question in small groups. You could tell them to discuss Exercise 22 at the same time, before opening up the discussion to include the class.

Suggested answer
Time and money may be saved that would otherwise be spent checking to see if the contract conforms to local regulations. In cases where businesspeople choose to draft the contracts themselves rather than consult a lawyer (e.g. for contracts of limited economic value), model contracts can help reduce the risks of bad drafting.

22 See Exercise 21.

Answers
Common provisions include:

○ identification of the parties
○ duration of contract
○ agent and principal responsibilities
○ payment of commission
○ indemnity/compensation
○ applicable law and jurisdiction

(A more complete list can be found at: http://www.londonchamber.co.uk/ docimages/1153.doc.)

23 Tell students to read the introduction to find out what Chance Computing does, and why it uses agents. It is essential that students are familiar with the details of this case study, as it will be important for the later listening and speaking exercises. You may need to check what a *budget laptop* is (= a very cheap one).

Then tell them to read the text to answer the four questions. When they have compared their answers with a partner, check with the class.

Answers

1 No. He can only change the conditions of sale with the consent of the principal.

2 As this contract is for an indefinite period, under clause 9 it can only be terminated following six months' notice (by registered letter) before the end of a calendar quarter.

3 The provisions of the EEC Council Directive of 18 December 1986 on the co-ordination of the laws of the Member States relating to self-employed agents (86/653/EEC), together with the law governing the agent's domicile (place of residence).

4 The competent court in the area where the agent has his residence or registered offices.

> **Background note**
> Although question 4 refers only to a breach by the principal, of course the text covers a breach by either party.

> **Language notes**
> ○ If you *endeavour* /en'devə(r)/ to do something, you try very hard.
> ○ The word *said* in paragraph 3 is a legalese device for referring back to the last previous mention of the same noun, in this case *Principal*, in order to make it absolutely clear that it refers to the same Principal, and not one of the other principals that the agent might work for. In this case, it seems superfluous, as the same effect is achieved by using capital letters (Principal = the one the contract is concerned with; principal = other principals, or principals in general) and articles (the Principal; a principal).
> ○ A *calendar quarter* is a three-month period ending on March 31st, June 30th, September 30th or December 31st. The six-month notice period starts after one of these four dates.
> ○ The phrase *party thereto* in paragraph 9 means 'party to that contract'.
> ○ The Agent's *domicile* is his/her permanent/official home address.

24 Elicit from the class some techniques for making legalese easier to understand (see Photocopiable worksheet 6.2). Go through the example with the class to elicit what changes have been made to it. Then tell them to work in pairs to try to rephrase the provisions. Finally, elicit some good explanations of each provision from the class. (See Optional extension below for examples of such rephrasings.)

> **Suggested answer**
> According to clause 3, the agent has to carry out his duties to the principal as well as he possibly can. The agent has to provide information to customers about the principal's business, and must tell the principal as soon as he has received a new order.
>
> Clause 4 says that the agent needs permission from the principal to change prices and conditions of sale, etc.
>
> Under clause 9, the contract is valid from 10 February 2006 and runs for an indefinite period. The contract can be ended by either the agent or the principal by registered letter. Six months' notice must be given, and this notice period must coincide with the end of a calendar quarter.
>
> Clause 10 states that the provisions of EEC Directive 86/653/EEC apply to the contract. If Directive 86/653/EEC does not cover a particular set of circumstances, the law of the country in which the agent is domiciled must be considered.
>
> Clause 11 says that any disputes concerning the contract must be heard before a court in the jurisdiction in which the claimant is resident or in which the claimant's business is registered.

> **Background note**
> Plain English is a type of English which non-specialists understand. It has grown out of the Plain English Campaign (http://www.plainenglish.co.uk/) and is used in a wide range of fields which have traditionally used lots of jargon and complex language, such as medicine, technology and law. Lawyers have often been accused of hiding behind language that only they understand, leading many to distrust lawyers, or to be over-dependent on them to explain what's going on.
>
> Plain English does not need to sound childish or unprofessional. Well-written plain English (or logically structured spoken plain English) treats readers and listeners with professional respect.
>
> It is important in law because clients need to be able to understand what they are agreeing to and signing. Indeed, if they are required to sign something which has been deliberately constructed to make it incomprehensible, they could argue that

such a contract is not binding. In other fields, plain English is equally important: an instruction manual written in IT jargon would be useless. If a doctor's instructions to a patient are incomprehensible, the results can be very dangerous.

The Plain English Campaign has support at the highest levels. The Plain English Campaign's website contains the following quotes:

○ United States: The National Conference of Commissioners on Uniform State Laws says: 'The essentials of good bill drafting are accuracy, brevity, clarity, and simplicity. Choose words that are plain and commonly understood. Use language that conveys the intended meaning to every reader. Omit unnecessary words.'

○ Canada: The Uniform Law Conference's drafting conventions say: 'An Act should be written simply, clearly and concisely, with the required degree of precision, and as much as possible in ordinary language.'

○ European Union: EU guidelines say that 'the wording of (an) Act should be clear, simple, concise and unambiguous; unnecessary abbreviations, "community jargon" and excessively long sentences should be avoided'.

The main features of plain English, apart from those mentioned in Photocopiable worksheet 6.2, include:

○ changing noun phrases into verb phrases, and adding human subjects and objects: *Your **notification** of your **intended termination** of the contract → You have **notified** us that you **intend** to **terminate** the contract.*

○ giving examples and explanations: *You must give notice six months prior to the end of a calendar quarter. Today is 7th May. The current calendar quarter ends on 30th June, so you could terminate the contract at the end of December.*

○ using simple conjunctions (*if, and, but, or*) rather than complex ones (*nevertheless, moreover, provided, whereupon*).

This highlights five techniques for turning complex legal English into simpler plain English, and focuses on the sentences in Reading 4. Although the text in Reading 4 is not especially complex, the techniques will be very useful when students want to understand or explain more difficult texts later (such as Reading 5).

Tell students to work through the exercises in pairs. With weaker classes, it may be necessary to stop and check with the class after every exercise; otherwise you can check all the exercises together at the end.

Suggested answers

1 a try   **b** must   **c** (nothing – the word can be deleted)   **d** as well as he can   **e** change   **f** permission   **g** an unlimited time   **h** is valid   **i** if / as long as   **j** before   **k** if   **l** to the contract   **m** apart from issues covered by that directive   **n** home   **o** coming from   **p** proper

2 a The Agent must try to get business for the Principal.
   b The Agent must also serve the Principal's interests as well as he can.
   c He will do his best to provide the Principal with all the information he needs in order to promote the business.
   d In particular, he must tell the Principal about every order he receives.

3 a The original presents what is impossible, with an exception. The plain English version presents what is possible.
   b The plain English version is intended to be clearer.

4 *The contract can either be for a fixed period or it can last for an unlimited time. With both options, the start date is 10 February 2006, and either the Agent or the Principal can terminate the contract. They have to give notice, by registered letter, six months before the end of a calendar quarter. The difference is that with the first option, the contract is valid only for the period of the contract, and automatically ends after that, while with the second option, it remains valid until one of the parties gives notice.*

5 The subject is: *The provisions of the EEC Council Directive of 18 December 1986 on the co-ordination of the laws of the Member States relating to self-employed agents (86/653/EEC).*

  a *This agreement **is governed by** the provisions of …*

  b ***There is an** EEC Council Directive **which** relates to self-employed agents (86/653/EEC). **Its provisions** apply to this agreement.*

  c ***If there are** any disputes which come out of this agreement, or which are connected with it, they must be decided by the proper court in the area where the claimant lives or has his registered offices.*

  d ***There may be** some disputes which come out of this agreement, or which are connected with it. **If that happens**, they must be decided by the proper court in the area where the claimant lives or has his registered offices.*

  Options a) and b) are both clear, but a) is perhaps more professional. Option c) is still rather complicated, so option d) is clearer.

(SB p.68) Reading 5: The Commercial Agents (Council Directive) Regulations 1993

Tell students to read the introduction on page 68 to find out how these regulations relate to the directive mentioned in Reading 4.

> **Background note**
> The Regulations are part of English law. They are based on (and implement the provisions of) the directive. Directives are not in themselves binding, but must be implemented into the legal systems of each Member State. For more on the Regulations, see http://www.opsi.gov.uk/si/si1993/Uksi_19933053_en_1.htm.

25 Point out that students do not need to read the text carefully, but only need to understand enough to answer the questions. Allow around two minutes for students to read the text, after which allow them to check with a partner. When you go through the answers with the class, make it clear that *indemnify* /ɪnˈdemnɪfaɪ/ has several related meanings (see Language

note below). Then tell them to read the first paragraph of the text carefully to answer the two questions. When they have finished, check with the class.

> **Answers**
> **1** The aim is to provide commercial agents with a level of protection and security by ensuring that they are compensated following termination of the agency contract.
> **2** Under Regulation 17, there are two alternative ways of calculating a lump sum payment following termination of an agency contract: *indemnity* and *compensation*. The circumstances under which an indemnity will be granted are outlined in 17(3), and the calculation of the indemnity is covered by 17(4). The rules for calculating the entitlement under the compensation option are vaguer. The parties can choose between the two options, but the compensation alternative will apply where there is no agreement for an indemnity. Both terms refer to the payment of a lump sum, the main difference being the circumstances under which each particular form of lump-sum payment will be granted and calculated.

> **Language note**
> *Compensation* means 'money paid to somebody in exchange for something that has been lost or damaged or for some inconvenience'. The term *indemnity* /ɪnˈdemnɪtɪ/ has several meanings. In the regulations, it refers to a specific form of compensation only available under certain circumstances. The verb *indemnify* /ɪnˈdemnɪfaɪ/ is used here to mean 'to make amends for something, or to pay compensation for something'. The term is more commonly used in legal English to mean 'to guarantee against any loss which another might suffer'.

26 Tell students to read the questions carefully, and then to read the rest of the text to find the answers. Allow plenty of time, as the text is rather difficult. When they have finished, tell them to discuss their answers with a partner and then check with the class.

Answers

1 If stated in the contract. (NB The text mentions that compensation is available except where the contract otherwise provides, so logically indemnification is available if it is stated in the contract.)

2 a) The agent has to have either brought new customers or significantly increased sales with existing customers and b) the payment of an indemnity has to be fair (this will depend on the surrounding circumstances).

3 The maximum amount of indemnity is one year's commission based on the agent's average earnings in the last five years. If the contract has run for less than five years, the indemnity will be calculated on the average for the period of the contract.

4 Yes (17(8)).

Language notes

○ Note that of the two options, *indemnification* is usually more attractive to agents, as it is worth a year's commission. According to the regulations, *compensation* is worth between six and nine months' commission (depending on when notice is given: around six months if just before the end of a calendar quarter, almost nine months if notice is given just after the end of a calendar quarter).

○ If something is *equitable* /ˈekwɪtəbl/, it is fair.

○ *Remuneration* /rɪˌmjuːnəˈreɪʃn/ is the financial reward for some work done.

○ *Proper performance of the contract* refers to the situation when a contract is not breached.

○ In a strict legal sense, *amortisation* /əˌmɔːtaɪˈzeɪʃn/ refers only to the reduction in the value of intangible assets over time. In this text, it is used in a looser sense to refer to the writing-off of costs over time from accounts. For example, if you amortise /əˈmɔːtaɪz/ costs, you write them off over time from your accounts. For example, you want to invest in a new computer costing £100 for your work. The computer brings £25 worth of benefits to you every year, which means after four years it has

paid for itself, so the cost has been amortised. In the case of an agent, he/she might invest in a marketing campaign to promote the principal's goods. If the campaign was some time ago, it may have paid for itself, but if it was recent, and the principal breaks the contract early, the agent may have a right to demand some money back. Amortisation is similar to, but not the same as, depreciation, which is the reduction of the value of property over time. A four-year-old computer is worth less than a new computer, regardless of how effectively it has been used.

Optional extension

Tell students to use the techniques from Photocopiable worksheet 6.2 to rephrase some sections of Reading 5 in plain English. The text is too long to rephrase it all, but students should take turns to choose a difficult section or subsection for their partner to explain, as if to a client.

27 Elicit from the class whether all the information needs to be included [**Answer**: No, because colleagues in the department may read the original if they need to; all they need at this stage is a summary of the main points]. Also, elicit whether they should use plain English or legal jargon [**Suggested answer**: For a summary, plain English is better, as it can be read quickly and easily. If lawyers need to analyse the regulations in detail, they may read the original].

The writing can be set in class or as homework. (See section on Writing, page 8.)

Suggested answer

Regulation 17 deals with the entitlement of a commercial agent to an indemnity or compensation on termination of the agency contract, stating that it 'has effect for the purpose of ensuring that the commercial agent is, after termination of the agency contract, indemnified [...] or compensated for damage'.

Regulation 17(2) goes on to state that 'except where the agency contract otherwise provides, the commercial agent shall be entitled to be compensated rather than indemnified'.

Regulation 17(3) deals with entitlement to the indemnity and Regulation 17(4) establishes a cap to the amount of the indemnity.

Regulation 17(5) provides the possibility for the commercial agent to seek damages in addition to the indemnity.

Regulation 17(6) deals with the entitlement to compensation for the damage suffered by the agent 'as a result of the termination of his relations with his principal'.

Regulations 17(7) and 17(8) deal with the circumstances in which this damage shall be deemed to arise.

Listening 2: Meeting with corporate counsel

SB p.70 *6.2 6.3*

Tell students to read the introduction to find out what they are going to be listening to. Point out that Chance Computing was introduced in Exercise 23.

28 Elicit from the class possible answers to the two questions, and then play the recording. Afterwards, allow students to discuss their answers with a partner, as well as anything else they understood/remember from the recording. Then check the answers with the class.

Answers

1 The company feels it no longer needs its agents in order to sell products in southern Europe. It is getting lots of repeat orders and relatively few new customers, and no longer wants to keep paying commission on all sales to its agents.
2 There is no maximum limit for compensation.

Transcript » STUDENT'S BOOK page 131

Language note
If an indemnity is *capped*, there is a maximum limit on how much can be paid.

29 Again, elicit from the class possible answers to the two questions. After you have played the recording, allow students to discuss their answers with a partner, as well as anything else they understood/remember. Then check the answers with the class.

Answers

1 No, compensation is also payable for any reasonable expenses incurred by the agents.
2 Two years.

Transcript » STUDENT'S BOOK page 131

Language notes
○ If you *reimburse* /ˌriːɪmˈbɜːs/ somebody, you pay them back the money they have spent.
○ A *restraint of trade clause* is a contract clause forbidding an agent from competing with the principal during the contract period and for a certain period of time after the end of the contract period.
○ If a clause is *struck out*, it is deemed invalid by a court, and therefore ignored.

30 Tell students to discuss the statements with a partner to try to remember whether they were true or false. Then play both parts of the recording again for them to check. Afterwards, allow them to discuss their answers with a partner before checking with the class.

Answers

1 F (They are not in breach of contract.)
2 T 3 F (The agreement doesn't provide for an indemnity.) 4 T 5 F (It is valid for two years.) 6 F (The clause must refer to both the geographical area *and* the type of goods.) 7 T

Speaking 2: Role-play: discussing options

SB p.70

31 Tell students to read the background information. You may need to check that students understand the term *shadowing* (i.e. working closely with an experienced colleague to observe how he/she works). Assign roles. If you have an odd number of students, the extra student in one group should be Jenny Miller, who may also advise Clive. Make sure students realise that their role-play must reach a conclusion as to what to actually do, as this will be essential for the writing task.

Set a time limit of around eight minutes for the role-play. Monitor carefully, and afterwards give and elicit feedback on the quality of the meetings, as well as the language used.

Writing 2: Summary

32 Remind students of the techniques for writing a summary (see notes to Exercise 27 above). Point out that they should write in the same character as in the role-play, and the summary should be aimed at the management board of Chance Computing. The writing can be set in class or as homework. (See section on Writing, page 8.)

Suggested answer

Dear Jenny

Compensation for early termination of agency contracts

Following our recent discussion, I understand that you would like to end the current agreements with your agents in France, Spain and Portugal. This should be done as quickly and inexpensively as possible.

As I confirmed during our meeting, your agents would be entitled to compensation should you choose to end the agreements without first giving notice. Under current regulations, each agent would be entitled to full compensation for lost commissions that they would otherwise have expected to receive under the agency agreement. They would also be entitled to recover any reasonable expenses incurred whilst performing their duties as agents.

The contractual notice period is six months prior to the end of the calendar quarter. Although you have just missed one calendar quarter, this does not necessarily mean that you would have to compensate for the (almost) full nine months. However, your agents might be more willing to accept less generous terms if they were first given some notice whilst still on full commission. I would suggest offering a compensation package based on the following terms:

- an initial notice period of three months under full commission, during which time they would continue to fulfil their duties under your agreement;
- a lump sum based on 50% of three months' lost commissions (calculated at the average monthly commission paid since the commencement of the agency agreements);
- reasonable expenses.

These terms should be enough to deter most agents from pursuing a more generous settlement. If you think that there would be a reasonable chance of your agents accepting a lower sum, I would be very pleased to discuss this with you further.

Please do contact me should you have any questions on this.

Kind regards

Clive Sanborn

Clive Sanborn

Language Focus

Answers

1 Word formation

noun	adjective
merchant	merchantable, mercantile
commerce	commercial
negotiation	negotiable
finance	financial
bankruptcy	bankrupt

2 Noun–adjective collocations

1 negotiable **2** commercial **3** mercantile/commercial **4** mercantile **5** mercantile/commercial **6** commercial/negotiable

3 Abbreviations

1 Uniform Commercial Code
2 World Trade Organisation
3 United Nations Commission on International Trade Law

4 Key terms in intellectual property law

The missing word in all the expressions is *patent*.

5 Prepositions

1 on **2** of **3** by **4** on; of **5** for **6** into

7 Real property law

Teacher's brief

In common-law jurisdictions, all property can be divided into two groups: personal property and real property. Civil-law jurisdictions make a similar distinction between movable (= personal) and immovable (= real) property. The term **real property** (or **real estate** / **realty** in the USA) comes from the Latin word *res* (meaning *thing* or *matter*), in contrast with *personal* (from Latin *persona* = *person*). The distinction is important because when you transfer title to a piece of land, you can keep your personal property, but you have to leave all the real property with the new owner of the land.

The word **estate** refers to a set of rights to use real property, and effectively means ownership, but does not give the 'owner' absolute power over the property: the government still has rights attached to the property, such as the right to tax the property and the right of **compulsory purchase** (also known as *eminent domain*, typically used when the government forces a landowner to sell in order that a road can be built on the land). The government also has a right to police a person's real property, and a power of **escheat** (/ɪsˈtʃiːt/) (i.e. a right to take possession of the property if there are no other owners, for example if the owner dies and does not leave the property to any heirs).

Reading 1 mentions four types of **freehold estates** (i.e. ownership of real property). The most common is a **fee simple**, which gives landowners full rights to use and sell the land as they wish (within the limits discussed in the previous paragraph), and to pass the land to their heirs when they die. Other types of freehold are less common. A **life estate** gives the owner the right to use and sell the land only during his/her own life, but ownership reverts to the previous owner (or his/her heirs) upon that person's death. For example, a man with grown-up children from an earlier marriage may marry a second wife. He makes arrangements to the effect that when he dies, he leaves his new wife a *life estate* over his house, so that she may continue to live there and benefit from it. But when she dies, she may not pass the house on to her own children; instead, it reverts to the man's children from his previous marriage. If, on the other hand, she decides to sell the house to a third party before she dies, she cannot sell it as a fee simple, but only as an **estate pur autre vie** (literally: *for another's life*), i.e. the third party only has rights to the house for the duration of the wife's life, after which again it reverts to the man's children. The fourth type of freehold estate, the **fee tail**, is very rarely used nowadays, but was traditionally used to keep land within a family: the land could be inherited from generation to generation, but not sold.

In contrast to freeholds, which effectively cover ownership of real property, **leaseholds** typically involve a **tenant** paying regular **rent** to a **landlord** (the owner) for the right to use the property. This key distinction between buying and renting real property is common around the world, although concepts such as freeholds and leaseholds will vary from one jurisdiction to another.

The first part of the unit focuses on two aspects of **real property law** in Ukraine. Of course, Ukraine is just used as an example, but many aspects of Ukrainian property law are very similar in other countries. Reading 2 includes an extract from an article on the rights and obligations of landlords and tenants when **terminating a lease agreement**. Both parties need special protection in this situation: the tenant risks losing his/her 'home', which can be a very traumatic experience, and the landlord will obviously be desperate to protect his/her real property, which in many cases represents years of investment, from irresponsible or destructive tenants. Listening 1 is a description of **foreigners' rights to buy real property** in Ukraine. Here, as in many other countries, foreigners have fewer rights than locals, especially with regard to buying farmland. This is to prevent, for example, rich foreigners buying up lots of attractive land when it is cheap in order to exploit it (or the people who live there) in the future. It is seen as especially important in countries like Ukraine to preserve local ownership of the countryside.

The second part of the unit covers several aspects connected with **fly-to-let**, a practice where someone buys a property abroad in order to make money by letting it to tenants, and perhaps selling it for a profit after some years. This is especially attractive in rapidly developing countries, where foreigners are often in a better position to afford high and rising property prices. At the time of writing, the countries of Central and Eastern Europe are especially attractive for fly-to-let investors, as many of them combine rapid economic development with EU membership, which simplifies the process of investment for citizens of other EU countries. The case study in this unit features an investor from Spain looking into a possible fly-to-let in Czech Republic. Firstly, we learn about various legal aspects connected with **buying a property**, such as liens, encumbrances, easements and restrictive covenants. Later, we learn about **letting a property**, focusing on the difference between a **shorthold tenancy** agreement (which expires at the end of a fixed period) and a **periodic tenancy** (which is automatically renewed at the end of each period), and we read a **sample tenancy agreement**.

The unit also focuses on several important language skills and techniques for lawyers and law students: understanding **formal writing**, **giving emphasis** in a presentation, and managing a **telephone enquiry**.

THE STUDY OF LAW

Lead-in
SB p.72

Elicit from the class what they understand by the term *property law*. Then tell them to read the introduction on page 72 to check their ideas. Draw attention to the fact that the term covers both personal property and real property, and elicit some examples of each.

Discuss with the class why real property law has to be different from the law on sale of goods.

[**Possible answer**: There seems to be no inherent reason for all the distinctions. It can be argued that real property tends to be more valuable than personal property, and therefore requires more regulation, but the same could be argued with regard to expensive items of personal property, such as specialist equipment, luxury cars, planes or rare minerals. In personal property transactions, the buyer and seller are responsible for taking necessary precautions, and the same could be true in terms of real property. On the other hand, there are, of course, important concepts which are only relevant to real property, such as easements.]

1a Discuss the question with the whole class.

▸ **Answer**
In common-law legal systems, property law distinguishes real property (land and immovable property, such as houses) from personal property (often referred to as *chattel*). Civil-law systems generally make a similar division between movable property (personal property) and immovable property (real estate).

b Tell students to work with a partner to decide which of the nine examples are personal property and which are real property.

▸ **Answers**
Real property: a, c, e, f, g
Personal property: b, h, i
A large outdoor sculpture (d) could be either real or personal property, depending on how permanent a fixture it is.

📖 **Background notes**
○ Students may be surprised to see *a business plan* described as personal property rather than intellectual property. In fact, intellectual property is a sub-category of personal property:

Property			
Personal property			Real property
Intangible property		Tangible property (e.g. a car)	(e.g. a house)
Intellectual property (e.g. a song)	Other types of intangible property (e.g. stocks and shares)		

○ The most difficult example to categorise is the *large outdoor sculpture*, which may be seen as a work of art (and therefore personal property) or as an improvement on the land it stands on (and therefore real property). This is important because an artist may retain rights over a work of art even when it belongs to another party (e.g. a right to prevent distortion or destruction of the piece, which might damage the artist's reputation). If the sculpture is considered to be 'site-specific art' (i.e. the location is an essential part of the art), it may be argued, therefore, that the owner of the land has no right to alter that land, as it would damage the art. See http://www.ca1.uscourts.gov/cgi-bin/getopn.pl?OPINION=05-1970.01A for a fascinating and fairly easy-to-read case study from the USA. In this case, the 'site-specific art' argument was rejected by the US Court of Appeals.

Reading 1: Real property law

SB p.72

2 With the class, read the four statements to make sure students understand the words (although you should avoid explaining *fee simple* and *life estate*, as these will be defined in the Reading). Elicit from the class the meaning of the word *estate* (see Teacher's brief on page 100 of this book and footnote 1 on SB page 72). You may also need to check *indefinite duration* (= an unlimited period of time), a *grantee* (= a person who receives title to real property, i.e. the owner), *heir* /eə(r)/ (= the person who inherits property when the owner dies) and *to confer title interest in a property* (= to pass ownership of the property to another party). Then tell students to read the text carefully to find whether the statements are true or false. When they have finished reading, allow them to discuss their answers with a partner before going through the answers with the class.

Answers

1 T **2** F **3** T **4** F

Language notes

○ The text refers several times to the concepts of *ownership* and *possession*. Ownership in a strict legal sense means legal title to property (whether real or personal). Possession is a more general term, meaning ownership, control or occupation of property. Thus ownership is a type of possession, but it is possible to possess property without owning it (e.g. under a lease agreement).

○ The terms *real property* and *real estate* are virtually synonymous. The difference is that real property includes interests such as a right to buy the property in the future. See http://dictionary.law.com/definition2.asp?selected=1727&bold=||||.

○ The text mentions that ownership of land includes ownership of the *airspace* above it. Of course, there are limits to this: the navigable airspace used by aeroplanes is considered to belong to countries, not individuals. In the USA, landowners have the right to the airspace up to a 'reasonable level', i.e. a level which they could reasonably take advantage of. See http://en.wikipedia.org/wiki/Air_rights.

○ Several of the terms in the text look more like French than English (e.g. *fee simple*, *estate pur autre vie*). They are pronounced, however, with a normal English accent: /fiː ˈsɪmpl, rˈsteɪt pər ˈɔːtrə ˈviː/. Note that *pur autre vie* (sometimes spelled *per autre vie*) is not a spelling mistake: the correct French spelling would be *pour* (meaning 'for'), but the English term comes from an older version of French, and has preserved that old spelling.

○ The text mentions *fee tail*. This was a device which allowed landowners to pass property to their heirs, but not to sell it. It was useful in medieval times as a way of ensuring land stayed within a particular family, but is now extremely rare (see http://en.wikipedia.org/wiki/Fee_tail).

○ Property can be *inheritable* (i.e. passed on to heirs), while genetic diseases can be *heritable*.

○ In the example of an *estate pur autre vie*, the text mentions that the landowner may *enjoy tax savings* as a result of giving her property to charity. An important tax saving associated with giving to charity comes from an exemption from inheritance tax (in the UK). When a landowner dies, inheritance tax is payable on the value of her estate over a certain threshold (currently £300,000 in the UK), but donations to charity from that estate are not subject to inheritance tax. This does not mean, of course, that her heirs receive more, but simply that the tax office receives less. It is also possible to reduce income tax payments by giving to charity, as long as the donation is classed as tax deductible. See http://www.charitynavigator.org/index.cfm?bay=content.view&cpid=31 for an example of how this works.

○ There is considerable confusion over the terms *lease*, *let* and *rent*. As nouns, a *lease* is the agreement, while the *rent* is the money to be paid. As verbs, the three terms are very often used interchangeably, and all can be used in both directions (i.e. you can lease/let/rent property *to* and *from* somebody). However, it is more common (and considered more correct) to *lease/let property to* somebody, and *rent property from* somebody. (It is also possible to *rent property out to* somebody.) *Letting* generally involves smaller properties, such as a single room, in contrast to *leasing*, which often involves whole buildings. It is also possible to *sublet* part of a property *to* or *from* somebody (i.e. the tenant of a house could charge rent to a subtenant for use of a room in that house).

○ In this text, *compensation* is used as a synonym for rent, and simply means 'money paid in return for something', in this case use of property.

○ A key difference between a *licence* and a *lease* is that a licence gives the *licensee* a right to use property for a specific purpose (such as staging a concert), while a lease tends to be for more general purposes.

○ The *Statute of Frauds* is a requirement in common-law jurisdictions that certain types of contract must be in writing. As well as covering real-estate contracts (deeds, etc.), it also includes marriage contracts and wills. See http://en.wikipedia.org/wiki/Statute_of_Frauds.

SB p.73 # Key terms 1: Instruments and people in real property law

3 Tell students to work alone to complete the matching exercise, and then compare their answers with a partner. When you have checked with the whole class, tell students to test each other in small groups by reading one of the definitions to elicit the terms in bold from their partners.

Answers
1 b   2 c   3 a   4 f   5 h   6 d   7 e   8 i
9 g

4 Explain the task to the class, using the example to illustrate. Make sure students realise that they can use words other than those highlighted in Exercise 3. When they have finished, elicit as many sentences as possible from the class.

Suggested answers
A tenant signs a lease when he/she rents property from a landlord.
A landlord signs a lease when he/she rents property to a tenant.
When he/she inherits property, an heir receives a deed granting title to property.
A grantor transfers a title to property to another person by means of a deed.
A grantee acquires an interest in property through a deed.
A licensee receives permission to enter another person's property through a licence.

SB p.74 # Language use 1: Forming adjectives with negative prefixes

5 Have the students search the text on pages 72–73 to find the two adjectives with negative prefixes.

Answers
indefinite (line 3), unlimited (line 11)
(Note that although the adjective *inheritable* starts with *in*–, in this case it's not being used as a negative prefix, i.e. it doesn't mean 'not able to be passed on to an heir'. See Language note after Exercise 2.)

Then elicit some more adjectives from the class. Encourage them to think of negative adjectives with all five prefixes (*un*–, *in*–, *im*–, *il*–, *ir*–). Discuss briefly any rules they know to help them form negative adjectives, but point out that such rules as exist are not especially reliable, and it is best just to learn negative prefixes one by one, in the same way that irregular verbs have to be learnt.

Language note
The confusing situation with negative adjectives has arisen mainly as a result of the complicated history of English, with many words coming from Latin or French and many more coming from old Germanic languages, such as Anglo-Saxon. As a

general rule, many Germanic adjectives form their negatives with *un–*, while Latin-based adjectives form their negatives with *in–/im–/il–/ir–*. This gives English many pairs of near-synonyms (*unsure/insecure, unbelievable/incredible, unlawful/illegal, unreadable/illegible, unlikely/improbable*). For Latin-based words, English has inherited from Latin and French a system where adjectives starting with *m–* or *p–* form negatives with *im–* (as in *impossible* and *immovable*), adjectives starting with *r–* form negatives with *ir–* (as in *irregular*), and adjectives starting with *l–* form adjectives with *il–* (as in *illegal*). Adjectives starting with other sounds form negatives with *in–* (such as *indirect* and *inaccessible*). These rules apply only to Latin-based words (although even here, there are plenty of Latin-based adjectives which form negatives with *un–* (such as *unfortunate*)). Unfortunately, most learners of English often have no way of knowing which words come from Latin and which are Germanic.

There are, of course, several other ways of making adjectives negative: *non–* (although this is mainly used for nouns, such as *non-smoker*, and adjectives derived therefrom, such as *non-smoking*); *dis–* (often connected with good and bad adjectives, such as *disrespectful*, *dishonest* and *disloyal*); and *mis–* (meaning 'wrongly', mainly used for nouns and verbs, such as *mistake*, and adjectives derived therefrom, such as *mistaken*).

6 Tell students to work through the exercise alone, using only their instinct / current knowledge, and then to compare with a partner. Encourage them to use a dictionary to check any prefixes they are unsure of. Then go through the answers with the class.

Answers
1 illegal; unsafe; unsanitary; illegal; unenforceable
2 unable; impossible
3 indefinite; unlimited
4 unspecified; uncertain

Language notes
○ If premises are *unsanitary*, they are unfit for human use because they may cause health problems, typically as a result of being dirty or neglected.
○ Sentence 3 mentions an *indefinite or unlimited period*. These two terms are synonyms.

SB p.74 # Reading 2: Real property investment law

Tell students to read through the introduction on page 74 quickly to find out a) who Mychajlo /mɪˈxaɪləʊ/ is; b) what his presentation is about; and c) what problems he has.

Answers
a Mychajlo is a Ukrainian graduate student of law.
b His presentation is about real property law in Ukraine.
c He has a problem understanding the English in the text.

7 Tell students to read the text to match the paragraphs with the headings. Make sure they realise that they will not need to use two of the headings. Allow them to check briefly with a partner before checking with the whole class.

Answers
1 e   2 c   3 d

Language notes
○ Note that the second and third paragraphs relate only to terminating *definite-term* lease agreements (i.e. ones with specified start and finish dates). *Indefinite-term* lease agreements, in contrast, are much easier to terminate, by giving the other party three months' notice.
○ *Capital repairs* are repairs to a real property with the aim of prolonging the life or productivity of the property. They contrast with day-to-day maintenance work.
○ *Compulsory purchase* is the situation when a government takes a piece of real property without the owners'

consent, typically in order to build a road through the land. In the USA, this power is called *eminent domain*. Note that the US term refers to the power, while the British term refers to the action. See http://en.wikipedia.org/wiki/Compulsory_Purchase.

○ *Alienation* means the complete transfer of title to real property.

8 Elicit from the class what they understand by the term 'features of the text' [**Answer**: Patterns affecting the choice of grammar, vocabulary, punctuation, etc.], with some examples of features that students find difficult in general (e.g. long sentences). Then tell them to read the excerpt quickly to identify the features that make this particular text difficult. When you go through the answers with the class, avoid explaining vocabulary (as much of this will come up in Exercise 9) or difficult sentence structures. Elicit examples to illustrate each of the features.

Suggested answers
○ Use of formal vocabulary, e.g. *terminated, commenced, in the event*
○ Many technical terms, e.g. *lease agreements, definite term, stipulated by law*
○ Non-colloquial use of *shall* and *may* (see Language note below)
○ Long sentences, complex sentence structure, e.g. most of the second paragraph is a single sentence

Language note
In colloquial (i.e. everyday) English, *shall* is mainly used to ask for suggestions (*What shall we eat?*) and *may* is mainly used for probability (*You may be right*) and permission (*May I use your phone?*). In legal English, *shall* is often used simply to refer to the future (*The landlord shall have the right to …*) or to state obligations, while *may* is often used to state a party's options in a contract (*Lease agreements may be terminated …*).

(SB p.76) Language use 2: Formal/informal style: synonyms

Elicit from the class what they know about the origins of words in English, and how this relates to formal and informal styles. Then tell them to read the box on page 76 to find four examples of formal Latin-based words and three of their less formal Anglo-Saxon equivalents.

Answers
Latin-based: demonstrate (Latin: *demonstrare*), retain (Latin: *retinere*), possession (Latin: *possessio*), terminate (Latin: *terminare*)
Anglo-Saxon equivalents: show (Old English: *sceawian*), keep (Old English: *cepan*), end (Old English: *ende*).
Source of etymologies: http://www. etymonline.com/. NB The Anglo-Saxon nearequivalent of *possession* is *ownership*, but in legal English these have slightly different meanings (see Language notes to Reading 1, pages 102–103).

9 Tell students to try the matching exercise alone and then compare their answers with a partner. Make sure they understand the term *common* (= *shared by both sides*). When you go through the answers with the class, make sure all students have understood all the terms in bold (and not simply made some lucky guesses) by asking concept-checking questions (e.g. *What does 'mutual agreement' mean?*; *When exactly is prior consent given?*; *Name three consecutive months*; etc.). Take this opportunity to check for any more vocabulary problems from the text.

Answers
1 prior consent 2 commenced
3 mutual 4 terminated 5 consecutive
6 comply with 7 contravenes
8 pursuant to 9 designation
10 compulsory purchase

Optional extension exercise
(Photocopiable worksheet 7.1)

This draws attention to the more difficult vocabulary and sentence structures from Reading 2, with a particular focus on legal English collocations. The aim is to move students closer to the stage where they can produce high-quality written documents themselves. Note that the content of the worksheet is almost identical to Reading 2, but the bullet points from the Reading have been expanded to make full sentences.

1 Make enough copies of the worksheet for students to work in groups of three or four. Cut up the worksheets along the dotted lines. There is no need to cut up the first column, as it is useful for students to have these in the correct order. It is also a good idea to give students a copy which has not been cut up, so they can test themselves later.

2 Students should work in groups to complete the matching exercise. Tell them to look out for collocations (such as *mutual agreement*) and to do the easier ones first. Monitor carefully and offer support and correction, as the exercise is rather difficult.

3 When the first groups have finished, go through the answers with the class, drawing attention to the collocations which have been split.

4 As a follow-up, students should test each other (or themselves) by reading the first column to elicit/work out how the sentence continues (especially the collocations).

Answers

1 o **2** f **3** e **4** a **5** p **6** u **7** r **8** d
9 s **10** l **11** n **12** m **13** j **14** b **15** h
16 t **17** i **18** q **19** v **20** c **21** k **22** g

10 Students should discuss the questions in groups first, and then as a whole class. The answer for most of the situations is likely to be 'it depends', in which case elicit what it depends on.

Suggested answers

1 Generally speaking, a formal style in writing and speaking is appropriate when dealing with official bodies and organisations, people you do not know well (such as a new client) or with your superiors (unless you know that they prefer a more informal style of speaking/writing). The factors that might affect the choice of a more formal style include the nature of the relationship of the people involved and the conventions of the text type in question (for example, a document to be submitted to the court would be written in a formal style).

2 Formal language would be most suitable for the seminar presentation and seminar paper. Both, however, would benefit from some paraphrases of technical language into plain English, as this will aid communication. A more neutral register would be appropriate for speaking and writing to a client (but see Background note below for further discussion of this).

Background note

Lawyers tend to use very formal and complicated language, especially in writing. In many cases, clients expect this, as it shows intelligence and professionalism, and it can also be a sign of respect, as it shows that the lawyer thinks the client is intelligent enough to understand. But many non-lawyers find this formal language difficult to follow, and this may lead to communication breakdowns. Less formal language can also enable lawyers to build better rapport with their clients – by showing their human side. For these reasons, it is essential for lawyers to be able to explain complex concepts using everyday language. This does not mean they have to use highly informal, colloquial/chatty language, but simply a 'neutral' register. Lawyers need to find a compromise between creating a professional impression and maximising communication, which in practice means they must master a range of registers, including very formal (e.g. for communicating with other lawyers) and neutral (e.g. for communicating with clients and colleagues). They need to listen carefully to the type of language that others use with them, and also pay attention to any misunderstandings, and adjust their language accordingly.

Listening 1: Property-law presentation

SB p.76 7.1

11 Make sure students remember who Mychajlo is (see Reading 2) and, as a class, predict what his presentation will be about. Discuss the question with the whole class. If students don't know the situation in their countries, discuss how they could find out. Play the recording once and allow students to discuss the answers with a partner before checking with the class.

> **Background note**
>
> It is very easy to find such information online by searching for 'real property' and the name of the country; there are hundreds of websites keen to help foreigners invest their money. For more general information, sites such as http://www.property-abroad.com/buyers-guide/ provide information on a range of countries.

Transcript » STUDENT'S BOOK **page 132**

> **Language note**
>
> *Settlement boundaries* refers to the official boundaries between settlements (cities, towns and villages) and the countryside.

12 Allow students to discuss the statements with a partner to try to remember whether they are true or false. Then play the recording for them to check. After they have discussed their answers with a partner, go through the answers with the class.

Answers
1 T
2 F (A foreigner must sell inherited agricultural land within a year.)
3 F (Foreign business entities may acquire buildings/structures on non-agricultural land.)
4 F (Foreigners can acquire land in Ukraine by buying shares in a Ukrainian company that owns land.)

Speaking 1: Giving emphasis to important points

SB p.77

13 Elicit from the class why it is important in a presentation to emphasise certain points, and get them to suggest some techniques for emphasising. Then tell them to read the introduction and the list of five points to compare it with their ideas. Make sure they understand the difference between repetition (= using the same words shortly after using them the first time) and rephrasing (= using different words). Also elicit some examples of sentence openers (e.g. *It is important to stress that …*) and intensifying adverbs and adjectives (e.g. *extremely important, absolutely crucial*). Then tell students to read and listen to the audio transcript on SB page 132 to underline examples of the five techniques. When they have checked with a partner, go through the answers with the class.

Answers
1 allowed to buy, exception, circumstances, ownership rights
2 And this one is particularly important …
So, it is not possible for foreigners to own farmland.
So, if they plan to do business and buy existing facilities or construct new facilities for business, they may have certain ownership rights to land.
… cannot buy farmland.
3 Let me stress that although foreigners can't *own* farmland, they *are* allowed to lease it.
The situation with *non*-agricultural land is quite different. In this case, it *is* possible for foreigners, …
Now let's turn to a very important point: the circumstances under which foreign ownership of land in Ukraine *is* possible.
4 But I must point out …
Let me stress that …
But I should stress that …
Now let's turn to a very important point: …
5 And this one is particularly important for …
But I must point out that there are some significant exceptions.

Elicit from the class more examples of useful expressions for each of the techniques (other than repetition) and write them up on the board. You may use these ideas:

- Rephrasing: *In other words …* ; *That is …* ; *So …* ; *I mean …*
- Using the voice to stress an idea (NB these phrases often accompany the stressed words): *However, …* ; *On the other hand, …* ; *In contrast, …* ; *… in fact …* ; *… actually …* ; *While …* ; *Whereas …*
- Sentence openers: *It's important to realise that …* ; *I'd like to stress that …* ; *The key difference is that …* ; *Remember that …* ; *Notice that …*
- Intensifying adverbs: *especially*; *particularly*; *really*; *absolutely*
- Intensifying adjectives: *essential*; *crucial*; *vital*; *important*; *significant*; *substantial*

Also, elicit the types of word that were stressed in Listening 1, and what each stressed word contrasted with:

- Auxiliary verbs: **are** allowed (contrasts with *can't*); it **is** possible (contrasts with *are not allowed*).
- Verbs with contrasting meanings: *can't* **own** farmland contrasts with **lease** it.
- Adjectives with negative prefixes: **non**-agricultural land (contrasts with *agricultural land*).

Elicit more types of word that may receive contrastive stress, e.g. modals (e.g. *may*, *must*); negative words (e.g. *not*, *under **no** circumstances*); nouns with contrastive meanings (e.g. *foreigners* vs. *Ukrainians*; *landlords* vs. *tenants*); adjectives with opposites (e.g. **new** facilities vs. **existing** facilities). Point out that positive sentences without auxiliaries may be contrasted with negative sentences by adding *do/does/did*: *Although foreigners may **not** own farmland in Ukraine, many **do** in fact own land in other countries.*

Tell students to work in small groups to make as many contrastive sentences as they can based on what they have learnt about Ukrainian real property law (from Reading 2 and Listening 1), in order to practise the various types of contrastive stress. Allow them to invent any details they don't know.

14 This will work best if all the students' presentations relate to different jurisdictions. Tell them to research foreign ownership restrictions in their chosen jurisdiction at home, and to prepare a short presentation (only one or two minutes) using the techniques from Unit 1 and this unit. If you would prefer not to wait until the next lesson, you could tell them to invent the details for the purposes of the presentation, as long as they practise the technique of emphasising important points. Ideally, each student should give his/her presentation to the whole class, but with large classes, it may be necessary for them to present to each other in groups. Remember to give feedback on their use of the techniques, and encourage students to comment on the effectiveness of each other's presentations.

LAW IN PRACTICE

SB p.77 Lead-in

Elicit from the class what they think *buy-to-let* and *fly-to-let* might mean, in the context of real property law. Then tell them to read the introduction on page 77 to check. Discuss briefly whether anyone in the class has any experience of such practices, either as one of the parties or as a lawyer.

15 Tell students to discuss the questions in small groups. Encourage them to consider the uncertainties connected with the three stages of the fly-to-let process: buying, leasing and selling at a later date.

Background note

One of the biggest considerations regarding buy-to-let or fly-to-let is tax. If the investor plans to sell the property after some years, without re-investing the money in the same country, there may be substantial taxes to pay (e.g. 10% of the sale price), which could easily wipe out any income made from the investment.

Key terms 2: Buying real property

SB p.77

16 Tell students to work in small groups to complete the exercise. Point out that there are likely to be many unknown words, but students should still be able to work out most of the answers. When you go through the answers with the class, briefly check students have understood all the words, not just the correct answers, as these words will be useful later. There will be a second chance for students to study these words after Listening 2.

Answers
1 deposit **2** rental income **3** mortgage
4 capital appreciation **5** purchase price

Language notes

○ A *lien* /liːn/ is an officially documented claim against property to guarantee a payment (e.g. a debt). See http://dictionary.law.com. A *mortgage* /ˈmɔːɡɪdʒ/ is a common type of lien which is secured against real property. It gives the lender (typically a bank) the right to sell the property if the borrower fails to repay the debt.

○ *Conveyance* /kənˈveɪəns/ is the transfer of real property from one party to another. A *conveyance* can also be the general name of the document transferring title to the property, also known as a *deed*.

○ An *escrow account* /ˈɪskrəʊ əˈkaʊnt/ is an account held by an independent third party (an escrow agent), which holds the funds and documentation (e.g. the deed) associated with a real property sale. The agent will only release the funds and documentation when both parties have fulfilled their obligations. This avoids the situation where, for example, a buyer transfers funds to the seller, but the seller then disappears without transferring the rights to the property.

○ An *easement* is a right over another party's real estate (e.g. a right to cross a neighbour's land in order to park one's car, or an electricity supplier's right to access a pylon situated on farmland).

○ A *cadastral* /kəˈdæstrəl/ register, also known as a *cadastre* /kəˈdæstrə/, is a complete list of all real property in a country, which documents ownership, dimensions, value, etc. See http://en.wikipedia.org/wiki/Cadastre.

○ A *chain of title* traces ownership of a piece of real estate over its entire history, from the first owner to its current owner. It is used by buyers (or their agents) to establish that title to the real estate is free from any claims. See http://dictionary.law.com.

○ *Capital appreciation* is the process whereby money invested (*capital*) goes up in value (*to appreciate*). If the capital loses value, it is said to *depreciate*.

○ *Stamp duty* is a tax on documents, based on the historical need for formal documents to carry an official stamp (see http://en.wikipedia.org/wiki/Stamp_Duty). In the context of real property, it is a type of *property transfer tax*.

○ A *notarial deed* /nəʊˈteərɪəl ˈdiːd/ is a deed which has been officially certified and witnessed by a *notary public*. Notaries public in common-law jurisdictions are considerably less powerful than notaries in civil-law jurisdictions, where they perform a much wider range of functions. See http://en.wikipedia.org/wiki/Civil_law_notary.

17 Tell students to work alone to complete the advertisement. Make sure they realise that one of the words is not used. When they have finished, let them check with a partner before going through the answers with the class. You may need to explain some of the abbreviations from the advertisement (e.g. *pcm = per calendar month; yr = year; @ 7% pa = at 7 per cent per annum* [= *per year*]).

Answers
1 purchase price **2** deposit **3** mortgage
4 rental income

18 Discuss this with the whole class. If necessary, refer students back to the uncertainties they discussed in Exercise 15.

Suggested answer

On the face of it, this seems like a good investment. Possibilities for checking include speaking to an independent financial adviser, running a search on an independent financial website (e.g. www.fool.co.uk) and comparing the figures quoted with those quoted by other agencies.

SB p.78 **7.2 7.3**

Listening 2: Telephone enquiry: buy-to-let

Tell students to read the introduction on page 78 to find out what the listening will be about, and who the two participants are.

19 Tell students to listen to the first part of the recording to answer the two questions. Point out that the recording is rather long, so they should try to understand and remember as much as they can from the dialogue. After listening, tell them to compare their answers with a partner, and to discuss what they can remember from the conversation.

Answers

1 From a colleague (Jordi Forrat)
2 No

Transcript » STUDENT'S BOOK **page 132**

Language notes

(NB Many of the technical terms from the audio transcript are explained in the Language notes after Exercise 16 above, and in Exercise 23 in the SB.)

○ The phrase *Should we go ahead ...* looks like it is a question, but is in fact a rather formal way of saying *If we go ahead ...*
○ If an insurance policy *matures*, it reaches an agreed time limit and becomes due for payment.
○ A *secondary residence* is a formal way of saying a 'second home'.
○ If a requirement has been *repealed*, the legislation covering it has been annulled, so it is no longer required.
○ If you *incorporate* /ɪŋˈkɔːpəreɪt/, you form a corporation.
○ If a tax is *levied* /ˈleviːd/ on something, there is a requirement that tax must be paid.

20 Students should discuss the questions with a partner first to see how much they remember, and then listen a second time to check. When they have had another chance to compare their answers with a partner, check with the class.

Answers

1 c **2** b **3** a **4** b

21 Tell students to work in small groups to go through the list of terms briefly to see which of them they can understand. Avoid explaining any of the terms yourself at this stage; point out that many of them are explained in the recording, and that you will clarify any remaining problems after the listening. Play the recording once for students to tick the terms that are mentioned. After listening, tell them to compare their answers with a partner, and to discuss what was said about each of the terms. Then go through the answers with the class. Avoid explaining the terms in detail, as this will undermine Exercise 23.

Answers

1, 2, 4, 5, 6, 8, 9, 12, 14

Transcript » STUDENT'S BOOK **page 133**

Language notes

○ If you buy a property *outright*, you buy it wholly and completely, i.e. without a mortgage from a bank.
○ If you *put down a deposit*, you pay a portion of the purchase price to guarantee that you will pay the remainder.
○ If a property is *under development*, it is being built or rebuilt.
○ A *facelift* literally means plastic surgery on somebody's face. In the context of real property, it is used to refer to a dramatic renovation to make the property look much younger.
○ A *title search* is an examination of all the local government records covering a property's history of ownership. See http://dictionary.law.com.
○ A *charge* is a legal claim to rights over another person's property.

Optional extension

Elicit from the class which seven terms were not mentioned in the recording. Then read the definition of each one in turn (from the list below), but in mixed-up order. Students have to guess which of the terms you are describing.

- **Gazump** /gə'zʌmp/: If you do this, you do not sell a property to another party even though you have promised to do so, because a third party has offered a higher price.
- **Foreclosure** /fɔːˈkləʊʒə(r)/: This is the situation when a lender requires the resale of a real property in order to return the money lent.
- **Planning permission**: This is required from local government bodies by property owners before they can build on land or make any alterations to current buildings.
- **Completion**: This refers to the final stage in a real estate sale, when ownership changes hands.
- **Survey**: This is a formal inspection of a building before its sale to assess its structural soundness and/or value.
- **Tenancy agreement**: The contract between a tenant and a landlord.
- **Boundaries**: Information about these is contained in the cadastral register and the deed of sale.

22 Tell students to discuss the six sentences with a partner to try to remember if they are true or false. You may need to check they understand some of the vocabulary in the questions (e.g. if you *incur* /ɪŋˈkɜː(r)/ debts, you have them as a result of your actions; if you are *liable* /ˈlaɪəbl/ for charges, you are legally responsible for them). Play the recording for students to check, and then allow them to discuss again with a partner before going through the answers with the class.

Answers
1 T   **2** T   **3** F (In reply to Ms Cervera's question about what happens if a developer goes bankrupt, Ms Fialová replies 'That's rare in the Czech Republic'.)
4 F (If someone has used a property as security for a loan, the lienholder would have a legal claim against the property if the lien has not been satisfied.)
5 F (Restrictive covenants limit the use of property.)   **6** F (She recommends her brother as a letting agent for finding tenants.)

SB p.79 **Key terms 3: Conveyancing**

23 Students should work alone to complete the matching exercise. Allow them to check with a partner before going through the answers with the class. As a follow-up, students should test each other by reading one of the definitions to elicit the key term from their partner.

Answers
1 c   **2** d   **3** g   **4** h   **5** i   **6** j   **7** a   **8** e
9 b   **10** f

Language notes
- *Successive* means 'one after another'. *Successive ownership* refers to the ownership passing from one party to another to another over a period of many years.
- A document can be *authenticated* in many ways, but it can only be *notarised* by an official *notary*, who confirms the document's legal validity with his/her signature and official stamp.

SB p.80 **Writing: Follow-up email**

24 The writing can be done as homework or in class. (See section on Writing, page 8.)

Suggested answer
See Optional extension below.

Optional extension (Photocopiable worksheet 7.2)
This contains a model answer for this writing task. Ideally it should be given after students have had a chance to write their own follow-up emails, but you may also decide to give it before they write their own versions, as it provides some useful language which they may copy. Of course, they should not copy too much from the model answer. If you feel that students would copy too much when doing

their own writing, change the writing task so that they have to write to Ms Cervera about a potential fly-to-let in their own countries.

The exercise focuses on the useful words from the listening, which are provided as anagrams.

1 Tell students to read the letter alone at first to solve the anagrams, and then to compare their answers with a partner. If they are struggling, allow them to listen again or read the audio transcript.
2 Go through the answers with the class.
3 Elicit from the class any useful phrases students could use in their own writing.

Answers
1 purchase   **2** conveyance   **3** completion
4 cadastral register   **5** repealed
6 incorporate   **7** advantages   **8** stamp duty
9 levied   **10** formation   **11** documentation
12 notarise   **13** purchase agreement
14 redraft   **15** deed   **16** recommend
17 escrow   **18** stipulated   **19** bankrupt
20 title search   **21** chain of title
22 encumbrances   **23** lien   **24** lienholder
25 restrictive covenants   **26** easements
27 letting agency   **28** confirmation

Reading 3: Draft tenancy agreement
(SB p.80)

25 Tell students to quickly read the introduction on page 80 to find out what has happened since the phone conversation in Listening 2. Make sure they understand the questions (e.g. *evict = to force tenants to leave the leased property, typically after a breach of the tenancy agreement*). Then tell them to read the text carefully to answer the questions. Tell them to ignore the gaps in the text for now. After one or two minutes, tell them to discuss the answers with a partner, and then check with the class.

Answers
1 A statutory periodic tenancy is automatically created.
2 The landlord can choose to evict the tenant, in which case he/she must first serve notice (of eviction).

Language notes
○ A *shorthold tenancy* is a tenancy for a fixed term (e.g. one year), in contrast to a *periodic tenancy*, which is automatically renewed at the end of each period.
○ A *dwelling house* is simply a house designated as a place for people to live (= *dwell*).
○ The phrase *at any point thereafter* means 'at any time after that time', i.e. after the expiry of the fixed term.
○ The agreement states that if the fixed term ends, a *statutory periodic tenancy* is *automatically* created. *Automatically* here does not mean that the parties have no control over whether such a periodic tenancy is created; it simply means that the parties may, by virtue of their actions (i.e. the tenants continuing to live in the property and pay rent and the landlord continuing to accept rent and taking no steps to recover the property), decide to take advantage of the convenience of a statutory periodic tenancy. *Automatic* simply means that they do not have to go to the trouble of drawing up a new tenancy agreement. Of course, the parties may agree they do not want this statutory periodic tenancy, in which case it is not automatically created.

Optional extension
As a comprehension check, tell students to decide what the function of each paragraph of the agreement is.

Suggested answers
1 duration of the agreement   **2** rent
3 the landlord's agreement   **4** deposit
5 tenancy deposit protection scheme
6 expiry   **7** breaches of the agreement

Listening 3: Telephone enquiry: tenancy agreement
(SB p.81) *(7.4)*

26 With the class, elicit what sort of information is required for each space in the tenancy agreement [**Answers**: **1** address; **2** number of months; **3** date; **4** amount of money; **5** an ordinal number, e.g. *5th*; **6** amount of money]. Then play the recording for students to

complete the gaps. Allow them to check with a partner, and also discuss what they remember from the phone conversation, before going through the answers with the class.

Answers

1 5   **2** six   **3** 1 September (year not given)   **4** 14,000 Czech crowns
5 28th   **6** 28,000 Czech crowns

Transcript » STUDENT'S BOOK **page 134**

> **Language note**
>
> If you *fall into arrears* with payments, you do not pay by the specified date. The expression suggests more than simply missing a deadline, but rather that late payment is becoming a habit.

Optional extension

1 Write the following questions on the board while students are listening.

  1   What is the difference between a periodic agreement and a short-term agreement?

  2   What is the advantage of a six-month agreement?

  3   What is the maximum amount that Ms Cervera could charge for the property?

  4   What two forms of protection are there in case the tenants fall into arrears?

2 Tell students to discuss the questions in pairs, based on what they remember, and then play the recording a second time for them to check their answers.

3 After they have checked again in pairs, discuss the answers with the class.

Answers

1 A periodic agreement is automatically renewed at the end of the tenancy period; a short-term agreement guarantees a fixed period, after which it expires and must be replaced by a new agreement. (But see Language note on *statutory periodic tenancies* after Exercise 25 above.)

2 It cannot be any shorter (because it's the statutory minimum), and any longer would make it more difficult to get rid of the tenants in the event of problems.

3 Ms Fialová's brother thinks a rent of 15,000 Czech crowns would be possible.

4 A deposit of two months' rent and Ms Cervera's insurance.

SB p.81 Text analysis: A telephone enquiry

27 Tell students to discuss with a partner which of the functions they remember being used in the listenings. You may need to check they understand all of the functions (e.g. *greeting* = saying 'hello'; *unavailable* = not there, or unable to talk; the difference between *leaving a message* and *taking a message*; *clarifying* = explaining after a misunderstanding; *apologising* = saying 'sorry'). Then tell them to look through the audio transcripts to audio 7.2, 7.3 and 7.4 to find examples of the functions. You can make this easier by telling students to work in groups of three, with each member of the group analysing only one transcript, and then comparing their findings with their groups. Point out that not all the functions appear in the listenings. When they have finished, go through the answers carefully with the class, making sure students have underlined all the useful phrases for telephoning. Point out that some people keep a list of such useful expressions on the wall next to their telephone, for quick and easy reference when they are talking on the phone.

Answers

 1 Novák and Fialová, how may I help?

 2 How can I help?
    I'd be very pleased to.

 3 Hello, can I speak to Ms Fialová, please?

 4 Can I tell her who's calling?

 5 It's Marta Cervera from Jacksons in Valencia.

 6 I'll put you through.

 7 Hello, Ms Cervera?

 8 I'm calling about my recent email.
    I wondered if it would be possible to discuss some of the points over the phone?
    … we wondered if you could handle the conveyance?
    I wonder if you wouldn't mind talking me through the essentials?
    I've just received the translated tenancy agreement and wanted to check on a couple of things.

10 Do you have a moment?

15 I thought so.
Of course.
So I'd heard.
Really?
That's right.
Great, thanks.
I'm pleased to hear that.
Really?

16 It's a buy-to-let property that you're interested in, is that right?
Right, so I don't need to form a limited company first to own property?
Why? Are there tax advantages?
Sorry, can you say that again, please?
I'm sorry, what was your question?
What, like no animals – that kind of thing?
The periodic is the one that is automatically renewed at the end of the tenancy period, right?

17 Yes, that's right.
That's right.
That kind of thing, yes.

18 I'm sorry.

19 I'm expecting a call in a few minutes, so don't have much time left.
Thanks very much for your help.

20 I'll be in touch nearer the time.
Not at all, and thanks for calling.
Goodbye.

28 Tell students to work in small groups to complete the exercise. Make sure they realise that there is no one-to-one relationship between the functions and the phrases: some functions may have several useful phrases, while some useful phrases may belong to more than one function. There may also be some disagreement as to the best function for some of the phrases. When they have finished, go through the answers with the class, and elicit any more such phrases that students know for each function.

▶ **Suggested answers**
a 19, 20 **b** 9 **c** 19, 20 **d** 16 **e** 10
f 15 **g** 13 **h** 7 **i** 15 **j** 16 **k** 12 **l** 8
m 16 **n** 2 **o** 7 **p** 14 **q** 11

(SB p.81) # Speaking 2: Using English on the phone

29 Students should discuss the questions first in small groups, and then as a whole class. Elicit from the class which is easier: talking over the Internet (e.g. via a webcam) or using a traditional phone.

30 Discuss this with the class. You may prompt the discussion with ideas from the answer key below. Try to discuss the advantages and disadvantages of each tip, and encourage students to use the tips in future.

▶ **Suggested answers**
○ Plan your call. Make notes on what you want to say and write out important phrases or questions.
○ Practise what you are going to say before you call. Do you need to speak more slowly?
○ As you make calls, write down any new expressions you hear and add them to a phrase book.
○ If the speaker talks too quickly, don't be afraid to ask him/her to slow down.
○ At the end of a call, summarise what you have agreed so that you can confirm you both understand.

31 Divide the class into pairs and allocate roles, A and B. If you have an odd number of students, the extra student in one group should be a senior lawyer supporting Student A. If you have only one student, you should play the role of Student B. Make sure all students read their role cards carefully to find out what they are doing before and during the role-play. Ideally, the role-play should be conducted using real phones (as this will prevent students from using body language to help them communicate), but it can also be done if students are sitting back to back. Make sure students know to use the useful language and tips from this unit. Allow about five minutes for the role-play itself. Afterwards, give and elicit feedback on their performance, in terms of language and telephone techniques, including praise for the successful communication you observed.

Language Focus

Answers

1 Word formation

verb	adjective	negative adjective	abstract noun
limit	limited	unlimited	limitation
define	definite	indefinite	definition
specify	specified	unspecified	specification
inherit	inheritable	uninheritable	inheritance
enforce	enforceable	unenforceable	enforcement
apply	applicable	inapplicable	application
complete	complete	incomplete	completion

2 Collocations

1 real estate, real property
2 prior agreement, prior consent
3 mutual agreement, mutual consent
4 exclusive agreement, exclusive possession

3 Formal/informal synonyms

2 b 3 g 4 c 5 a 6 d 7 f

4 Telephoning language

2 j 3 e 4 g 5 h 6 d 7 b 8 a 9 f 10 c

8 Litigation and arbitration

Teacher's brief

This unit deals with the range of ways of handling legal disputes. Lawyers are often perceived as spending all their time in court, involved in **litigation** (**lawsuits** and **criminal trials**), but of course that is only a small part of what they do. They are far more likely to try to avoid litigation, either by reaching an **out-of-court settlement** with the other party, or by using one of the methods of **alternative dispute resolution** (ADR).

There are two main types of ADR: **mediation** and **arbitration**. **Mediation** involves an independent third party working with the **disputing parties** to help them negotiate and reach agreement. The disputing parties have to find their own compromise: the mediator has no power to impose decisions. This is especially useful if, for example, the parties are keen to preserve a good working relationship during and after the dispute (e.g. an employer and employee, or a supplier and customer). The mediator can help by bringing up ideas and suggesting compromises that the disputing parties would be too guarded to mention. He/She can also defuse potential conflicts, and help the parties to remain focused on the aim of the negotiation: to find a solution which is acceptable to both parties.

Arbitration also makes use of an **impartial third party**, but in this case the **arbitrator** (or **arbiter**) has the power to impose binding judgments on the parties. This procedure is more formal and confrontational than mediation, but less so than litigation. Arbitration is useful when the disputing parties are more interested in the rights and wrongs of the case than in reaching a compromise. The hearings are generally quicker and less bureaucratic than full trials.

Litigation is the most formal option, and also potentially the most expensive and time-consuming. Reading 4 highlights the **costs of litigation** to business, to illustrate the importance of avoiding litigation if at all possible.

The first part of the unit contains a case study: a student invites a Chinese law professor to take part in a **simulated arbitration**. Simulations are very common in law schools, as they enable students to practise the procedures and techniques that they need to know when they start working. In this case, the simulation concerns a famous Chinese arbitration case: the peanut kernel case (see notes to Reading 2). Listening 1 is an extract from the professor's talk on various aspects of **Chinese arbitration law**. This focus on Chinese law may seem irrelevant to some students, but the point is that China is used as an example, to show how the same concepts apply in both English-speaking and non-English-speaking jurisdictions.

Students will have an opportunity to compare what they hear with the situation in their own countries.

The second part of the unit deals with **avoiding litigation**, a less glamorous but extremely important part of lawyers' work. Reading 3 suggests ways to prevent disputes from arising in the first place and ideas for managing them when they do arise.

Reading 5 introduces a case study of an employee threatening to sue her employer for **constructive dismissal** (i.e. being effectively forced to resign as a result of an employer's unfair actions). The employee's lawyer sends a **letter before action** to her employer's lawyer. Letters before action are very formal documents warning the other party that legal action (e.g. litigation) is planned, and giving the other party a chance to avoid litigation, typically by agreeing to an **out-of-court settlement**. Later in the unit, we hear an initial lawyer–client interview, in which the employer and his lawyer discuss the issues arising from the employee's letter. Based on the interview, the lawyer recommends that the employer should make a generous **offer of a settlement** in order to avoid the potentially crippling costs of a tribunal hearing and payment of damages.

The unit also focuses on several useful language areas for lawyers: writing a **letter of invitation** and a **letter before action**, and taking part in a **question-and-answer session** and an **initial lawyer–client interview**. There is also a focus on **future forms** and techniques for **formal writing**.

Further information

○ There is plenty of good **advice on litigation** available online. For example, http://law.freeadvice.com/litigation/litigation/120/ is a very thorough and readable introduction to all types of dispute resolution. See also http://people.howstuffworks.com/lawsuit.htm.

○ For more on **Chinese arbitration law**, see http://en.wikipedia.org/wiki/Judicial_system_of_the_People%27s_Republic_of_China#Arbitration_System. The Beijing Arbitration Commission (http://www.bjac.org.cn/en/about_us/index.html) has some good information to support this unit.

○ For **background information on the case study** in the second part of the unit, see http://www.bbc.co.uk/consumer/guides_to/employment_unfairdismissal.shtml, which explains many of the concepts mentioned in Listening 2.

○ The UK's **conciliation and arbitration service**, ACAS (http://www.acas.org.uk/) has a very user-friendly website, outlining ways of resolving employment disputes in the UK.

Discussion

Use these questions to generate a discussion with the whole class.

○ What sorts of issues do people have legal disputes over? [Use this question to encourage students to think not just in terms of simple breaches of contract, but also things like rival claims to ownership of some property, alleged crimes and torts, etc. You could use the unit headings from this book to generate lots of ideas.]

○ As a lawyer, is it better to resolve disputes quickly and cheaply, or to prolong disputes in order to make more money? [Use this to provoke students to question where their loyalties lie: with their client (and therefore costs must be minimised) or with themselves (and therefore their income must be maximised). Although many clients suspect their lawyers deliberately prolong disputes in order to make more money, this would be a short-sighted policy, as clients would learn to use the services of another, more honest, lawyer.]

THE STUDY OF LAW

(SB p.83) Lead-in

Tell students to read the introduction to find four examples of disputes. Then discuss with the class what these four examples might involve.

📖 **Background notes**
○ **Disputes over people's behaviour** may involve conflict between neighbours over anti-social behaviour (such as loud parties or verbal abuse). See for example http://www.adviceguide.org.uk/index/family_parent/housing/anti_social_behaviour_in_housing.htm for more examples, together with the legal procedures in place to deal with them.
○ **Business disputes** can involve different interpretations of the terms of a contract, or questions over whether a contract has been breached, and what remedies/damages are appropriate.
○ **Planning disputes** include situations where, for example, a property owner

plans to construct a new building, or improve an existing building. In many countries, planning permission is required from a local government body, and disputes often arise when a property owner is refused permission, or when a neighbour is unhappy that the property owner has been granted permission, or when the property owner does the construction work without first seeking permission.
○ **Environmental disputes** include disputes over resources and questions over who has the right to exploit those resources, and at what cost to the environment. See http://greenomics.blogspot.com/2007/01/how-do-we-resolve-environmental.html for some interesting examples.

1 Discuss the questions with the whole class. Avoid confirming students' suggestions at this stage, as the questions are fully answered in Reading 1.

(SB p.83) Reading 1: Litigation and arbitration

2 Tell students to read the four statements to check they understand all the words. You may need to check some words (e.g. *settle* = *resolve*). Then tell them to read the text carefully to find the answers. When they have finished, tell them to discuss their answers with a partner. As you check the answers with the class, discuss any problems they have had with difficult words and phrases.

➡ **Answers**
1 F **2** T **3** T **4** F

📖 **Background notes**
○ *Government agencies* are bodies controlled and funded by government ministries. See http://en.wikipedia.org/wiki/Government_agency. In the UK, they include agencies such as Companies House, the Courts Service, Prison Service, and the Driver and Vehicle Licensing Agency.

- The text mentions *litigation between governmental bodies*. This is very rare, as government bodies usually prefer to keep their disputes internal, or resolved through mediation. But a famous example is the case of Ellis Island in the USA, which was claimed by both New York and New Jersey. The case was finally resolved in the Supreme Court in 1998 (which concluded that the island belonged to New Jersey). See http://en.wikipedia.org/wiki/Ellis_island#Federal_jurisdiction_and_state_sovereignty_dispute.

- The text mentions both *hearings* and *trials*. While these are often treated as synonyms, there are important differences: *hearings* are more general and can take place before arbitration panels, tribunals, etc., as well as courts. See *hearing* at http://dictionary.law.com.

- A *pleading* is the general name for many types of formal document submitted to a court as part of a lawsuit, such as a *complaint* or *answer*.

- If you *enforce judgment*, you force the other party to do what the court has already ordered them to do. Normally, this is not necessary, but if a party refuses to follow the court's order, the winning party must take steps to enforce the judgment, by obtaining, for example, a *warrant of execution*. See http://www.hmcourts-service.gov.uk/infoabout/enforcement/judgment/ for a very clear explanation.

- The terms *arbitrator* and *arbiter* are interchangeable, although *arbiter* often refers generally to someone who makes decisions for other people, while an *arbitrator* is usually used for a person involved in the legal process of arbitration.

1 Students should work in pairs. Hand out one copy of the worksheet to each pair for them to complete.
2 Point out that the first letter of each gapped word is given, and the boxes are numbered in the order the information appears in the text. Point out also that where two boxes have the same number, it means they both contain the same information.
3 Allow plenty of time for this, and then go through the answers with the class.
4 As a follow-up, students should take turns to explain to their partner one type of dispute resolution, as they would to a client, using only the worksheet to guide them.

Answers
1 settled 2 judge; jury 3 Pre-trial 4 solicitor
5 claimant; defendant; barrister 6 attorney
7 Enforcement 8 settlement 9 lawsuits; pleadings 10 Discovery 11 judgment
12 order 13 Counsel; enforce
14 Alternative Dispute Resolution
15 Arbitration 16 Mediation 17 Impartial; arbitrator; arbitral tribunal 18 Bound
19 Disputing 20 binding 21 facilitates negotiation; agreement 22 disputes; commercial 23 International
24 Online dispute resolution 25 Claim
26 Proceedings

(SB p.84) Key terms: Parties and phases in litigation and arbitration

3 Students should work alone to complete the exercise. Allow them to check with a partner before going through the answers with the class.

Answers
1 claimant; defendant; solicitor; barrister; court
2 arbitrator; arbitration tribunal
3 third party; disputing parties

4 Tell students to quickly do the matching exercise alone, and then compare with a partner. After you have checked, students can test each other by reading one of the definitions to elicit the phase of litigation from their partner, or by reading one of the phases to elicit an explanation.

Background note
Description c) mentions that the winning party has the task of *collecting the judgment*. This is similar to *enforcement* (mentioned in Reading 1), although *enforcement* usually has the more specific meaning of 'compelling through legal action', as opposed to *collecting* simply through sending a letter, etc. See http://www.nycourts.gov/Ithaca/CITY/webpageJudgement.html for a range of options available to the winning party if the losing party fails to make a payment that has been ordered by a court.

5   Elicit from the class the three main types of dispute resolution which were mentioned in Reading 1 [**Answers**: litigation, arbitration and mediation]. Then tell students to read the outline quickly and then discuss with a partner which form of dispute resolution is referred to.

Answer
The website text refers to mediation.

Optional extension
To extend the discussion, tell students to discuss each bullet in turn to decide a) how exactly mediation confers the four advantages, and b) whether the advantages are in contrast with other forms of dispute resolution. Afterwards, discuss the answers with the whole class.

Suggested answers
1 a Mediation encourages co-operation because the two parties have to decide on their own resolution to their dispute, which usually involves compromise from both parties. Without a co-operative attitude, the parties will be wasting their time and money by going to mediation. Relationships are preserved because the parties have to resist the temptation to be hostile towards each other, so the dispute does not grow into a broader battle.
   b This contrasts with litigation especially, but also with arbitration, where a third

party (either the court or the arbitrator) makes the decision, thus encouraging the parties to take extreme positions, and to resist compromises.

2 a In mediation, the parties have a say in resolving the dispute because it is they, in partnership with the other party, who must find the resolution.
   b In litigation and arbitration, the decision is taken out of the disputing parties' hands.

3 a Mediation allows parties to look at issues which are not directly relevant to the case, but still relevant to their long-term relationship with each other (such as their desire to do business with each other in future, or their co-operation in other areas). The actual rights and wrongs of the case may be less important than the need to preserve a good long-term relationship between the parties.
   b In litigation and arbitration, there may be pressure to stick strictly to the details of the case.

4 a Because the parties can communicate more freely during mediation, there is a better chance to get to know the other party's side of the story. For example, if a party has failed to pay money owed to the other party, it may be caused by financial problems resulting from a personal tragedy. In this case, an awareness of such circumstances might enable the parties to reach an understanding.
   b In litigation and arbitration, the parties are expected to stick to the facts of the case, so underlying reasons for problems may not be considered relevant.

6   Elicit from the class some of the phrases from Unit 5 for talking about advantages and disadvantages, and write them on the board. Tell students to check on page 54 of the SB to find more of these phrases, and write these on the board as well. Then tell students to discuss the question in small groups, using the phrases from the board. Encourage them to discuss both *litigation* and *arbitration*, and to structure their discussions along the lines of their discussions on *mediation* above.

ADR is often much quicker than litigation (in the USA, the average contract-based lawsuit takes two years; similar cases in arbitration can be as short as five or six months). This can mean that arbitration is also much cheaper than litigation. Parties can stipulate that the arbitrator must have specific experience in the matter under dispute. Judges may be experienced in law, but may not have specific experience in the field that is being litigated. Employing ADR methods often means that parties are more likely to continue to do business with each other, and is a good option if litigation is likely to cause public embarrassment. However, ADR may not be an option where one party wants a test case to set a precedent or is seeking injunctive relief. It may also be the case that one party is hoping to drive another out of business, an outcome that is often better achieved through the time and expense of litigation.

One party may see a strategic advantage to litigating, rather than attempting ADR. This can be particularly true if one party has greater financial resources, or if it is perceived that one party would be likely to win a more substantial award should it go to trial. Litigation may also be a preferred option if the case involves unsettled legal issues, rather than purely factual ones. However, litigation will often have a negative impact on the relationship between parties, and can be bad for business.

⒮⒝ Reading 2: Letter of invitation
p.85

Elicit from the class why a law student might write a letter of invitation to a Chinese law professor. Then tell them to read the introduction to compare it with their ideas. Elicit also whether the students have ever had to write a letter of invitation in English (in a professional context), and why they may need to do this in their careers.

7 Tell students to read the letter to answer the three questions. After they have found the answers, check the answers with the class. Elicit from the class what the simulation might involve [**Suggested answer**: a formal role-play with two parties presenting their arguments to

a panel of arbiters, who must find a resolution to the dispute].

➠ **Answers**
1 Nicholas invites Professor Zhang to take part in a simulated arbitration at the Law Faculty and to join the members of ELSA as their guest at a dinner.
2 The simulated arbitration will be about a Chinese case called the 'peanut kernel' case.
3 Nicholas offers to send Professor Zhang relevant information about the planned simulation.

📖 **Background note**
Peanut kernels are the edible parts of peanuts, i.e. the peanuts without their shells. The case is summarised in fairly simple terms at http://cisgw3.law.pace.edu/cases/990600c1.html. It revolved around a Dutch importer of peanuts from China. According to the contract, the buyer agreed to issue a Letter of Credit (an instrument for international trade transactions) to pay for the peanuts before shipment from China. Over the course of a long business relationship, the buyer had established a pattern of inspecting the peanuts in China before issuing the Letter of Credit. On one occasion, the peanuts were assessed as failing to meet the required quality standards, so (after various negotiations between the parties) the buyer refused to issue the Letter of Credit, claiming the seller was in breach of contract. The buyer argued in court that its pattern of inspecting the peanuts before issuing the Letter of Credit constituted an implied contract. The seller argued that the actual written contract between the parties did not permit the buyer to choose not to issue the Letter of Credit. By failing to issue the Letter of Credit, the buyer was in breach of contract, and was liable for the value of the peanuts. The mediation tribunal agreed with the seller that the written contract took precedence over any contract implied by the parties' habitual behaviour. The actual damages awarded were calculated as the value of the peanuts according to the contract, minus the current

market value for peanuts (i.e. the seller was expected to mitigate its losses by selling the peanuts at the market price).

Optional extension

Tell students to read the letter again to underline useful phrases for letters of invitation, which they could use if they had to write their own letter.

You may also ask students to write their own letters of invitation to a specialist in an area they are interested in, using the useful phrases. You could even send out the invitations to see if any of them are accepted.

Suggested answers

○ I am a …
○ (Person) has informed me that you are visiting …
○ On behalf of (organisation), I would like to invite you to take part in (event), which will be carried out by (people).
○ We are holding the (event, time) and very much hope that you will have time to participate.
○ If you would like, I can send you more detailed information about the (event).
○ I would also like to invite you, on behalf of (organisation), to be the guest of honour at (event) we are hosting on (date).
○ I very much hope that you will be able to accept this invitation.
○ I look forward to your reply.

SB p.86 Language use 1: Future forms

Tell students to read the information in the box, and check they understand the implications of the second sentence (i.e. that for most uses other than those listed in Exercise 8, different future forms should be used). Elicit from the class some other ways of speaking about the future in English (e.g. present simple, *shall*, *may*, *might*, *going to*), but try to avoid explaining too much about these, so as to remain focused on the two forms highlighted in this section.

8a Tell students to work alone to find six examples of the present continuous in the letter of invitation, and to label them according to whether they refer to the present or the future.

You may need to explain *ongoing* (= still in progress), and check what exactly is meant by *fixed arrangements* (see Language note below). When you go through the answers with the class, elicit how it is possible to tell whether present continuous refers to the present or the future (see Language note below).

Answers

am taking **(B)**
are also learning **(B)**
are visiting … and giving **(A)**
are holding **(A)**
are hosting **(A)**

Language notes

○ The difference between present continuous for future arrangements and *going to* for future plans is rather subtle. Plans with *going to* tend to exist only in the speaker's head, and can often be changed easily, simply by changing one's mind. Arrangements with present continuous tend to be more concrete, as they could not be changed without disrupting other people's plans, etc.

○ When present continuous refers to the future, the context contains a specific reference to a future time (e.g. *on March 11, tomorrow, next week*), usually, but not always, in the same sentence. When there is no such reference to a future time, present continuous typically has a present meaning.

○ It is often said that present continuous refers to the near future. This is only true in the sense that people tend not to make firm arrangements more than a year in advance. But an arrangement for the distant future would also use present continuous.

b Tell students to work alone again to find six examples of *will* + verb, and to identify which of the three labels is appropriate for each. Allow them to discuss their answers with a partner before checking with the class. Again, discuss what clues enabled them to label the examples.

⏩ **Answers**

will advertise **(C)**

will attend **(D)**

will be carried out **(E)**

will have time **(E)**

will use **(E)**

will be able **(E)**

✎ **Language notes**

○ English has many ways of referring to the future, and learners of English often struggle to decide which is appropriate in which case (or simply overuse the *will* future, because it is easy).

○ *Will* is usually used to convey a sense of subjectivity, from the point of view either of the speaker or of the subject of the sentence. So the sentence *I'm certain that many students will attend* is a subjective prediction based on the writer's opinion, in contrast to *Many students are going to attend*, which is a prediction based on more objective evidence (such as ticket sales). It is often said that predictions with *going to* are more certain than predictions with *will*, but this example suggests otherwise: the writer actually claims to be certain, and his subjective prediction may turn out to be more accurate than one based on objective criteria like ticket sales.

○ Similarly, the sentence *I hope you will be able to accept this invitation* is about the attitude/willingness of the subject (you, i.e. Professor Zhang) to attend, in contrast to *I hope you are able to accept this invitation*, which is simply about his objective ability.

○ In formal writing such as this, *will* can be a powerful way for the writer to create a professional impression (i.e. *you can trust/believe me*), and to take personal responsibility for future events (i.e. *I'll make sure this happens*). Other future forms are more useful to distance the speaker from statements about the future.

9 Tell students to read the letter quickly to see if the professor accepts or rejects the invitation [**Answer**: He rejects the invitation to the arbitration, but will try to come to the dinner]. Students should then try the exercise alone, and then check with a partner before going through the answers with the whole class.

⏩ **Answers**

1 are holding **2** am flying **3** am meeting **4** will try **5** will contact **6** will be

SB p.87 / 8.1 / **Listening 1: Question-and-answer session**

10 Elicit from the class when they would expect to take part in a question-and-answer session [**Suggested answer**: after a lecture, formal presentation or panel discussion]. Then do the matching exercise quickly with the class and elicit what may be asked about each term in the question-and-answer session.

⏩ **Answers**

1 c **2** a **3** b

💬 **Pronunciation notes**

arbitral /ˈɑːbɪtrəl/

bilateral /baɪˈlætərəl/

frivolous /ˈfrɪvələs/

signatory /ˈsɪgnətrɪ/

✎ **Language note**

An *arbitral tribunal* can also be called an *arbitrational tribunal*. The word *arbitral* also collocates strongly with *award* (so *enforcement of an arbitral award*, not *an arbitrational award*).

11 Students should read through the list of topics and then listen to the recording to tick the topics that were mentioned. After the recording, tell students to discuss their answers with a partner, including as much information as they can remember about each of the topics. Then discuss what was said about each topic with the class.

⏩ **Answers**

He talks about topics 2, 3 and 5.

Transcript » STUDENT'S BOOK **page 134**

Language notes

○ A *legal person* is a group of individual people treated as a single legal entity (e.g. a corporation) which has many of the same legal rights and obligations as a *natural person* (i.e. an individual), such as the capacity to be sued.

○ A *substantive* legal issue relates to essential legal principles, not to matters of procedure and practice.

○ If an agreement *excludes recourse to judicial decision*, it makes it impossible for the parties to choose litigation to resolve disputes.

12 Play the recording again for students to tick the question openers they hear. Afterwards, elicit how each question continued, and as much detail about the professor's answer as possible. Discuss with the class any similarities and differences between the Chinese arbitration system and that in their own jurisdictions.

Answers
1, 2, 5, 6

Speaking 1: Talk on litigation/arbitration
SB p.87

13 Tell students to do the research for this as homework, but make sure they realise they are not expected to speak for more than a few minutes, which may make the task less daunting. Suggest some sources of information (e.g. search the Internet for 'arbitration' or 'litigation' or 'dispute resolution' and the jurisdiction's name, or look for sites dealing with 'landmark cases' such as http://www.landmarkcases.org/. An excellent source of light-hearted 'stupid lawsuits' can be found at http://www.power-of-attorneys.com/stupid_lawsuit_collection.asp?wacky=0). Point out that the purpose of the exercise is to practise the question-and-answer session, so the presentations can be very simple.

Students should take turns to make their presentations to the class, after which there should be a question-and-answer session for each presentation. If you have a very large class, it may be necessary for students to present to each other in groups. Make sure students realise they are expected to use the question openers from Exercise 12. Afterwards, give and elicit feedback on the presentations and especially on the effectiveness of the question-and-answer sessions.

Optional alternative
Rather than getting students to choose their own aspect of litigation/arbitration to talk about, you could get them to research and present on the peanut kernel case, which was mentioned several times in the preceding exercises. The website is provided above (page 120), but the case can also be found easily

by searching the Internet for 'peanut kernel case'.

Students should work in groups of three: one should research the seller's position, another should research the buyer's position, and the third should research the reasoning of the arbitration tribunal in reaching a verdict. This research can then provide the basis for a question-and-answer session, either in groups of three or with the whole class.

You may also want to try to hold a simulation of the peanut kernel case, as the students mentioned in Reading 2 were planning. One student (or group) should present the buyer's arguments. Another should present the seller's arguments. A third student or group should represent the arbitration panel, and manage the simulation. You will need to decide on a suitable procedure first (e.g. presentations by the two parties, followed by cross-examination and closing arguments, and then deliberation by the tribunal and presentation of a reasoned decision). You will also need to decide the level of formality and rigidity of the procedures, and make sure all the students are aware of what is expected of them. The simulation is best conducted with the whole class if possible, and you should set a time limit of around 20 minutes.

LAW IN PRACTICE

(SB p.88) Lead-in

Elicit from the class what the three main stages of litigation might be, and then tell them to read the introduction to check. Elicit what is involved in each stage, and which is likely to take the longest amount of time. [**Suggested answer**: Of course this will vary from case to case and from one jurisdiction to another, but, given the costs and inconvenience of a court case, it would make sense to spend more time preparing and filing the claim and then preparing the case than actually appearing in court. On the other hand, court cases often involve lengthy formal procedures and delays, so they may take a long time. The second and third stages of a long case may overlap.]

14 Ideally, elicit some examples of famous lawsuits, in students' own jurisdictions or internationally, in order to prompt the discussion. You may help this by preparing a list in advance (see ideas for searching the Internet in Exercise 13 above), and if necessary printing out some short texts outlining the cases. Tell students to work in small groups to discuss what they know about the cases. Then open up the discussion to include the whole class.

(SB p.88) Reading 3: Avoiding litigation

15 After students have discussed the questions in pairs, open up the discussion to include the whole class. Make a note of the answers on the board, as this will make Exercise 17 work more smoothly.

▶ **Suggested answer**
See Reading 3.

16 Tell students to work alone to read the text. Allow a short time (two minutes), and then tell students to work together to do the matching exercise. When they have finished, discuss the answers with the class.

▶ **Answers**
1 c   2 d   3 e   4 a   5 b

📖 **Background notes**
○ A *'loser pays' rule* simply states that the loser in any litigation is responsible for paying the other party's legal fees. According to http://www.pointoflaw. com/loserpays/overview.php, the USA is one of the few jurisdictions in the world where this is not automatic, which is perhaps one reason why the USA has a reputation for frivolous lawsuits (see next point).
○ For plenty of examples of *frivolous lawsuits*, see http://www.power-of-attorneys.com/stupid_lawsuit_collection. asp?wacky=0.

17a Discuss this quickly with the class, using the notes you wrote on the board for Exercise 15.

b Students should discuss this in pairs and then feed back to the class.

Optional extension

As a follow-up, tell students to test each other by reading one of the examples from Reading 3 to elicit the explanation from their partner.

You could also turn this into a mini-role-play, which will help to set up the role-plays at the end of the unit: one student should be a client who wants to avoid litigation, and the other should be a lawyer giving the advice from the article. If you have an odd number of students, one group should have two lawyers. The client should ask for explanations and examples for each piece of advice. When they have finished, they should swap roles.

(SB p.89) Reading 4: Cost of litigation

18 Tell students to read the article quickly to answer the two questions. Set a time limit of around a minute. Avoid explaining the word *burden* in advance, as students may be able to work out its approximate meaning by reading the text. After the time limit, tell them to compare their answers with a partner, and then check with the whole class.

Answers
1 A burden is a heavy load that you carry. It is also used to mean something difficult or unpleasant that you have to deal with or worry about.
2 The most common types of litigation are employment and contract disputes.

Language notes
○ A *burden* is, literally, something that must be carried/tolerated. It has the same origins as the verb *to bear* (as in *I can't bear it*).
○ When the text says that *US and UK firms faced average costs of $12m and $1m respectively*, it means US firms had costs averaging $12m, and UK firms had costs averaging $1m.
○ The text mentions that *insurers have paid out $36m on average*. This does not refer to the money they have paid out to cover their clients' litigation costs, which is considerably higher, but rather to their own costs connected with litigation initiated by and against them.

19 Tell students to read the text again more carefully and to discuss the three questions with a partner. When you go through the answers with the class, focus on the words and phrases in the text that led students to the answers. You could also elicit from the class why they think construction firms, insurers and manufacturers have such high litigation costs. Students should think of examples of litigation that these three types of company might be involved in, either as claimant or as defendant.

Answers
1 F (They are 12 times higher in the USA.)
2 T **3** F (They consider arbitration to be quicker, but see little difference in cost.)

20 Elicit from the class which paragraph explains the increased costs of litigation [**Answer:** the third paragraph]. Then tell students to read the paragraph quickly to identify the reason it gives. Elicit examples of regulations that may lead to more litigation.

Answer
Increased regulation

Background notes
The UK, like most countries, has *regulations* on a wide range of issues, including environmental requirements, health-and-safety standards and procedures to prevent discriminatory behaviour. While regulation has undoubted benefits (e.g. increased fairness and predictability), bad regulation can have the opposite effect, especially if it is too complicated for people to understand, or changes frequently. It also opens the door to more litigation: the more rules there are to break, the more individuals and companies will break them, knowingly or otherwise. See http://www.betterregulation. gov.uk/private/casestudies.cfm for some examples of bad regulation, and the UK's strategy for dealing with it.

21 Tell students to quickly do the exercise alone. When you have checked with the class, tell students to test each other, by giving a definition to elicit one of the words from their partner, or by giving a word to elicit a definition.

SB p.89 Reading 5: Letter before action

22 Elicit from the class a range of ways in which a person's employment can end, and write these on the board. Then tell students to work in small groups to discuss whether and how each of these might result in litigation or arbitration. When the first groups have finished, open up the discussion to include the whole class.

Suggested answers
They could come to the end of their contract (and not have it renewed).
They could hand in their notice and leave at the end of the period of notice.
They could be dismissed (fired), i.e. lose their job because they have done something wrong or badly. They could also be made redundant, i.e. lose their job because their employer no longer needs them.
They could be made redundant because the position they held no longer exists.
They could leave as a result of the employer's breach of contract and sue for constructive dismissal.

23 With the class, elicit what they think *constructive dismissal* and *defamation* might mean. Avoid explaining *constructive dismissal* yourself at this stage, as this would undermine the reading task, but make sure students know what *defamation* means.

Language note
Defamation is the tort of damaging a person's reputation by making an untrue statement about them.

Then tell students to read the letter to answer the two questions, and then discuss their answers with a partner. Encourage students to treat the two questions as discussions, rather than simply answering them as quickly as possible. After you have opened up the discussion to include the whole class, elicit or explain what *constructive dismissal* means.

Answers
1 When an employee resigns due to his/ her employer's behaviour and brings an action against the employer. The employee must prove that the employer's actions were either in serious breach of contract or unlawful.
2 The allegations were untrue (so the client claims) and were made in front of another person.

Language notes
Note that most of the difficult words and phrases from the letter are explained in Exercise 28 below.

○ If you *strenuously deny* /ˈstrenjʊəslɪ dɪˈnaɪ/ something, you say, in the strongest and most vigorous way, that accusations against you are untrue.
○ *Exemplary damages* /egˈzemplərɪ ˈdæmɪdʒɪz/, often called *punitive damages* /ˈpjuːnətɪv ˈdæmɪdʒɪz/, are designed to punish a defendant for particularly nasty behaviour, and to set an example to deter others from such behaviour in future. Exemplary damages are often requested by claimants in addition to the main claim for damages, but rarely awarded. See http:// dictionary.law.com. The claimant must prove that the behaviour was *wilful* (i.e. deliberately intended to make the claimant suffer) and either *malicious* / məˈlɪʃəs/ (i.e. driven by hatred for the claimant) or done with reckless disregard for the claimant's rights.

24 Students should read the text again and then discuss these questions in pairs. Point out that the first two questions both have a simple answer (i.e. What is the *stated* purpose of the letter? What, *according to the claimant*, are the facts of the case?), as well as a more subtle answer (i.e. What is the *unstated* purpose of the letter? What, *according to the defendant*, might be the facts of the case?). Open up the discussion to include the whole class.

Answers

1 To inform the recipient that one of his employees has left his firm and intends to sue for damages.

2 Mr Tyler accused Ms Loushe of stealing confidential information.

3 A tribunal claim for constructive dismissal and a defamation suit (both are claims for damages).

4 Suggest an acceptable settlement (*satisfactory proposals*).

Optional extension

The letter contains many useful adverb–adjective, adverb–verb and adjective–noun collocations.

1 Tell students to read the letter again to work in pairs to find three adverb–adjective collocations. (NB You should do the first together to make sure everyone is clear about what adverbs and adjectives are. In this exercise, all the adverbs end in –*ly*.)

2 They should also find two adverb–verb collocations and nine adjective–noun collocations.

3 When they have finished, go through the answers with the class. There may be some disagreement as to what exactly constitutes a collocation, and what is simply a pair of words used in this particular letter. This will be a good opportunity to check some of the difficult vocabulary from the letter.

Suggested answers

adverb–adjective	strictly private and confidential fully entitled shortly (be) forthcoming
adverb–verb	strenuously denies recently informed
adjective–noun	confidential information previous criticism a positive asset a substantial increase constructive dismissal excellent prospects exemplary damages alternative means satisfactory proposals

---

4 As a follow-up, students should test each other in pairs: one student should read the first part of a collocation to elicit the second part from their partner.

SB p.91 Text analysis: Letter before action

25 Make sure students realise that only five of the nine points should be included in a letter before action. Therefore students' first task is to identify the four points that should not be included, and only then should they match the remaining five with the paragraphs of the letter. They should complete the exercise in pairs. When you check the answers with the class, point out that this five-paragraph plan will be useful if ever they have to write a letter before action.

Answers

1 h 2 e 3 i 4 a 5 c

Optional extension

Tell students to work in pairs to identify useful phrases that they could use in their own letters before action. (NB They will have a chance to write such a letter in Exercise 36.) Point out that since most of the letter consists of such useful phrases, it may actually be quicker to identify the sections of the letter which would *not* be used for other letters before action.

Suggested answers

○ All of paragraph 1 can be copied.

○ From paragraph 2: *We understand that our client ...*; *Our client strenuously denies these accusations.*

○ From paragraph 3: *We are informed that ...*; *In fact, ...*

○ From paragraph 4: *In light of your actions of* (date), *it is clear that our client would be fully entitled to ...*; *Due to the circumstances under which the allegations against our client were made, we have also advised* (client) *that* (he/she) *would stand excellent prospects of success should* (he/she) *decide to pursue a claim for ...*

○ All of paragraph 5 can be copied.

26 Tell students to discuss the questions in small groups, and then open up the discussion to include the whole class.

Language use 2: Formality in legal correspondence

(SB p.91)

27 Discuss this with the class, and make a list of features of very formal writing on the board.

Language notes

The 'cold' tone of the letter before action is achieved in a range of ways:

○ When stating the facts of the case, references to *we* and *our client* tend to be indirect, to suggest *we* are innocent and passive victims: *We are instructed ...; We*

understand ...; ... she was accused .... The only active action directly attributed to the claimant is *Our client strenuously denies these accusations.*

○ In contrast, the phrase *Following **your** actions ...* portrays the employer as the active and guilty party.

○ Several sentences have abstract impersonal subjects, in order to present the facts in a clinical/impersonal manner: *... there had been no previous criticism ...; a promotion ... would shortly be forthcoming; ... it is clear that ...; ... the allegations against our client were made ...; our instructions are to ...*

○ The options and proposals to resolve the dispute are more direct and active, but use modal verbs to convey a sense that these are considered hypothetical options (*would/ should/ might,* rather than *will/ may/ can*), in order to make the threat less aggressive but more businesslike.

28 Students should work with a partner to find the 11 phrases. After you have checked with the class (paying attention to any difficult vocabulary or pronunciation), tell students to test each other in pairs: one should read a formal phrase to elicit the informal equivalent, or vice versa.

1 Elicit from the class what other types of letter a lawyer might write, and write these on the board.

Suggested answers

a An internal memo from one partner to another partner

b An internal memo to all employees of a legal firm

c A demand letter from a lawyer

d A letter written by one lawyer to another lawyer in response to a demand letter

e An email from one associate to another associate working on the same case

f A letter from a lawyer to his/her client

g An email from an associate to a partner

2 Then tell students to work in small groups to grade the types of letter from most formal (1) to least formal (5).

3 They should also discuss the typical features of each type of letter, and the ways in which each type differs from a letter before action (e.g. in terms of purpose, style, level of formality and information included).

4 When some groups have finished, open up the discussion to include the whole class.

Suggested answers

1 (most formal) c, d **2** b, f **3** g **4** a
5 (least formal) e
NB other orders will also be acceptable, depending on the particular situation.

SB p.91 · 8.2 8.3 Listening 2: Lawyer–client interview

29 Discuss this question with the whole class and write the suggestions on the board. This will enable you to compare the class's ideas with the topics the lawyer and client actually discuss. Play the recording for students to see which of their ideas were mentioned in the interview. After listening, students should discuss in pairs which of their ideas were mentioned, before feeding back to the whole class.

Suggested answer
Full details of exactly what happened (including the circumstances of the alleged theft, what evidence Mr Tyler has and how he might have defamed Ms Loushe).

Transcript » STUDENT'S BOOK **page 135**

30 Tell students to discuss the five statements with a partner to check they understand everything and to try to remember some of the answers. Then play the recording again. Allow students to compare their answers with a partner before checking with the class.

Answers
1 F (Ms Loushe has not come into work, but has not resigned or been dismissed.)
2 F (He fired her for professional negligence.)
3 T
4 T
5 T

Language notes

○ If you *allege* /əˈledʒ/ something, you claim formally that it is true. An *allegation* /æləˈgeɪʃən/ is a formal accusation against somebody.

○ *Professional negligence* is a tort in English law, where the defendant has failed to fulfil a duty of care towards the claimant. In the case of normal negligence, the defendant's actions are assessed in comparison with those of a reasonable person in order to judge whether the defendant has neglected his/her duties. But in professional negligence, the defendant has claimed to have some professional skills (e.g. a surgeon claims to have a certain level of medical knowledge and skills). So his/her actions are assessed in comparison with professional standards. See http://en.wikipedia.org/wiki/Professional_negligence_in_English_Law.

○ A *lucrative contract* is one which is expected to generate a lot of money.

31 Tell students to discuss this question in small groups. Point out that they should discuss the strengths and weaknesses of Mr Tyler's case. Then discuss the question with the whole class, including the following: the credibility of Mr Tyler's accusations; any mistakes he has made in his handling of the case; and the likely outcome of legal action. Play the recording so students can check their answers.

Suggested answer
On the face of it, not very convincing. Mr Tyler's suspicions are based purely on circumstantial evidence, conjecture and rumour. A lawyer would probably advise him to settle as soon as possible.

Transcript » STUDENT'S BOOK page 135

32 Make sure students understand all the words in the five questions. Tell students to discuss the questions with a partner first to see if they can remember the answers, then play the recording again for them to check. Allow them to discuss in pairs again before checking with the whole class.

Answers
1 Concrete evidence of the alleged theft
2 To take Mr Tyler to a tribunal (for constructive dismissal)
3 He should offer a generous settlement.
4 The damages consist of two separate awards, the basic award and the compensatory award. The basic award is calculated according to a formula based on age, length of service and gross pay. The compensatory award is to compensate for the loss suffered through being unfairly dismissed.
5 £58,400

Language notes
○ A *repudiatory* /rɪˈpjuːdɪˈeɪtərɪ/ *breach of contract* is also known as a fundamental breach. It is so fundamental that it allows the non-breaching party to terminate the contract and sue for damages. See http://en.wikipedia.org/wiki/Fundamental_breach.

○ The *burden of proof* is the duty of one party to prove disputed charges. The other party does not normally have to disprove the charges, but merely to convince the court that the charges cannot be proved.
○ The *statutory dismissal and disciplinary procedures* are procedures governed by statute (i.e. legislation) which determine the steps an employer must follow when disciplining or dismissing an employee. See http://www.acas.org.uk/index.aspx?articleid=906 for information about these procedures in the UK, and a comprehensive downloadable guide.
○ *Gross pay* /grəʊs ˈpeɪ/ means a person's salary before tax has been deducted.
○ If you *allude* /əˈluːd/ to something, you refer to it indirectly.

SB p.92 Language use 3: Establishing the facts

Tell students to read the introduction on page 92 to find three things that a lawyer must do during an initial interview with a client.

Answers
Show understanding; establish the relevant facts of the case; give informed legal advice.

33 Tell students to work alone to find the useful phrases, and then compare their ideas with a partner before you check with the whole class. Write the useful phrases up on the board, as this will make the role-play in Exercise 35 easier.

Suggested answers
Before I can give you any advice, I need to establish the relevant facts.
Please do give as much detail as possible, and try not to avoid any facts which may be uncomfortable. It's better I hear everything now in order to avoid any unfortunate surprises later.
It's probably best just to stick to the facts surrounding …
And you think that this is in some way connected with …?
I think you'd better tell me just what you suspect …

And do you have any *proof* ...?
So these are just suspicions?

**Optional extension
(Photocopiable worksheet 8.2)**
This contains examples of useful phrases
for a lawyer–client interview, taken from both
parts of the listening. The phrases have been
split in the middle.

1 Make enough copies of the worksheet so
   there is one copy for every pair of students,
   and cut them along the dotted lines into
   slips. Do not cut along the solid lines.
   (Also make an additional copy for each
   student, not cut up, which they can use
   later as a reference list of these phrases.)

2 Give each pair a set of slips, and tell them
   to match the two halves (see 'Matching
   games' on page 9). With weaker classes,
   you may want to do the exercise with
   phrases from part 1 of the listening first
   (the top half of the worksheet) followed by
   the phrases from part 2 (the bottom half).

3 The first pair to finish is the winner.

Answers
1 c **2** d **3** j **4** b **5** a **6** i **7** g **8** f **9** h
10 e **11** n **12** t **13** k **14** m **15** q **16** s
17 o **18** p **19** l **20** r

4 As a follow-up, tell students to role-play the
   interview between Mr Tyler and his lawyer,
   using only the phrases on the worksheet
   to help them remember the details of the
   interview. They should use as many of the
   phrases as possible. If you have an odd
   number of students, the extra student in
   one group should be a second lawyer.

5 At the end of the interview, they should
   swap roles, so both students have a
   chance to play the lawyer.

6 At the end of the activity, do not clear away
   the slips of paper, as these will be useful
   for the role-play in Exercise 35 (see 'First
   use' activity on page 9).

Writing 1: Responding to a letter before action

SB p.92

34 Discuss with the class what the best tactics
   would be for the letter of response (i.e. should
   Mr Tyler's lawyer strenuously deny all the
   charges in order to negotiate from a position
   of strength later, or should he/she accept
   some or all of Ms Loushe's demands?).
   Discuss also whether these tactics might
   change depending on the type of dispute
   resolution chosen, i.e. litigation, negotiation,
   arbitration and mediation. [**Suggested answer**:
   It would be unusual for an initial response to
   accept the other side's demands completely.
   Although at the end of the listening exercise
   the advice seems to be to make a generous
   offer, it is fairly standard tactics to begin
   with a strenuous denial. A more conciliatory
   approach would put the potential defendant at
   an immediate disadvantage when it comes to
   negotiating an out-of-court settlement (i.e. the
   other party would probably sense weakness
   and go after as much as they could possibly
   get – this is exactly why mediation and
   arbitration are often preferable to litigation).]

Then tell students to work in pairs to go
through the bullet points and decide what
would need to be included in the response
letter. The writing may be set as homework,
but it might be better if it is done in class
in groups (see section on Writing, page 8).
Ideally, you should give feedback on the
strengths and weaknesses of students'
writing before moving on to Exercise 36. This
will enable students to learn from their first
attempt and make improvements in the final
writing task.

Suggested answer
Dear Sirs
Re: Jaycee Loushe
Thank you for your letter of 29 February
2008.
We cannot accept the allegations your client
makes against Mr Tyler. With regard to the
specific points you raise:
1 It is clear that Ms Loushe has
   misunderstood Mr Tyler's concern over
   the possible misuse of confidential
   information. Mr Tyler has certainly taken
   Ms Loushe into his confidence on this
   issue, but it had not occurred to him
   that the difficulties currently faced by
   David Tyler Construction Ltd could have
   anything to do with your client.

2 Our client denies ever having made any reference to Ms Loushe's possible promotion.

3 Our client denies ever having made any defamatory statements concerning Ms Loushe.

Should your client choose to pursue these allegations, Mr Tyler will have no option but to file a counterclaim against Ms Loushe for recovery of damages arising from her sudden departure without notice.

Yours faithfully

Tong, Nelson and Yarbrough Solicitors

Tong, Nelson and Yarbrough Solicitors

(SB p.92) Speaking 2: Lawyer–client interview

35 Allocate roles and tell students to read their role cards carefully to find out what they have to do before and during the role-play. If you have an odd number of students, the extra student in one group should be a second lawyer (role B). With weaker classes, put students together with others with the same roles so they can plan together. Monitor the planning stage carefully to make sure everyone has understood what they are expected to do.

After around three or four minutes' preparation time, set a time limit for the role-play (e.g. five minutes) and make sure the lawyers know to use the useful language from Exercise 33. During the role-play, monitor carefully in order to give feedback at the end. At the end, give and elicit feedback on the role-plays in terms of language and the general effectiveness of the interviews.

(SB p.92) Writing 2: Letter before action

36 This writing should be set as homework. See section on Writing, page 8.

(SB p.93) Language Focus

Answers

1 Collocations

1 to reach an agreement, an outcome, a settlement
2 to file a lawsuit
3 to deliver a judgment
4 to decide on an outcome, a settlement
5 to settle a dispute, a lawsuit

2 Word formation

verb	abstract noun	personal noun
settle	settlement	
resolve	resolution	
arbitrate	arbitration	arbitrator, arbiter
mediate	mediation	mediator

3 Collocations with *dispute*

2 resolve/settle   3 legal
4 alternative; resolution

4 Question openers

2 You mentioned that …
3 Could you go back to the point about …
4 I'm afraid I didn't understand what you said about …

5 Sentence collocation

1 d   2 c   3 e   4 a   5 b

Case study 3: Litigation and arbitration: an employment law case

(See page 10 for step-by-step instructions to case studies.)

The facts of the case

The legal issue is: Does Redlin and Orbison's treatment of Ms Johnson amount to sex discrimination and/or constructive dismissal?

> ✎ **Language notes**
> ○ If you *allege* /əˈledʒ/ something, you claim it is true.
> ○ Your *counterparts* are people who are in an equivalent or similar position.

Comprehension questions

1. Who are the parties? [A law firm, Redlin and Orbison, and a former employee, Chiara Johnson.]

2. What do you know about each of them? [R&O has a head office in New York and offices around the world. Johnson is an IP lawyer with two children.]

3. What is the dispute? [Johnson left her job because she claims her employer treated her unfairly because she is a woman.]

4. What evidence has each side produced to support their case? [Johnson alleges that she was forced to spend an unreasonable amount of time at work (unlike a male colleague), that she was passed over for promotion, and that she was paid less than men in similar positions. R&O argues that it has a high number of female partners, and that Johnson's position was not one which led to promotion to become a partner.]

Relevant legal documents

○ **Text 1** is part of an authentic UK law, the Equal Pay Act 1970. The phrase *on like work with men* means 'in similar work to men'. *Regard shall be had to the frequency or otherwise* means that employers have to take into consideration how often (if at all) the differences occur. This text seems to support Johnson, who claims that she was paid less than men in similar positions.

○ **Text 2** offers a practical example of the law from Text 1, and again should support Johnson's claim, although this particular case was supported by statistical evidence of gender-based salary disparity (i.e. differences between men's and women's salaries). Johnson therefore needs to show that the jobs of the two higher-earning male colleagues were not just *comparable*, but *substantially equal* to her own.

○ The relevant section of **Text 3** is the phrase *unlimited career growth opportunities*. This seems to conflict with the R&O spokeswoman's assertion that it was a non-partnership job. However, the question is how literally a phrase like this should be taken.

9 International law

Teacher's brief

This unit deals with the three branches of international law: **public international law** (e.g. the law governing treaties and disputes between countries), **private international law** (e.g. avoiding and resolving disputes involving individuals and companies from more than one jurisdiction) and **supranational law** (e.g. EU law). A related area, **comparative law**, is covered in Unit 10.

Public international law, also known as **law of nations**, was traditionally a question of **custom**, i.e. countries behaved towards each other as they chose, and rights came from military power. Countries had **treaties** with each other, but since breach of a treaty could only be remedied by **diplomatic pressure**, **sanctions** and the threat of war, they were often ignored. Public international law grew enormously during the 20th century, particularly after World War II, when there was a widespread desire to manage trade and disagreements between countries in a more civilised manner. Early examples of public international law were the **Hague Conventions** (1899 and 1907, dealing with the rules for declaring war) and the **Geneva Conventions** (begun in 1864, completed in 1949, dealing with humane treatment of prisoners, civilians and the sick and wounded in times of war). Countries **submitted to** these conventions, and many others that came later, voluntarily, and in theory could **withdraw** (or breach the conventions and be expelled), but in practice the advantages of being inside such legal frameworks often outweigh the limitations they impose. But if enough countries (and especially powerful countries) choose to ignore a particular international law, the law will cease to have any force.

The creation of the **United Nations** (1945) was a huge step in the development of international law. In addition to **military** and **international trade** issues, public international law also regulates the **law of the sea**, **of space**, **of the environment** and, most recently, **international criminal law**.

Private international law, also known as **conflict of laws**, aims to solve disputes involving individuals and businesses from more than one jurisdiction. Listening 2 introduces a case study of a Scottish–American client involved in a conflict with a Turk living in Slovakia and an Italian living in Russia, about a restaurant business in Austria. The client's lawyer outlines the stages in determining which jurisdiction should hear such a case, and what laws it should apply. An important concept here is **renvoi**, which is when a court in one jurisdiction applies the laws of another.

A second case study involves another aspect of private international law: a **patent dispute** involving two American companies. One of the companies had a US patent to prevent other companies from copying its invention (voice compression software), but the second company copied the software onto disks only in its overseas manufacturing plants, where the patent had no protection. This case study highlights an area where private international law intersects with public international law: companies are increasingly making use of tools like **international patents** from the **World Intellectual Property Organisation**, one of the specialised agencies of the United Nations.

The third branch of international law, **supranational law**, currently is relevant mainly for the **European Union**, where EU laws may override the laws of Member States. Reading 2 introduces a wide range of issues in EU law, connected with **labour law** and **company law**. One of these areas, labour law, forms the background to Listening 1, which deals with a case of so-called **wage-dumping**: replacing high-cost employees from one country with lower-cost employees, often immigrants from poorer countries.

Further information

- An excellent starting point for public international law is http://en.wikipedia.org/wiki/Public_international_law.
- The websites for many of the international organisations mentioned in the unit are given below (see Background notes after Exercise 2).

THE STUDY OF LAW

SB p.94) **Lead-in**

Elicit from the class what international law is, and what it might include. Then tell them to read the introduction on page 94 to find out.

1 Tell students to read the three questions to make sure they understand all the words. You

may need to check they understand the verbs *compel*, *obey* and *violate*. Note that question 2 could be highly controversial: where countries have been accused of violating international law, there may be strong nationalist or political opinions – this is probably not the place to discuss the rights and wrongs of recent wars, human rights abuses and sanctions. If necessary, tell students to focus in question 2 on less controversial issues, such as violations of trade or environmental commitments.

Tell students to discuss the three questions in small groups. After a few minutes, open up the discussion to include the class.

Suggested answers

1 Public international law refers to the corpus of legal rules that apply between sovereign states and international organisations (e.g. the United Nations and the International Court of Justice). Private international law is that part of law that deals with cases involving a foreign law element where different judgments may result depending on which jurisdiction's laws are applied.

2 The two main weapons available to the international community when a state refuses to comply with international law are sanctions (agreements among states to cease trade with a state that has violated international law) and the threat of war. It is sometimes said that most states follow most international law most of the time, and countries have often stretched or violated international law. Common justifications for such violations include the claims that important national security and foreign policy goals are at stake.

3 If the case goes to trial, the court will first decide whether or not it has jurisdiction. The legal questions will then be identified, and choice of law rules will determine what laws should be applied. The case will then proceed according to these laws.

Reading 1: International law
SB p.94

2 Students should read the text carefully to answer the three questions. Allow around three minutes for them to read, after which they should discuss their answers with a partner. Then go through the answers with the class.

Answers

1 Custom, legislation and treaties
2 1 In which jurisdiction may a case be heard?
  2 Which laws from which jurisdiction(s) apply?

3 A supranational legal framework is one that involves more than one country and has power or authority that is greater than that of single countries. The laws of a nation state are not applicable if in conflict with those of a supranational legal framework.

Background notes

○ The full text of the *Vienna Convention on the Law of Treaties* is available at http://untreaty.un.org/ilc/texts/instruments/english/conventions/1_1_1969.pdf.

○ In the context of international treaties, there is no significant difference in meaning between the terms *convention, agreement, charter, framework convention* and *outline convention*. See http://en.wikipedia.org/wiki/List_of_treaties for a fascinating list of treaties throughout history, which nicely illustrates trends in their terminology. *Framework conventions* and *outline conventions* are treaties dealing with very broad areas, with the intention of leaving details for other procedures. Examples include the United Nations Framework Convention on Climate Change (UNFCCC: http://unfccc.int/2860.php) and the European Outline Convention on Transfrontier Cooperation between Territorial Communities or Authorities (http://www.conventions.coe.int/Treaty/EN/Treaties/Html/106.htm). A famous example of a *charter* is the United Nations Charter (http://www.un.org/aboutun/charter).

○ The *Geneva Conventions* deal mainly with prisoners of war and non-combatants (see http://en.wikipedia.org/wiki/Geneva_convention).

○ The *Universal Declaration of Human Rights* is a declaration adopted by the United Nations General Assembly in 1948. For a good summary, see http://en.wikipedia.org/wiki/Universal_Declaration_of_Human_Rights.

○ The *World Health Organisation* is a specialised agency of the United Nations, whose mission is to combat disease and to promote good health. See http://www.who.int/en/.

- The *World Intellectual Property Organisation* is a United Nations specialised agency responsible for developing a balanced intellectual property system. See http://www.wipo.int.
- The *World Trade Organisation* is an international organisation whose mission is to promote the welfare of the people of its member countries, specifically by lowering barriers to international trade. See http://www.wto.int/.
- The *International Monetary Fund* is an international organisation which offers financial and technical support to its members in macroeconomic and financial matters.
- A *sovereign state* is a state which has a legal right and/or the ability to exercise power over a territory. There are complications when a state has rights but no power over a territory (*de juris sovereignty*) or vice versa (*de facto sovereignty*), in which case sovereignty in international law becomes a question of whether a state's sovereignty is recognised by other sovereign states. See http://en.wikipedia.org/wiki/Sovereign_state#Sovereignty_in_international_law.
- At the time of writing, the *East African Community* consists of five countries: Kenya, Uganda, Tanzania, Burundi and Rwanda. See http://www.eac.int/.

Optional extension
(Photocopiable worksheet 9.1)
This is a visual presentation of the information in Reading 1, designed to help students understand the relationship between the various concepts, and encourage them to read the text very carefully and learn some of the information in it.

1 Distribute copies of the worksheet, and tell students to work in pairs to complete the chart using key words from Reading 1. Point out that the key words are usually, but not always, the terms in bold in the Reading. Point out also that the answers are numbered in the same order as the key words appear in the text.

2 When the first pairs have finished, go through the answers with the class.

3 As a follow-up, tell students to retell the information in Reading 1, using only the chart as a prompt.

Answers
1 widest   2 Public international
3 Private international   4 Supranational
5 Narrowest   6 Conflict   7 Custom
8 Legislation   9 Treaties   10 Conventions
11 Agreements   12 Charters   13 Framework
14 Outline   15 Customary   16 war
17 Geneva Conventions   18 institutions
19 Inter-governmental organisations
20 United Nations   21 Universal Declaration; Human   22 Norms   23 WHO, WIPO, WTO, IMF   24 Rights; duties; sovereign states
25 jurisdiction   26 laws   27 Regional
28 applicable, supranational; framework
29 European   30 East African; customs

Key terms 1: Prepositions and prefixes

3 Students should complete the exercise alone, and then check with a partner before feeding back to the class. As a follow-up, students should test each other in pairs: one should read one of the collocations, saying 'blank' where the preposition should be (e.g. *parties blank a treaty; be bound blank the treaty*), to elicit the preposition from their partner.

Answers
1 to; by; in   2 to   3 Under; to   4 to   5 on

Background note
The Convention on the Rights of the Child is a treaty ratified by almost all members of the United Nations (except the USA and Somalia). See http://www.crin.org/resources/treaties/CRC.asp?catName=International+Treaties&flag=legal&ID=6.

4 Tell students to complete the exercise, and then check with a partner. As you check the answers with the class, elicit words with each prefix, preferably with some connection with legal English.

Answers
1 c   2 d   3 f   4 a   5 e   6 b

Language notes

Here are some more general and legal English examples for each prefix.

- *bi-*: *biannual*, *bifurcation* (= when a judge splits two issues before a trial in order for a decision to be reached on one issue before hearing evidence on the other. See http://dictionary.law.com)
- *inter-*: *inter alia* (= legal Latin: among other things), *intervene* (= to obtain a judge's permission to join a lawsuit as an additional party after the lawsuit has already started. See http://dictionary. law.com)
- *intra-*: *intranet*, *intra vires* (= legal Latin: within an individual's or company's legal power or authority)
- *multi-*: *multi-cultural*, *multifarious* /ˌmʌltɪˈfeərɪəs/ (= when a series of causes of action are improperly joined in a single lawsuit. See http:// dictionary.law.com)
- *non-*: *non-breaching party*, *non-binding agreement*, *non-negotiable*
- *supra-*: *supraprotest* (= an acceptance or a payment of a bill by a third person after protest for non-acceptance or non-payment by the drawee. Source: http:// dictionary.com). Note that *supra-* is mainly used in medical English. In other varieties of English, the prefix *super-*, which has essentially the same meaning, is much more familiar (e.g. *supervisory board*, *superpower*)

5 Students should complete the exercise alone, and then check with a partner. When you check the answers with the class, elicit a typical context for each of the words (see Background note below for an important example of *non-aligned*).

Answers
1 f **2** a **3** c **4** b **5** e **6** d

Background note

The Non-Aligned Movement (NAM) is an international organisation of countries which are not aligned to the major world powers, and was influential during the Cold War (see http://en.wikipedia.org/wiki/Non-Aligned_Movement).

Reading 2: Developments in EU law

SB p.96

Elicit from the class how practising lawyers keep their knowledge up to date. Then tell them to read the introduction on page 96 to compare it with their ideas.

6 Tell students to discuss the three questions in small groups. With pre-experience lawyers, rather than asking them about their experiences with CPD in question 2, get them to predict what sorts of topics such courses might cover. After a few minutes, open up the discussion to include the whole class.

7 Allow one minute for students to read the two course descriptions quickly to answer the questions. Afterwards, tell them to discuss their answers with a partner, and then check the answers with the class.

Answer

The topic of the first seminar is 'Recent developments in European labour law'; it is intended for lawyers in private practice, in-house counsel or civil servants specialised in labour law or working with businesses, associations or trade unions at national or European level. The topic of the second seminar is 'Recent developments in European company law'; it is intended for lawyers in private practice, in-house counsel, officials in tax administrations, accountants and academics.

Background notes

- An *in-house counsel* is a lawyer who works as an employee of a company doing that company's legal work. Unlike outside counsel, who are usually employed by a law firm and have various different clients, an in-house counsel has no other client besides the employer company.
- *Flexicurity* is a model of economic development developed in Denmark in the 1990s, combining flexibility (e.g. easy to recruit and dismiss employees) with security (e.g. strong welfare protection for the unemployed). See http://en.wikipedia.org/wiki/Flexicurity.

○ For more on the *Laval* case, see Listening 1.

○ The *Viking* case is similar to the Laval case, in that it involved a trade union from a high-labour-cost European country (in this case, Finland) attempting to stop workers from a country with cheaper labour (in this case, Estonia). A Finnish ferry company, Viking Line, attempted to re-flag its Tallinn–Helsinki ferry so it could be crewed by Estonians. The Finnish Seamen's Union attempted to use its influence with its affiliates to refrain from cooperating with Viking Line. For full details of the case, see http://www.nieuwsbank.nl/en/2007/12/11/R011.htm.

○ Directive 2007/36/EC (see http://www.eurosif.org/eu_eurosif/lobbying/shareholders_rights/eu_directive_on_shareholders_rights) removed the requirement for *expert reports* in *mergers* (i.e. when two or more companies join together to become one) and *divisions* (i.e. when one company splits into two or more separate companies). Previously, an expert had to assess the impact of any proposed merger or division on third parties.

○ At the time of writing, the *European Private Company Statute* is still an idea for EU legislation to make cross-border operations within the EU easier, and may or may not become reality. See http://commercial-law.blogspot.com/2007/07/european-private-company-statute.html for some good background and analysis.

8 Tell students to discuss with a partner the suitability of the courses for the five lawyers. When you check the answers with the class, elicit why each course is suitable for particular lawyers. Also, discuss which of the two courses would be most useful for students in your class.

Answers
1 B 2 A 3 N 4 B 5 N

SB p.98 **Key terms 2: Legal instruments**

9 Elicit from the class what they understand by the term *legal instrument* (= legally binding legal document, whether in private law, such as a contract, or public law, such as a statute). Then tell them to read the second extract again quickly to find four different legal instruments. When you go through the answers with the class, avoid explaining the instruments, as this will spoil the next exercise.

Answers
Directive 2007/36/EC on …
… the 3rd and 6th Company Law Directives …
… the Commission published its Communication COM(2007)394 …
A recommendation on …
… for the European Private Company Statute.
… the proposal for a Directive on …

10 Tell students to work with a partner to complete the exercise. When you check the answers with the class, elicit why one instrument might be chosen for a particular function rather than another.

Answers
1 Recommendations and opinions
2 Regulations   3 Directives   4 Decisions
5 Communications

11 Do this quickly with the class. As a follow-up, elicit more legal English meanings and collocations for each of the five words, and write these up on the board, in the form of mind maps. Encourage students to copy the mind maps into their notebooks, and to add more collocations for each word as they come across them.

Answers
1 fully binding, binding on*
2 Member State
3 achieve a goal, reach a goal (*The two collocations mean the same.*)
4 leave something to the discretion of
5 course of action
* The term *binding upon* is also used, although is increasingly less common in contemporary legal texts.

Listening 1: CPD seminar on labour law

Elicit from the class what the course outline said about the Laval case [**Answer**: It was mentioned as an important example for the relationship between social rights and internal market rules]. Then tell them to read the introduction on page 98, and to use the limited information they know (social rights, internal market, labour laws) to predict what it might involve. Avoid confirming or rejecting their suggestions.

12 Tell students to read the three questions, and then play the recording for them to find the answers. After listening, students should discuss their answers with a partner, and then feed back to the class.

Answers

1 A landmark case (or *landmark decision*) is one that establishes a precedent which either substantially changes the interpretation of the law or establishes new case law on a particular issue. This case is considered to be a landmark case because it will have an impact on countries that do not have a minimum wage but who rely on collective bargaining.

2 a Laval: a Latvian construction company employed to carry out some renovation work on a school in Sweden; Laval gave the work to one of its subsidiaries (see below).

b Vaxholm: the Swedish town where the school was located

c L. and P. Baltic Bygg: the subsidiary company of Laval who actually carried out the renovation work on the school in Vaxholm

3 The case was heard in the Swedish Labour Court and the European Court of Justice.

Transcript » STUDENT'S BOOK **page 136**

Language notes
See Optional extension after Exercise 14 for explanations of useful vocabulary.

13 Students should discuss the four statements with a partner to decide whether they are true or false. Avoid checking the answers with the class until you have played the recording a second time (i.e. for Exercise 14).

Answers

1 F (They called for the blockade because the Latvian workers were being paid less than they should have been.)

2 T **3** T **4** T

14 Tell students to read through the lawyer's notes with a partner to try to remember the missing information, but tell them not to write until they have listened a second time. You may need to check some of the vocabulary from the notes (e.g. *dumping*, *incompatible*). Play the recording for them to complete the exercise, and then tell them to discuss their answers with a partner before going through the answers with the class (as well as the answers to Exercise 13 above).

Answers

1 wage **2** bargaining **3** Latvia **4** lower
5 bankruptcy **6** Justice **7** 2007 **8** right
9 services **10** Posting **11** disappointed

Optional extension
This quiz follows up on several useful words and phrases connected with law that occurred in Listening 1, as well as many other useful legal English expressions. Tell students to read the audio transcript on page 137 to underline any such useful/difficult/interesting expressions. Note that the questions are numbered in the same order as they appear in the audio transcript, which will make it easier for students to find the answers.

1 Which expression refers to a case which has had a considerable impact on the decisions in other cases? [a landmark ruling]
2 What is the procedure where the European Union admits new members? [enlargement]
3 What verb means *to charge less than a competitor*, and often suggests an unfair advantage? [to undercut]
4 What is the expression for the practice of getting rid of expensive employees and replacing them with cheaper employees from other countries? [wage-dumping]

5 What is the name for the lowest amount that an employer is legally allowed to pay employees for work? [a minimum wage]

6 What is the name for the practice where an organised group of employees negotiates wages and salaries on behalf of the group? [collective bargaining]

7 What is the name for a company which is owned by another company? [a subsidiary]

8 What is the name for the practice of physically preventing employees from getting to work? [to blockade]

9 What is the name for the negotiated wage settlement between an employer and a group of employees? [a collective wage agreement]

10 What is the situation where you are unable to pay your debts and your property is taken to pay those debts? [bankruptcy]

11 What two verbs are used in the third paragraph to talk about a court's decision? [ruled, held]

12 What is the general name for a group of employees acting together to influence their employer's decisions? [collective action]

13 What is the name for the process where striking employees form a line in front of a place of work, which members of the union are expected not to cross? [picketing]

14 What adjective is used to say that two things cannot work together? [incompatible (with something)]

15 What verb means *to be* or *to have the status of?* [to constitute]

16 What adjective describes something that is fair in the circumstances? [justified]

17 What is the name for a country to which immigrants have moved? [host state]

18 What adjective is used for a reason or argument which is stronger or more important than all others? [over-riding]

19 What verb means *to get involved in something, and make it more difficult for others?* [to interfere (with something)]

20 What is a two-word expression meaning *it doesn't matter what?* [regardless of]

SB p.99 **Speaking 1: Debate**

Elicit from the class how a debate works, and whether it is similar in terms of format or language to any real-life situations students might encounter in their work as lawyers.

Background notes

Typically, in a debate, there are two sides arguing one motion. One side argues in favour of the motion, while the other side argues against. At the end, a judge (or members of the audience) decides who has won the debate. It is traditional for the competitive nature of debates to focus on the debating skills themselves, rather than on participants' private opinions regarding the motion. In other words, a skilled debater should be able to argue successfully in favour of a motion which he/she privately opposes (or vice versa). This has obvious relevance to the role of lawyers in prosecuting or defending a client to the best of their ability, regardless of their private opinions about the client's guilt or otherwise. The typical highly structured format of a debate (proposer's arguments, followed by opposer's counter-arguments, then opposer's arguments and proposer's counter-arguments) is similar to the stages in a court case, as well as similar legal procedures (e.g. unfair dismissal tribunal, patent application hearing, etc.), and the language used is very similar. It is essential in all of these situations for the speakers to address their arguments to the chair (i.e. the person chairing the process), and under no circumstances to start arguing with their opponents directly.

Optional lead-in
(Photocopiable worksheet 9.2)

This includes some useful phrases for students to use in the debate (and in similar real-life situations).

1 Divide students into groups of three or four, and give each group a set of cut-up slips of paper from the worksheet.

2 In their groups, they should find one extra word on each slip of paper and delete it. They should also sort the phrases into the three categories.

3 When the first groups have finished, go through the answers carefully to make sure all students know which word to delete: it is essential that they use the correct phrases during the debate later.

4 You may also give out complete copies of the worksheet (i.e. not cut up) to each student so they have a permanent record of the phrases.

Answers
1 a to **b** must **c** would **d** be **e** like **f** you **g** to **h** have **i** my **j** his **k** in **l** to **m** a **n** like **o** have **p** Why **q** about **r** to **s** or **t** be
2 1 b, d, h, k, l
  2 o, p, t
  3 a, c, e, f, g, i, j, m, n, q, r, s

When you are setting up the debate (see Exercise 15 below), tell students to use as many of the phrases as they can during the debate. Of course, they may need to change the phrases slightly to suit their needs. Every time they use one of the phrases, they should take the slip containing that phrase from the set nearest to them. If a slip has already been claimed (by themselves or another person in their group), they may use the phrase, but cannot claim the slip again. At the end of the debate, the person who has collected the most slips is the winner. Make sure students realise not to overdo the phrases in a cynical attempt to win the game; the phrases must be used naturally and logically as part of a genuine debate.

15 Divide the class into groups for the debates. The ideal group size is three or five: one or two students to propose the motion, one or two to oppose it, and one to chair the debate. If you have a class size which does not divide into threes or fives, there can be an extra chairperson in one or two groups. If there are only two students in the class, you should be the chairperson. If you have only one student, hold the debate without a chair – you will have to be one of the debaters.

Get each group to decide quickly which of the three questions to debate and which members of the groups are arguing for and against. If they can't decide quickly, decide for them. Point out that it doesn't matter what their private opinions are: they will be judged on their ability to argue a difficult case convincingly, whichever side they are on.

Allow students a few minutes to prepare their arguments and to plan who is going to say

what (i.e. is one student going to present arguments while the other presents counter-arguments to their opponent's points, or will they each contribute to both sections?).

Make sure the chair(s) understand the procedure of the debate (see Background notes above), and set a strict time limit for each section (say, three minutes for each, giving a total of 12 minutes for the debate). During the debate, monitor carefully for successful and less successful language, and be ready to step in if the chair is having problems controlling the debate. At the end of the time limit, ask the chair(s) to decide which side is the winner (based on their debating skills rather than on the chair's opinion of the Laval case). Finally, give and elicit feedback on the quality of the debate in terms of accuracy, appropriateness and sophistication.

LAW IN PRACTICE

SB p.100 Lead-in

Elicit from the class what the purpose of a patent is, and why international law is important for patents. Then tell them to read the introduction on page 100 to compare it with their ideas.

16 Tell students to discuss the questions in small groups. After a few minutes, open up the discussion to include the whole class.

➡ **Suggested answers**
1 Ideas emanating from one jurisdiction can be developed by individuals or companies from other jurisdictions, leading to possible issues concerning international law, e.g. open source software, often developed collectively by programmers from many jurisdictions, sometimes infringes registered patents.
2 A case involving parties from different jurisdictions will often involve questions of a) what court has jurisdiction to hear a case, and b) what laws (from which jurisdictions) apply to which aspects of the case.

Background note

Obtaining and maintaining a patent is an expensive and time-consuming business, as the patent office must research each invention thoroughly to ensure that it is sufficiently different from existing inventions, whether patented or not. It is normal for business competitors to challenge patent applications, by demonstrating that their own inventions are part of the 'prior art' (i.e. they existed before the application was filed, and therefore the application knowingly or otherwise copied their ideas), or that the applicant's invention is not sufficiently inventive, etc. to deserve protection. Traditionally, inventors have had to file (and pay for) an application in every country for which they wanted protection. In recent decades, it has become increasingly popular for inventors to apply for international patents through the Patent Cooperation Treaty (PCT) of the World Intellectual Property Organisation (WIPO). See http://www.wipo.int/portal/index.html. en. It is also common to submit a single application to the European Patent Office (EPO) to get a patent for 34 European countries. See http://www.epo.org/. Because international patents are very expensive, inventors and their companies often try to save money by applying for patents in only a few countries. However, as the case study in Readings 3 and 4 shows, this can allow rivals to ignore the patent when manufacturing and selling goods in other countries.

Reading 3: US patent laws

17 Tell students to read the text quickly to answer the question. When you check the answer with the class, elicit also what the dispute was about, and any other details they know about the case (from either the text or their own knowledge).

Answers
Headline 2

Background note

There is plenty of information about the case online (e.g. search for *Microsoft AT&T voice compression*), including a very clear analysis of the two sides' arguments, at http://www.law.cornell.edu/supct/cert/ search/display.html?terms=patent&url=/ supct/cert/05-1056.html.

18 Students should work in pairs to complete the exercise. When the first groups have finished, go through the answers with the class.

Answers
1 d   2 a   3 c   4 b

Optional extension

Elicit from the class how they managed to work out which sentence goes where, and why an awareness of such cohesive devices might be useful.

Suggested answers

○ Sequence of tenses (present perfect in first sentence, followed by past simple in second sentence, followed by past perfect in third sentence)
○ Articles (*a* in early paragraphs: *a long-running case*, *a software patent dispute*; *the* later: *the infringement*, *the judges*)
○ Chains of related concepts, linking the middle or end of one sentence with the beginning of the next: *Microsoft ... the US Supreme **Court** ... . The **court** ... US telecoms operator **AT&T**. AT&T ... **patent** in voice-compression software. Microsoft ... **patent** violations ...*

Cohesive devices are important especially in students' writing. They help the reader to follow the writer's arguments. Students should pay attention to such devices when they read, and try to use them when they write. A quick test of good writing is to cut it up (as in Reading 3) to see if somebody else can put it back together again easily. Cohesion is also important in speech (most obviously in highly structured speech situations like presentations, debates and court cases).

19 Tell students to work with a partner to complete the matching activity. When they have finished, check the answers with the class. As a follow-up, students should test their partners by reading one of the definitions to elicit the term, or by reading a term to elicit a definition.

Answers
1 presumption   2 governs (to govern)
3 rigid   4 entitled (to entitle)   5 narrow
6 infringement   7 ruling
8 extended (to extend)   9 test

20 Tell students to discuss the question in small groups, and then open up the discussion to include the whole class. Note that the question includes a 'third conditional' about the imaginary past. You could encourage students to use this structure in their answers or, with weaker students, allow them to treat the question as a discussion about the hypothetical future (*How would … rule in this case?*).

Reading 4: Microsoft v. AT&T

21 Tell students to read the questions. You could elicit suggested answers from the class before reading (based on Reading 3 and students' knowledge of the words in question 2), but avoid confirming or rejecting their ideas. Allow two or three minutes for them to read the text carefully, and then tell them to discuss their answers with a partner before feeding back to the class. Elicit from the class a simple example of a patented invention with components which are combined (e.g. a bicycle, whose wheels, frame, seat, pedals, etc. are all components, which may be made in one country and assembled in another), and elicit why such a definition is more problematic for a computer program.

Answers
1 AT&T holds a patent on its voice-compression software (referred to as *AT&T's speech-processing computer* in the decision).
2 Sending a part of a patented invention overseas to be incorporated into another product.

Language notes
○ *Certiorari* /ˌsɜːtɪəˈrɑːrɪ/ is the name for a writ allowing a case to be heard by a higher court. See http://en.wikipedia.org/wiki/Certiorari#Federal_courts. Before a case can be heard by the US Supreme Court, at least four of the nine judges must vote to grant the writ of certiorari.
○ In the USA, the *Federal Circuit* /ˈfedərəl ˈsɜːkɪt/ is a circuit which has jurisdiction over the whole country in certain kinds of case, such as patent cases. A circuit is the territory over which a court has jurisdiction.
○ The ruling includes the abbreviation *35 U.S.C. s.271 (f)(1)*. This means United States Code Title 35, section 271, paragraph (f), part (1). See http://www.law.cornell.edu/uscode/35/271.html for the relevant section of the USC. The USC is a compilation of the law of the USA (see http://en.wikipedia.org/wiki/United_States_Code).
○ *Unincorporated software* means software which is not a part of any actual component of a computer. In this case, the software existed in the USA on master disks, or was transmitted electronically, but was incorporated in physical disks only outside the USA.

22 Students should read the text again to answer the three questions. They should discuss the questions with a partner before feeding back to the class.

Answers
1 Section 271(f) of the Patent Act provides that infringement occurs when one 'suppl[ies] … from the United States', for 'combination' abroad, a patented invention's 'components'.
2 1 Unincorporated software is not a 'component' of an invention under s.271(f) because it is intangible (not material or physical) information.
   2 Copies of Windows made overseas and installed abroad were not 'supplie[d] … from the United States' under s.271(f).

3 Microsoft was not liable under s.271(f) because it did not export the copies of Windows installed on the foreign-made computers in question from the United States, and therefore did not 'suppl[y] … from the United States' 'components' of those computers.

23 Tell students to discuss the question with a partner. They could also discuss Exercise 24 at the same time. Note that the question in Exercise 23 is in the form of a third conditional about the imaginary past. With stronger classes, encourage students to use the same structure in their answers.

Answers

The software at the centre of this case was first sent from the United States to the foreign manufacturers either on a master disk, or by electronic transmission. It was then copied by the foreign recipients for installation on computers made and sold abroad. The ruling may have been different had Microsoft physically supplied *each* copy of Windows (i.e. by post on CD or DVD) that was then installed on the foreign computers.

24 See Exercise 23 above.

Background note

Dissent /dɪˈsent/, or a *dissenting opinion*, is an opinion of one or more judges which disagrees with the majority ruling. It does not create case law, but can often be influential in highlighting areas of the law which need compromise or clarification. See http://en.wikipedia.org/wiki/Dissenting_opinion.

(SB p.102) (9.2 9.3) ## Listening 2: Multiple jurisdictions

25 Tell students to read the introduction and the question to find out who they are going to listen to and what they have to do. Then play the recording for them to complete the exercise. Allow them to check their answers quickly with a partner, and to discuss what they remember about each country/nationality, before going through them with the class.

Answers

countries: Scotland, Austria, Germany, Slovenia, America (the term *USA* is also mentioned), UK, Italy, Russia
nationalities: Austrian, Turkish, British, American, Italian

Transcript » STUDENT'S BOOK page 136

Language notes

○ An *amicable settlement* /ˈæmɪkəbl ˈsetlmənt/ is the situation when the parties to a dispute reach a settlement without any bad feeling between them, typically because they have not had to go to court.

○ *Ljubljana* /ljuːˈbljɑːnə/, the capital of Slovenia, where Mr Kundakçi lives, is around 300km from Innsbruck in southern Austria, the location of the restaurant.

○ If you *execute* a contract, you sign it.

○ A *hard copy* of a contract is the paper version, in contrast to the soft copy, which exists and can be sent electronically (e.g. as an email attachment).

○ If you *jump at an opportunity*, you take advantage of it very enthusiastically.

○ If a court is *competent*, it is an appropriate court (in a legal sense), that is, it has lawful jurisdiction to hear a particular case.

26 Tell students to discuss the four questions with a partner. You may need to check they understand the term *fall through*. With stronger classes, you may decide to check the answers without listening, as there will be another opportunity to listen in Exercise 27. With weaker classes, play the recording for them to check their answers, and then go through the answers with the class.

Answers

1 A restaurant in Austria (Innsbruck)
2 The joint purchase of a restaurant from Mr Piombo
3 As a Turkish national, Mr Kundakçi can't buy property in Austria.
4 Which court is competent to hear the case (has jurisdiction)

27 Tell students to work with a partner to decide what information should go in each space.

28a Elicit from the class what the lawyer might advise the client to do, and what might happen next in the case. [**Suggested answers**: Mr Jones may try to sue Mr Kundakçi to recover the money he has lost, on the grounds that they had an implied contract (a series of online conversations). Mr Piombo may keep the deposit, and may try to sue Mr Jones and/or Mr Kundakçi for the remainder of the cost of the restaurant they agreed to buy. They may reach an amicable settlement: for example, they may find a way for Mr Jones to buy the restaurant using Mr Kundakçi's money.]

Tell students to listen to make notes of the five stages. They should note not just the names of the stages, but any further information about each stage that they could pass on to their own clients. After playing the recording, tell students to compare their notes with a partner before discussing the answers with the class.

> **Answers**
> **1** Court must decide whether it has jurisdiction in each of the possible legal actions in the case.
> **2** Break down the cause of action (the facts that give rise to the legal claim) into its component legal categories.
> **3** Once the legal issues have been determined, decide which laws should be applied.
> **4** Apply the appropriate law to reach a judgment.
> **5** Secure cross-border recognition of any award.

Transcript » STUDENT'S BOOK **page 137**

📖 **Background notes**
○ For more on the stages in a conflict of laws case, see http://en.wikipedia.org/wiki/Conflict_of_laws#The_stages_in_a_conflict_case.
○ Mr Connor mentions that there may be *several possible legal actions*, e.g. Mr Jones may sue Mr Kundakçi, Mr Piombo may sue Mr Jones or Mr Kundakçi (or both), depending on who signed the original contract.
○ By the *measure of damages*, Mr Connor simply means the amount of damages awarded.
○ A *cause of action* is the legal basis for a court case, i.e. the key legal facts which fulfil the necessary criteria to justify bringing a case.
○ A *legal category* is a category as defined by law. In other words, if a document falls under the legal category of 'treaty', it must have certain characteristics.
○ If a court *adjudicates* /əˈdʒuːdəkeɪts/, it hears and judges a case.
○ *Renvoi* /ˈrɒ̃vwʌ/ comes from the French for 'sent back'. It is a technique designed to ensure the same outcome is achieved no matter where a case is heard, and involves a court in one jurisdiction applying the laws of another. See http://en.wikipedia.org/wiki/Renvoi.

b Tell students to read the six statements to make sure they understand (although if you have to explain any words, avoid giving the answers to questions 2, 3, 4 and 5). Then play the recording again for them to check. They should discuss their answers with a partner before feeding back to the class.

> **Answers**
> **1** T **2** T **3** F (It is the facts that give rise to a legal action.) **4** F (It is a question that arises in connection with the main claim.) **5** T **6** F (Cross-border recognition needs to be secured separately.)

29 Tell students to work with a partner to analyse the interview. After a few minutes, open up the discussion to include the class.

Answers

Welcome the client: Yes
Acquire information: Yes
Supply information and advise: The lawyer supplied a lot of information on the stages of a conflict of laws case, although he gave little actual advice. Presumably this will be included in his follow-up letter once he has had the opportunity to research the possible legal claims and issues in more depth.
Part: Yes

Language use: Explaining legal terms to non-lawyers

SB p.103

Elicit from the class what sort of language is useful for explaining legal terms to non-lawyers, with some examples of the types of phrase for each function (see Exercise 30 for examples). Then tell them to read the information in the box on page 103 to compare it with their ideas.

30a Tell students to do this quickly alone, and then check with the class.

Answers

1 rephrasing
2 giving examples
3 simplifying
4 giving further details

b Discuss this with the class, and encourage students to write down any useful phrases for each function. As a follow-up, students can test each other by giving a function to elicit from their partner as many phrases as possible for that function.

Suggested answers

rephrasing: *to put it another way …*; *this actually means …*
giving examples: *for example*; *for instance*
simplifying: *in essence*; *really*
giving further details: *specifically*; *in particular*

Optional extension

There are many other useful phrases for lawyers in the audio transcript.

1 Tell students to look through the audio transcript on page 137 to find examples of the following functions: welcoming, reassuring, structuring, and checking.

2 When they have finished, check the answers with the class.

Suggested answers
Welcoming
Good morning, Mr Jones. Please come in.
Reassuring
I realise you must be very concerned at the moment, but I'm hoping we'll be able to work out some kind of amicable settlement that all parties can accept.
It's not normally in anyone's interest to go to court if it can be avoided.
I'm sure we'll be able to settle this before things go any further.
Structuring
I think it would be useful if I could outline what I understand the facts of the case to be. Then I'll explain the legal issues.
Please do stop me if I've misunderstood anything.
Let's start with your current circumstances.
OK, to pick up where I left off.
There are essentially five stages to a case involving a conflict of laws.
I can take you through them if you'd like.
First, there are several possible …
Anyway, the second stage is to …
As I said, there are several …
But let's worry about that later.
A key element in this may be …
I'll put all of this in a letter outlining the various potential causes of action and how they would most likely be resolved.
Checking
Right, so …. Is that right?
Can I ask why you decided … ?
Can I just check, … , is that right?
And I think you said in your email that … ?
Is there no chance that you could … ?
OK, I think I'm clear on the facts now. Unless I've missed something?
I'm assuming you don't have … ?

Speaking 2: Definitions/Role-play: explaining legal terms to non-lawyers

31 Assign roles to students. If you have an odd number of students, there will have to be one group of three, in which case there must be two Student As in that group. Tell them to turn to the appropriate page, and to take turns to explain their words to their partner. The explanations should be in the form of mini-role-plays, where the explainer is a lawyer, and their partner is a client with very limited knowledge of legal English. The lawyer should use phrases from the box on pages 103–104 to explain the terms. The client should ask for clarification if the lawyer's explanation is insufficiently clear. Do the first one together with the class as an example, e.g. A: *I need to check your nationality. In other words, the country where you were born, or of which you have become a naturalised citizen.* B: *What do you mean by 'naturalised'?* A: *That's the process by which you gain the same rights as people born in a particular country.*

Point out that the purpose of the exercise is to practise the phrases for explaining, so it is not essential that students have a deep understanding of the terminology. However, if you feel students will struggle with the exercise, you could prepare them by either going through all the words first with the class, or setting as homework the task of researching the words in their lists. Note that the words are also defined in the answer key (copied below), which you may allow your students to look at.

While students are completing the role-play, listen for successful and less successful language, and give and elicit feedback at the end. Also check the explanations of some of the more difficult terms, such as *renvoi* and *competence*.

Suggested answers
Student A
1 nationality: the official right to belong to a particular country
2 dual citizenship: the state of being a member of two particular countries and having rights in both because of this

3 competent: a court is competent (or has *competence*) if it has jurisdiction to hear a particular lawsuit
4 forum shopping: the practice of filing a lawsuit in the jurisdiction thought most likely to provide a favourable outcome for the claimant
5 expat (= expatriate): a person who has decided to live in another country, often for work purposes or to retire
6 cause of action: the fact or facts that give a person the right to seek a legal remedy through litigation

Student B
1 joint purchase (of land): to buy land together with one or more other people or business entities
2 residence: the place where you live (a person may have his/her state of *domicile* elsewhere for tax or other purposes, especially if the residence is for convenience or temporary)
3 domicile: the place where a person has his or her permanent principal residence (home) to which he or she returns or intends to return
4 renvoi: the choice of law rules that may be applied whenever a court is directed to consider the law of another jurisdiction
5 cross-border recognition: for something (e.g. a judicial decision) from one jurisdiction to be accepted in another
6 adjudicate: to act as judge in a legal dispute; to make a formal decision about something

32 Tell students to work in the same pairs (although if you have an odd number of students, it is fairer to change the groups), and direct them to the relevant page to read their notes. If there is an extra student in one group, he/she should be a second lawyer (so Role A). Monitor carefully while they are reading, as they may have some problems with the terminology on the cards. Tell Students B to prepare for the role-play by deciding what information they will need from the lawyer, and what questions they will need to ask.

Make sure Students A know to follow the WASP approach in their interviews, and to use as much of the language from the unit as possible. Allow up to around ten minutes for the role-plays. If some pairs finish early, tell them to swap roles and act out the role-play again. Monitor carefully during the role-plays, and give and elicit feedback at the end on the quality of the language and the effectiveness of the meetings.

Language notes

○ A *class action suit* is a lawsuit brought by a group of litigants (claimants) against a single defendant, because they claim to have suffered a common injury as a class. Any damages awarded are shared by all members of that class, and not just to those who have brought the lawsuit.

○ The phrase *choice of law and statutory interpretation intersect* simply means that in, for example, class-action cases involving litigants from different jurisdictions, lawyers and judges have to worry about both issues: *choice of law* (i.e. which jurisdiction's law should be used to judge the case) and *statutory interpretation* (i.e. what did the drafters of the relevant statute intend when they made the statute).

○ *Class certification* is the process where a court agrees that a group of plaintiffs can represent a class in a class action suit. See http://en.wikipedia.org/wiki/Class_action#United_States.

○ An *extraterritorial litigant* is a litigant (claimant) from outside the territory in question (in this case, California).

(SB p.104) **Writing: Follow-up letter**

33 The writing can be done at home or in class (see section on Writing, page 8). Make sure students realise they are writing as the lawyer to the client from Exercise 32 (regardless of the role they played in the role-play).

(SB p.105) # Language Focus

Answers

1 Collocations

1 binding **2** advisory **3** customary
4 enforceable **5** governmental **6** intellectual

2 Vocabulary

1 bilateral **2** non-governmental
3 supranational **4** inter-state

3 Explaining legal terms

1 c **2** d **3** a **4** b

10 Comparative law

Teacher's brief

Comparative law has grown enormously in importance in recent decades, as **globalisation** and **internationalism** have made it increasingly necessary for lawyers to relate their legal systems to those of their clients and colleagues from around the world. There are two ways around the problem of dealing with several legal systems. As a short-term, small-scale solution, lawyers (or their colleagues) have to **translate legal terms**, and to understand and explain untranslatable terms. A larger-scale, longer-term project is to **harmonise or unify** the laws of various countries to minimise or eliminate the differences. International organisations such as the **European Union**, **UNIDROIT** and the **Hague Conference on Private International Law** have made progress in harmonising and unifying the laws of many different countries, but of course a great deal remains to be done.

Much of the world can be divided into two **families of legal systems**: **common law** and **civil law**. Common-law jurisdictions, which correspond closely with the countries of the English-speaking world, derive most of their detailed law from legal decisions of judges in earlier court cases (**precedents**). Historically, **codified law** (in the form of **statutes** passed by the **legislature**) played a very minor role in the body of laws in these countries, although in recent decades there has been a marked growth.

Much of the rest of the world belongs to the **civil law** family, which derives its laws from **statutes**, and these laws are collected together in **codes**, which judges must apply when making decisions. There are also many **mixed systems** (e.g. common law and civil law, as in Scotland). Some jurisdictions also make use of **religious texts** in their law (mainly Muslim countries), in which case the religious text acts rather like the US Constitution: an unchanging reference text on which to base all legal decisions, but which must be **interpreted**, as it cannot provide detailed guidance on all technical legal matters. As in common law, **religious-law** systems (such as **Islamic law**) make considerable use of interpretation and precedent.

A key issue in this unit is **legal translation**: in Listening 1, a Mexican lawyer outlines some problems with **false friends** (terms which look like terms in another language, but whose meaning is different) and other difficult-to-translate terms. This problem is developed further in Listening 2, where a term from English law, **equity**, presents problems because it does not exist in other jurisdictions. (Equity has several meanings in financial and legal English, but here it refers to a subsidiary legal system which existed in England and which attempted to overcome the harshness and rigidity of the common law.) In spite of the particularly English nature of this system, the speakers nevertheless find broad comparisons with concepts in their own jurisdictions. This provides a good example of the importance of the language of **similarities and differences**, highlighted and practised in this unit.

A further example of concepts which occur in one jurisdiction and not others is provided around the end of the unit: **asset protection entities** in Liechtenstein. These entities (the Stiftung and Anstalt) enable clients to protect their assets from **creditors** (people to whom they owe money) and others who may want to seize those assets (such as tax authorities, if they suspect **tax evasion** (deliberate non-payment of taxes) or the police, if the money has been stolen). The unit includes a **letter of advice** from a lawyer to a businesswoman who is considering taking advantage of the asset protection entities. The letter of advice presents a lot of complex information clearly by making use of **discourse markers** (e.g. *consequently*, *furthermore*).

The issue of asset protection in so-called **tax havens** such as Liechtenstein is a delicate one, depending on whether one sees things from the side of the asset owner or the creditor. There is a perception that it is possible for powerful people to avoid their legal obligations by taking advantage of the different laws in another country, and this perception is one of the driving forces behind harmonisation and unification of laws.

Further reading
○ For a very good guide to **comparative law**, see http://www.nyulawglobal.com/globalex/Comparative_Law.htm.
○ The **legal systems of the world** are presented in both a series of maps and as a table at http://chopin.cc.uottawa.ca/droitcivil/world-legal-systems/eng-monde.php.

THE STUDY OF LAW

SB p.106 Lead-in

Elicit from the class what they understand by the term *comparative law*, and what they know / can guess of the legal systems in different countries. (You could prompt them by naming some countries in various parts of the world.) Then tell them to read the Lead-in text to compare it with their ideas.

📖 **Background notes**

○ For an excellent list of the legal systems in the countries of the world, see http://chopin.cc.uottawa.ca/droitcivil/world-legal-systems/eng-monde.php, which contains both a comprehensive list and a map. There is also a useful list and map at http://en.wikipedia.org/wiki/Legal_systems_of_the_world.

○ The lead-in text mentions different *classification systems*. Several such classifications split the civil-law group into a French group (i.e. countries whose systems are based on or influenced by the Napoleonic Code), a German group and a Scandinavian group. Several systems also put Muslim law and Hindu law in separate families. See http://en.wikipedia.org/wiki/Comparative_law#Classifications_of_legal_systems.

○ The *common-law* and *civil-law* systems are described in Reading 2. For more information, see http://en.wikipedia.org/wiki/Common_law and http://en.wikipedia.org/wiki/Civil_law_%28legal_system%29. Note that the term *civil law* has two common meanings: as well as referring to the world's most widely used legal system, it is used within common-law jurisdictions to refer to those areas of law dealing with disputes between individuals and organisations (e.g. tort law, commercial law, etc.), in contrast with criminal law (in which the disputes involve the state).

○ The most widespread system of religious law is *Shariah* (Islamic law), which is used (either in a pure form or in a mixture with other legal systems) in around 16 countries, including Iran, Saudi Arabia, Afghanistan and Pakistan.

However, there is considerable variation in the way it is used: in most Muslim countries, Shariah courts are limited to matters of marriage and inheritance, while secular courts are used for all other legal issues. Shariah is based on the Koran and the Sunna (the actions and teachings of the prophet Mohammed). It also draws heavily on analogy and precedent, rather than a codified set of laws, and as such was an important influence on common-law and civil-law systems, as well as on international law. See http://en.wikipedia.org/wiki/Sharia. As a result of these influences, the three most popular bodies of law (civil, common and Islamic) have a great deal in common in terms of legal principles, although of course there are differences in how those principles are applied.

○ *Hindu law*, one of several legal systems used in India, is concerned mainly with family law and rituals, and applies only to the country's Hindu population. India also has Muslim and Christian courts. However, these three bodies of religious law are of limited importance in modern India, whose legal system is mainly common law (based on English law). See http://en.wikipedia.org/wiki/Law_in_India. An important concept in Hindu law is *Dharma*, which includes both legal and religious duties (e.g. connected with hygiene and rituals). See http://en.wikipedia.org/wiki/Hindu_law.

○ *Jewish law* (Talmudic law or *Halakha*) is also mainly concerned with family and rituals, but in modern Israel, the legal system is very much a mixture of British-influenced common law and German-influenced civil law. Judges are encouraged to interpret laws in the spirit of ancient Jewish law. See http://en.wikipedia.org/wiki/Law_of_Israel.

○ The term *Chinese law* in the classification of legal systems refers to traditional Chinese law. The modern law system of the People's Republic of China is a combination of civil law and socialist law, with influences from this traditional system. The Republic of China (Taiwan) uses a combination of traditional law with a German-style civil-law system. Hong Kong and Macao, now both part of the People's Republic of China, retain substantial elements of the English common law and Portuguese civil law respectively. See http://en.wikipedia.org/wiki/Law_of_the_People%27s_Republic_of_China. Within traditional Chinese law, the two biggest influences are Confucianism and Legalism. Confucianism is based on the idea that the state should lead by example, and the people will follow because they will be ashamed of doing wrong. Legalism was a system of standard law that bound even the Emperor. Both systems shared the idea that the state knows better than its citizens and creates laws to protect them. See http://en.wikipedia.org/wiki/Chinese_law.

○ *Socialist law* is very similar to civil law, although in place of civil law's emphasis on private property, socialist law deals extensively with property belonging to the state and co-operatives. Since the collapse of the Soviet Union, and market-oriented reforms in China, socialist law has ceased to be one of the world's major law systems, although it still plays a significant part in Chinese law, alongside civil law and traditional Chinese law. See http://en.wikipedia.org/wiki/Socialist_law. Other countries with communist governments (at the time of writing, North Korea, Cuba, Laos and Vietnam) tend to be classified as civil-law countries.

1 Tell students to discuss the three questions in small groups, and to think of examples for questions 1 and 3. Point out that the term *English-speaking* may be interpreted loosely to include countries where English is one of the official languages (such as India, Nigeria and Singapore). After a few minutes, open up the discussion to include the class.

Answers
1 A system that combines two or more aspects of different legal systems. Mixed systems include those based on

civil law and common law (e.g. Scotland, the Philippines and jurisdictions based on South African law), civil law and religious law (e.g. Egypt, Indonesia and Morocco), common law and religious law (e.g. India, Pakistan and Singapore).
3 The majority of English-speaking jurisdictions have common law or mixed systems based on common law.

Background notes
If we interpret the term *English-speaking* very loosely to include those countries where English has some status as an official or 'linking' language, mixed systems include several former British colonies (e.g. India, Bangladesh, Nigeria, Pakistan, Malaysia, Singapore, etc.) which have common-law systems with elements of religious law. There are also many examples of mixed common- and civil-law countries, such as South Africa, Zimbabwe, Botswana, the Philippines and Sri Lanka. Scotland (in the UK), Quebec (in Canada) and Louisiana (in the USA) are all also mixed systems, with elements of common and civil law.

SB p.106 Reading 1: Comparative law

2 Tell students to read the text quickly to answer the three questions. Allow around three minutes, after which tell them to compare their answers with a partner. As you go through the answers with the class, elicit what, if anything, students know about the various topics (especially those mentioned in the Background notes below).

Answers
1 The importance of comparative law is growing due to the globalisation of world trade, which means that lawyers often have to work with more than one jurisdiction, and as a result of the increasing harmonisation of laws worldwide. Internationalism and democratisation have also led to the growth in importance of the study of comparative law.
2 HCC stands for the Hague Conference on Private International Law. It is a global intergovernmental organisation

which aims to work for the progressive unification of private international law.

3 The Uniform Law on the International Sale of Goods, 1964.

📖 **Background notes**
- ○ *Harmonisation* means adjusting the laws of various jurisdictions so they have the same effect as each other. *Unification* means replacing the laws in various jurisdictions with a unified law which covers all the jurisdictions.
- ○ At the time of writing, the *Union of South American Nations* is still a planned project to unite two free-trade organisations, Mercosur and the Andean Community. See http://en.wikipedia.org/wiki/Union_of_South_American_Nations.
- ○ For more on the *Hague Conference on Private International Law*, see http://www.hcch.net/index_en.php. Its 65 members include the USA, China, all EU members and Russia.
- ○ For more on the *International Institute for the Unification of Private Law (UNIDROIT)*, see http://www.unidroit.org/english/home.htm. Like HCCH, its members include the world's biggest economic powers.

Key terms: Expressions used in comparative law
SB p.107

3 Tell students to work in pairs to come up with a definition of each term, as if they had to explain them to a client. Afterwards, elicit some explanations from the class.

➡ **Suggested answers**
1 *Applicability of laws* refers to the question that arises when a case involves parties from more than one jurisdiction: which set of laws applies to the case?
2 *International civil procedure* refers to the process that courts will follow when hearing civil cases that have an international element.
3 *Enforcement of judgments* means the efforts that are made to make sure that a legal decision is obeyed (e.g. ensuring

that an award for damages is paid, or that a contract is performed).
4 The phrase *progressive unification of law* is used to talk about the process by which laws from different jurisdictions are made more similar.

Optional extension
Tell students to work in groups to write quiz questions for other teams. (See 'Quiz game' in the section on Games and activities, page 9.)

Reading 2: Course reader
SB p.107

Elicit from the class what a course reader is, and then tell them to read the introduction on page 107 and the instructions for Exercise 4 to find out what this particular course reader will be about.

4 Tell students to read the questions. Allow two or three minutes for them to read, and then tell them to discuss their answers with a partner. As you go through the answers with the class, check for any problems with understanding (see Language notes below for some potential problems).

➡ **Answers**
1 Civil law originated in ancient Rome and was later developed in continental Europe.
2 Precedent is at the core of common-law systems. The term refers to decisions that establish legal principles, or which reverse the decision in an earlier case. These precedents are then applied in future cases.
3 *Stare decisis* is the doctrine that compels lower courts to follow decisions made by higher courts.
4 codified law, enacted law
Note: The term *written law* is also used. These terms contrast with the terms *uncodified law*, *unenacted law* and *unwritten law* (all used to refer to precedent).

📖 **Background notes**
- ○ The *Commonwealth of Nations* consists of most countries of the former British Empire, which corresponds fairly closely

with both the English-speaking world and common-law jurisdictions (one important non-Commonwealth exception being the USA).

○ A *legislator* is somebody who makes laws, i.e. a member of a legislative body, such as an MP in the UK.

○ *Stare decisis* /ˈstɑːrɪ dəˈsaɪsɪs/, as explained in the text, literally means 'standing by a decision'. See http://dictionary.law.com.

Language notes

○ *For the most part* (paragraph 2) means 'generally speaking'.

○ Paragraph 4 states that *judges must then apply [abstract rules] to the various cases **before** them*. In this case, *before* means 'in front of' or 'facing' them. In other words, judges apply these rules to the various cases which they (the judges) face / have to deal with.

○ The final paragraph introduces some sets of synonyms: *codified law* = enacted law = written law; *uncodified law* = unenacted law = unwritten law.

○ In the last paragraph, we learn that codified law is paramount but differs in importance in the two systems. This may seem contradictory, but it depends on the meaning of *paramount*, which here means 'more powerful'. Within the common-law system, most law is created by precedent, so in this sense, codified law is less important. But in the limited (but growing) areas of law where statutes exist, judges are expected to base their judgments on these statutes, rather than earlier precedents, so in this sense, codified law is paramount.

5 Students should complete the exercise in pairs, and then feed back to the class. Elicit from the class situations in which the more formal words would be more appropriate (e.g. formal writing, formal meetings with colleagues and clients in which you want to make a professional impression), and in which situations the more everyday terms are better (e.g. informal writing and speaking, especially where clear communication is more important than creating a professional impression).

Answers
1 subsequently   2 compels   3 rendered
4 paramount
In each pair, the second word (the one in the original text) is more formal.

Optional extension
(Photocopiable worksheet 10.1)
This focuses on some of the useful prepositional phrases from Reading 2.

1 Tell students to close their books. Distribute the worksheets and tell students to work in pairs to put the prepositions from the boxes into the extracts from the text (note that the extracts have been shortened slightly to fit the exercise).

2 Set a tight time limit (around three minutes), after which go through the answers with the class.

3 Point out that prepositions are especially important in legal English, as they enable readers and writers to manage complex relationships within a text.

Answers
1 as; in; as; in; as; in; around
2 on; of; for; in; of; in; to; in
3 between; on; in; in; through; of
4 Under; of; in; at; of
5 In; at; in; on; on; to
6 in; of; in; in; In; to; over
7 of; by; in; in; in; of

4 As a follow-up, students can test each other by reading the words before or after a gap (e.g. *Civil law may be defined* blank ...; blank *the world*) to elicit the missing preposition.

6 Students should work in pairs to complete the table. Point out that they should try to find a succinct word or short phrase for each box. They should, however, make sure they would be able to expand on the information in the box during a presentation.

SB p.109

Language use: Explaining, comparing and contrasting

7 Tell students to work alone to complete the exercise, and then to compare their answers with a partner before feeding back to the class. Check students understand the grammatical difference between *while/ whereas* and *conversely / on the other hand* (see Language notes below).

Answers
Contrasting
... is much more detailed than ...
A major difference between ... is ... ,
   whereas ...
This difference in ... can be explained by ...
... while ...
on the other hand
rather than
... it differs in ...
Conversely, the opposite is true ...

Expressing similarity
... share similar ...
... in both ...

Language notes
○ *While* /waɪl/ and *whereas* /weəˈræz/ are both used to join two clauses in the same sentence. The two clauses are normally separated with a comma. *While/whereas* can come at the beginning of either the first or the second clause:
While/Whereas England has a common-law system, Scotland's is civil law.
*England has a common-law system, **while/whereas** Scotland's is civil law.*

○ *Conversely* and *on the other hand* are both normally used to show a contrast between two separate sentences. They are used in the second sentence, typically at the beginning (followed by a comma) or after the part of the sentence to be contrasted (marked off by a pair of commas). Sometimes the two ideas may appear in the same sentence, in which case a semi-colon is needed:
*England has a common-law system. **On the other hand / Conversely**, Scotland's is civil law.*
*England has a common-law system. Scotland's, **on the other hand / conversely**, is civil law.*
*England has a common-law system; Scotland's, **on the other hand / conversely**, is civil law.*

8 Students should work with a partner to complete the sentences. As you go through the answers with the class, elicit ways of paraphrasing the same sentences using other linking expressions.

Answers
1 differ in; On the other hand / Conversely
2 while the opposite is true
3 In both
4 A major difference between; On the other hand / Conversely

Suggested paraphrases
1 A major difference between civil law and common law concerns their origins. Common law was developed by custom, beginning before there were any written

154

laws, **whereas** civil law developed out of the Roman law of Justinian's Corpus Juris Civilis.

2 In civil-law systems, court-made law is almost unknown. In common-law systems, **on the other hand**, large areas of law are created and shaped by court decisions.

3 Civil law and common law **are similar in** the enormous importance they place on statutory law.

4 Common law and civil law **differ in** the method of argument. **While** in the civil law, the principal method of argument is by deduction from general principles or from statutes towards particular cases, in the common law, the principal method of analysis is induction and analogy.

Language notes
○ In question 4, the noun *deduction* is derived from the verb *deduce* (= calculate by logic), and not, in this case, from the verb *deduct* (= to subtract from a total).
○ Note the difference in question 4 between *principle* as a noun (= a basic truth or generalisation) and *principal* as an adjective (= most important).

9 Tell students to work with a partner to take turns to present the information from Exercise 6. Encourage them to use a wide range of expressions for contrasting and expressing similarity. Afterwards, elicit some good examples from the class.

Optional extension
As a homework research task, tell students to complete the information in Exercise 6 for another of the world's legal systems (e.g. Islamic law, Chinese law). When they are giving their presentations, they should present the legal system they have researched.

Sample answer (for Islamic law)
○ Origin: religious texts (Koran and Sunna)
○ Countries found in: most Muslim countries, either in a pure form or, more commonly, mixed with elements of common or civil law
○ Importance of case law: precedent and analogy, as interpreted by judges, are central

○ Importance of enacted law: not part of traditional Islamic law, but very important in countries with mixed systems

Alternatively, students could focus on a particular aspect of law which differs between various systems (e.g. how 'fixed' are the laws?; who do the laws apply to?; importance of individual compared to the state; property ownership; balance between personal rights and obligations), and research and present their findings to the group, using the language from Exercise 7.

SB p.109 10.1 10.2 # Listening 1: Legal translation

Elicit from the class whether they have any experience of legal translations, either as translator or as someone reading translated texts.

10 Tell students to discuss the three questions in small groups. After a few minutes, open up the discussion to include the whole class.

Suggested answers
1 The translator can translate a term incorrectly. This is often due to interference from another language (i.e. the translator wrongly thinks that a similar sounding word from his or her own language means the same). It could also be because there is no equivalent concept in the language of the jurisdiction into which the text is being translated. In the latter case, the translator might choose a wrong word, leave out the unknown term or fail to provide an adequate paraphrase.

2 These problems can best be avoided if the translator has a good knowledge of both legal systems of the source language and the target language, or if the translator works together with someone who knows the legal system with which the translator is not familiar, or if the translator is fully aware of the problems that can occur and researches the unfamiliar terms very carefully.

3 A practising lawyer should be aware of these problems when making use of texts which have been or need to be translated so that he/she can make sure the quality of the translated text is good before

relying on it. This is especially true when dealing with clients, documents and/or laws from another jurisdiction.

11 Tell students to read the instructions to find out who they are going to listen to, and what they have to do. Then play the recording for them to find the answer. Afterwards, tell them to compare their answers with a partner, and to discuss anything else they understood/ remember from the recording.

Answer

They need to be aware of the differences between different legal systems, which involves having a high level of familiarity with the legal systems of the countries 'originating and receiving the translated message'.

Transcript » STUDENT'S BOOK **page 138**

Optional extension

As a second listening task, write the following questions on the board. You may need to elicit/explain the meanings of the underlined terms before playing the recording again. After listening, allow students to compare their answers with a partner before going through the answer with the class.

1 Why is international trade <u>booming</u>?
2 What forces previously independent and <u>alien</u> legal systems to <u>interact</u>?
3 What two divides does a legal translator need to <u>bridge</u>?

Answers

1 Because of advances in transportation and communication technologies
2 The boom in international trade
3 Different languages (*different ways they express meanings*) and different legal systems (*whole new worlds of complexity*)

12 Ask students if any of them are familiar with the term *false friends*. Avoid confirming or rejecting any explanations at this stage. Play the recording, then ask students if the explanation given there was the same as theirs. You could also ask them to give examples of different types of false friends, either from the recording or of their own.

Answer

False friends are words that appear to be the same as other words in the target language, but which actually have a different meaning.

Transcript » STUDENT'S BOOK **page 138**

13 Tell students to read the three questions to check they understand. You may need to check some of the words: *distinguish* (= describe as separate), *pose a problem* (= cause a problem). Then play the recording again for students to answer the questions. Allow them to discuss their answers with a partner before checking with the class.

Answers

1 The first category includes concepts that have a nearly identical equivalent in the target language.
2 The translator should research carefully and avoid misleading the reader or distorting the message when choosing terms.
3 The problem posed by the third category is when there are legal concepts with no near or rough equivalent in the target legal system. They should be explained to the degree necessary to the particular context.

Language notes

○ *Compensatory damages* are damages recovered for actual loss or injury. See http://dictionary.law.com.
○ *Loss of anticipated profits* is a type of consequential damages, i.e. damages which may be awarded as a result of a breach of contract.
○ *Non-pecuniary damages* are damages other than money. They include specific performance (= an order to perform some action) or an injunction (= an order not to perform an action).
○ The verb *pertain to something* means 'be relevant to / connected with something'. The related adjective *pertinent* means 'relevant / appropriate in a given context'.

- If land is *encumbered*, there is a legal claim (e.g. a mortgage) on it, which must be resolved before the land can be sold.
- A *final severance payment* /faɪnəl 'sevrəns 'peɪmənt/ is paid to compensate an employee who loses his/her job.
- *Liquidated damages* are damages calculated by the parties when a contract is drawn up. If and when there is a breach of contract, the liquidated-damages clause should make it unnecessary for the parties to fight in court.

14 Discuss this with the whole class. If you need inspiration, tell students to look through the Glossary on pages 155–160 to find examples of such problems.

(SB p.110) Language skills: Finding and choosing legal terms

15 Tell students to discuss the question in pairs. After a few minutes, open up the discussion to include the class. Note that there are some good ideas in the following exercises.

16 Discuss the sources of information with the class, eliciting examples of good websites/ dictionaries, etc., that the students recommend.

⇒ Suggested answers / Background notes

- Law firms' glossaries can be very useful, but may be smaller and less powerful than some of the more sophisticated search tools (e.g. Google, OneLook – see below). Some examples of law firms' glossaries: http://gradrec.law-now.com/opportunities/glossary.aspx, http://www.bpmlegal.com/patgloss.html.
- Advantages of online legal dictionaries include the fact that their definitions are reliable and appropriate. Disadvantages include the fact that they generally do not have pronunciation information. Some good examples: http://dictionary.law.com/, http://www.nolo.com/glossary.cfm, http://legal-dictionary.thefreedictionary.com/.
- Legal dictionaries in book form will always be useful, and it is often possible to get reliable bilingual legal dictionaries only in book form. The disadvantage is that they are limited by their physical size, and they are not free.
- Important international organisations' glossaries tend to be the most reliable, but may suffer the same disadvantages as law firms' glossaries. For example, the European Patent Office's glossary of patent terminology (http://www.epo.org/help/glossary.html) may be considered as the definitive glossary on that subject. Other examples of glossaries of terms on the websites of public organisations include Her Majesty's Court Service (UK): http://www.hmcourts-service.gov.uk/infoabout/glossary/legal.htm.
- Google's definition search is an extremely useful tool. A search for *misdemeanour*, for example, generates 29 definitions, most of which lead to useful online legal glossaries. A similar function is played by OneLook (http://www.onelook.com/), which generates links to 13 dictionary definitions of *misdemeanour*, including some with pronunciation, etymology, etc. The disadvantage is that it can be difficult to select the correct definition, and to check the reliability of the definitions given.
- As a last resort, an Internet search for a document containing a term can be time-consuming and frustrating, but the advantage is that, if a term exists, it should be possible to find a document presenting it in context.
- An excellent tool is http://www.google.com/language_tools, which will generate a list of web pages containing translations of a given term.
- One option which is not mentioned in the SB is specialised sites for translators, such as ProZ (http://www.proz.com/), a searchable forum where translators discuss tricky translations and evaluate each other's suggestions.

17 Set this research task as homework. Point out that the actual definitions of these particular words are less important than the techniques, so encourage them to experiment with techniques they would not normally use. Make sure they know to find a translation / comparison with their own jurisdiction, not just an English-language definition. Note that you could include the example (*good faith*) in the homework task. Note also that these words will be useful for Listening 2, so if possible try to go through the answers before you begin that section. When you go through the answers, concentrate on the successes and failures of the techniques, and any conclusions to be drawn, as well as on the definitions themselves.

▐▶ **Suggested answers**
(NB These are definitions, but of course students' answers will be tailored to their own situations.)

1 Equitable remedies are the remedies developed by the old courts of equity, such as the Court of Chancery in England. These remedies are still available today in common-law jurisdictions and include injunction, specific performance, rescission and estoppel.

2 The doctrine of promissory estoppel prevents one party from withdrawing a promise made to a second party if the latter has reasonably relied on that promise and acted upon it to his detriment.

3 Some jurisdictions have different general categories of crime depending on their seriousness. In US jurisdictions, a misdemeanour is a lesser crime punishable by a fine and/or county jail time for up to one year. Misdemeanours are distinguished from felonies, which are more serious crimes and can be punished by a state prison term.

4 The thing of value that induces another to enter into a contract, including money payment, services offered in return and promises, is referred to as *consideration*. In common-law systems, consideration must be found in order for a contract to be legally binding. Consideration must not be from the past, which means that a contract cannot be based upon consideration that was given before the contract was made. For example, if A promises to reward B for an act that B has already performed, the performance of that act is *past consideration* and therefore not good consideration.

5 The Lord High Chancellor of Great Britain (or Lord Chancellor) is responsible for the efficient functioning and independence of the courts.

💬 **Pronunciation notes**
equitable remedy /ˈekwɪtəbl ˈremədɪ/
misdemeanour /ˌmɪsdəˈmiːnə(r)/
promissory estoppel /ˈprɒmɪsərɪ ɪˈstɒpl/

LAW IN PRACTICE

(SB p.110) **Lead-in**
Tell students to read the lead-in text quickly to see if they agree, and if they have any experience of the situation it describes.

18 Students should discuss the questions in small groups. After a few minutes, open up the discussion to include the class.

▐▶ **Suggested answer**
Wikipedia (http://en.wikipedia.org/wiki/Main_Page) is increasingly reliable and comprehensive, and has lengthy articles about the legal systems of most, if not all, countries. However, with very specific questions, or when you need to be 100% sure of the reliability of the source, legal directories are excellent (e.g. http://www.law.cornell.edu/world/).

(SB p.111) (10.3–10.5) **Listening 2: In-company course**
Tell students to read the introduction on page 111 quickly. Elicit from the class what they know about the ILEC exam.

19 Elicit from the class what they understand by the term *equity*. Then tell them to read the three definitions to check. Note that all three definitions are correct. Elicit what, if anything, students know about the three types of equity. Then play the recording for them to find which of the three meanings is being discussed. Afterwards, allow them to check with a partner, and also to discuss anything else they understood/remember from the listening. Then check with the class.

Language note

For more on the meanings of equity, see
http://dictionary.law.com and http://
en.wikipedia.org/wiki/Equity.

20 Tell students to read the three questions and
to listen again to find the answers. After you
have played the recording, allow students to
check with a partner before going through the
answers with the class.

Answers

1 Michael asks Gareth what the term means.

2 Because she took her first degree in the
UK. She also wrote her dissertation on
the topic of equity.

3 Equity developed as a way of dealing
with the inflexibility of the English legal
system.

21 Students should read the statements first to
check they understand, but avoid explaining
any of the terms that are explained in the
listening (*Lord Chancellor* /ˌlɔːd ˈtʃɑːnsələ(r)/,
equitable remedy /ˈekwɪtəbl ˈremədɪ/, *Court of
Chancery* /ˈkɔːt əv ˈtʃɑːnsərɪ/). After you have
played the recording, tell students to discuss
their answers with a partner, including anything
else they understood from the listening, and
then go through the answers with the class.

Answers

1 F (It removed the Lord Chancellor's
judicial roles.)

2 F (The examples of equitable remedies
given in the text are injunction and
specific performance.)

3 T

4 F (The Court of Chancery was abolished
by the Judicature Acts 1873–1875.)

Language notes

○ If somebody *petitioned* the king, he/she
made a formal written request for the
king to intervene in a problem.

○ The *British cabinet* consists of the most
senior ministers. It is the key decision-
making body in the British government.

○ For more on the *Constitutional Reform
Act*, see http://en.wikipedia.org/wiki/
Constitutional_Reform_Act_2005.

○ An *injunction* is an order from a court to
perform an action, or to stop performing
an action.

○ *Specific performance* refers to an order
from a court for a party to perform the
action which that party was specifically
required to perform under a contract.

○ If equity *prevails over* common law, it
takes priority in any legal judgment.

Optional extension

1 If you feel students need to listen a
second time, write the following words
and phrases on the board: *petition,
claimant and defendant, British cabinet,
efficient functioning and independence of
the courts, harsh or severe, injunctions
and specific performance, Earl of Oxford,
prevail, Judicature Acts, clean hands*.

2 Tell students to listen again to find out
exactly what was said about each of the
words or phrases. After you have played
the recording, tell students to discuss their
answers in pairs, and then go through the
answers with the class.

Answers

○ Litigants could **petition** the king.

○ The litigants in a case are the **claimant
and defendant**.

○ The Lord Chancellor is a senior member
of the **British cabinet**.

○ The Lord Chancellor is responsible for the
**efficient functioning and independence of
the courts**.

○ The new system made the common law
less **harsh or severe**.

○ **Injunctions and specific performance** are
examples of equitable remedies.

○ The **Earl of Oxford**'s case was important
in English legal history.

○ Where there is a difference between the
common law and equity, equity **prevails**.

○ The Court of Chancery was abolished by
the **Judicature Acts**.

○ For equity to prevail, you have to have
clean hands.

22 Tell students to read the two statements to make sure they understand. You may need to check they understand *abuse* /əˈbjuːs/ (= improper use). Then play the recording for them to check. Afterwards, allow them to compare their answers with a partner before going through the answers with the class.

Answers
> **1** F (It is similar to the English concept of good faith.)
> **2** T (It has the effect of softening the harshness of the law in the same way as equity does in England.)

Background note
> The German doctrine of *Treu und Glauben* /ˈtrɔɪ ʊnt ˈɡlaʊbən/ translates roughly as *loyalty* (≈ equity) and *belief* (≈ good faith).

Optional extension
1 As a second listening task, write the following words and phrases on the board: *equitable defence, unethically or in bad faith, burden of proof, influence, softening.*
2 Tell students to listen again to find out exactly what was said about each of the words or phrases.
3 After you have played the recording, tell students to discuss their answers in pairs, and then go through the answers with the class.
Answers
○ The clean hands doctrine is an **equitable defence**.
○ The claimant is not entitled to an equitable remedy if he/she acted **unethically or in bad faith**.
○ The defendant has the **burden of proof** to show that the claimant is not acting in good faith.
○ Similar concepts in the French Code Civil have had less **influence** than the *Treu und Glauben* doctrine in Germany.
○ The French doctrine of the abuse of rights has the effect of **softening** the law.

23 Tell students to work in pairs to find phrases for describing a legal system. Do the first with the class as an example. Afterwards, go through the answers with the class and write

the useful expressions on the board, as these will be necessary for the next exercise.

Answers
Is that **the equivalent of** *Treu und Glauben*? From what Beate said, it's **basically the same as your concept of** good faith. **It has a similar effect to** equity in certain cases. I think that equity **corresponds to certain concepts in** the French Code Civil, but **these haven't had quite the same amount of influence that** the concept of good faith has had in Germany. Still, they're **comparable to** each other.
What they do have is something similar called the doctrine of the abuse of rights. That has the effect of softening the harshness of the law **in the same way as** equity does in England.

Speaking 1: Describing, comparing and contrasting

SB p.111

24 Tell students to work in pairs or small groups. The first student should describe an area of the law in his/her jurisdiction, as if they were describing it to a client. Suggest that they look in the Glossary (SB pages 155–160) for inspiration, although obviously the Glossary will not be directly relevant to their own jurisdictions. The other student(s) in the group should then contrast the area described with a near-equivalent in another jurisdiction (i.e. their own, in a mixed-nationality class, or perhaps UK/US law if all students are from the same jurisdiction). Make sure they know to use the language for describing, comparing and contrasting from Exercises 7 and 23.

You could turn this into a game, where the first student explains an area related to one from the Glossary, and the second student has to guess which term in the Glossary the first student chose.

Afterwards, elicit from the class some difficult-to-explain areas of law (i.e. those with no simple equivalent), and any solutions students can come up with.

Reading 3: Asset protection

25 Tell students to read the introduction and the four questions. Allow them five minutes to discuss the questions, then conduct a feedback session with the whole class to ensure that students understand the concepts, as this will enable them to deal effectively with the reading text that follows.

Answers

1 A *tax haven* is a country or independent region where certain taxes are levied at a low rate or not at all.
2 There are many tax havens throughout the world, including Andorra, the Bahamas, Jersey, Monaco and Panama.
3 *Tax avoidance* refers to legal measures that can be taken to minimise a person or business entity's tax burden. *Tax evasion* refers to unlawful measures to achieve the same ends as tax avoidance.
4 *Asset protection* refers to methods by which individuals or entities protect their assets from legal problems (e.g. judgments) and/or taxes through the use of multiple business entities, trusts, insurance and estate planning.

26 Students should read the three descriptions to make sure they understand all the words. You may need to check *tax burden* (= the amount of tax somebody has to pay) and *safeguard* (= protect). Then tell students to read the first paragraph to find out which description is best. When you check the answer with the class, elicit how students worked out the answer.

Answer

a

27 Tell students to read the four statements with a partner to predict what the answers might be. You may need to check some words (e.g. *a trust* = an entity which holds assets for the benefit of certain beneficiaries; *a hybrid entity* = an entity that is a combination of two or more types of entity; *a holding company* = a company whose only business is to own and manage other companies). Then give them about four minutes to read the text to find the answers. At the end of the time limit, tell them to discuss their answers with a partner, and then feed back to the class.

Answers

1 Stiftung 2 Anstalt 3 beneficiaries
4 contempt

Language notes

○ Paragraph 4 lists four taxes: *income tax* (levied on somebody's salary), *capital tax* (levied on capital holdings), *transfer tax* (levied when title to land is transferred to a new owner) and *inheritance tax* (levied on money and assets inherited when somebody dies).

○ A private foundation is a non-profit organisation, typically used for charitable purposes or to support a family purpose (see http://en.wikipedia.org/wiki/Foundation_%28nonprofit_organization%29). It may hold assets separately from its founders, but has no shareholders. It may have *beneficiaries*, i.e. people who benefit financially from the foundation.

○ To *endow* /ɪnˈdaʊ/ means to provide with money.

○ To *conceptualise* /kənˈseptʃəlaɪz/ here means 'to imagine'.

○ If assets are *repatriated* /riːˈpætrɪeɪtɪd/, they are sent back to their country of origin.

○ A *settlor* /ˈsetlə(r)/ is a person who creates a trust, and usually transfers money into the trust.

Text analysis: Discourse markers for text cohesion

Elicit from the class what they understand by the terms *discourse markers* and *text cohesion*, and then tell them to read the introduction and language box on page 112 to compare it with their ideas. Afterwards, check they have understood the information in the box by asking for more examples and why discourse markers are important.

Language notes

○ In written English, *discourse markers* mark the boundaries between stretches of language (e.g. between sentences), but are not an integrated part of the structure of the main sentence. In the example in the SB, the word *furthermore* could be removed from the sentence, and the sentence would still work. Its function is to show the relationship between separate sentences. Other discourse markers show the relationship between the writer or reader and the text (e.g. *apparently, unfortunately, obviously*). As the examples show, they are often in the form of adverbs, but can also be longer fixed expressions (e.g. *in fact, apart from this, as a matter of fact, as you know, what is more, that said*, etc.). Discourse markers typically come at the beginning of a sentence, and are separated from the sentence by commas.

○ *Text cohesion* /ˈtekst kəˈhiːʒən/ refers to the way a text holds together, especially links from one sentence to other sentences, and from one paragraph to other paragraphs. Discourse markers are an important device for achieving cohesion, alongside things like use of pronouns, elision of words, and use of synonyms and word families within a text.

28 Tell students to look at the highlighted discourse markers and put them into the table. Point out that the categories in the table are rather broad, so discourse markers within a category may still have different meanings/functions. Point out also that there may be some disagreement as to the correct category for some discourse markers.

Suggested answers
(NB Examples in italics are not included in the text)

Function	Examples
Giving extra information	Besides, Furthermore, *In addition, On top of this, Similarly, Moreover, What's more*
Comparing, contrasting and qualifying	Although, Instead, While, That said, Despite this, Nevertheless, *However, On the other hand, In contrast, Alternatively*
Introducing the result of previous information	Consequently, Because of this, *As a result, Therefore, As a consequence, It follows from this, For this reason,* So, Thus, Accordingly
Emphasising	Notably, The fact that, *In fact, In particular, Of course, Clearly, Ultimately, Indeed*

SB p.113

Speaking 2: Advising on asset protection

29 Tell students to read through the instructions to find out what they will be discussing. Check that they realise that the role-play is between groups of lawyers, and is not a lawyer–client meeting. Check also that they know which entities they should be discussing (i.e. *Stiftung* and *Anstalt*).

Tell students to work in small groups. Allow about five minutes for the role-play. Monitor students as they work for language problems, as well as the success of the meetings from a practical point of view. Afterwards, give and elicit feedback, and discuss the advantages and disadvantages of the two entities with the class.

Optional extension
You could follow up the role-play with a further role-play between the lawyer and client, presenting the best form of asset protection as decided in Exercise 28. For this role-play, students should work in pairs. If you have an odd number of students, there should be two lawyers in one group.

Writing: Letter summarising options

30 Tell students to read the information on page 115 carefully to identify potential advantages and disadvantages for the American client. Allow around two minutes for them to read, and then to check with a partner before feeding back to the class. NB If you feel your students can read and understand the text without checking with you, you may set the reading and writing as a joint homework task.

Language notes

○ The text mentions that the *frustrating time difference* between the USA and Liechtenstein can be an advantage to the client, as creditors seeking to recover money from the client will find it difficult to speak with their legal adviser (counsel) in Liechtenstein.

○ A *discretionary payment* /dɪsˈkreʃənərɪ ˈpeɪmənt/ is a payment that is not governed by rules, but which the payer may pay if and when he/she chooses.

○ Panama has a *three-year statute of limitation for fraudulent transfer challenges*. In other words, creditors can challenge fraudulent transfers of money only up to three years after they occur. After this *three-year window* (i.e. period when a challenge may occur) has closed, the transfer cannot be challenged.

○ *Gifting* here means 'giving money to a foundation', officially as a gift to the foundation, but since the eventual beneficiary of the foundation is often the person who made the gift, it is often merely a device for transferring money. If a gift is *voided*, the foundation may be legally required to pay it back to the donor (in order that the donor can pay creditors).

○ A *for-value transfer* method is a way of transferring money to another entity other than a gift (i.e. where the transfer is in exchange for something of value).

○ An *instalment note* is a promissory note (i.e. an official written promise to repay a debt) in which repayments are made in regular instalments (e.g. every month).

○ An *annuity* /əˈnjuːɪtɪ/ is an agreement where one party transfers a sum of money to another party, and the second party agrees to make regular payments to the first party for the remainder of the first party's life. A *private annuity* is one which does not involve a company which deals with annuities as part of its normal business activities, such as an insurance company. Source: http://www.answers.com/annuity?cat=biz-fin.

Suggested answer

Dear Ms Radford

Asset protection entities in Panama

Thank you for your phone call of 5 June 2008. As I outlined briefly during our conversation, I believe the Panamanian foundation (hereafter the *foundation*) might be a suitable alternative asset protection mechanism. I have now had the opportunity to research this more fully, and am pleased to provide the following summary of the foundation.

The foundation is largely based on Liechtenstein's *Stiftung*, as described in my letter of 2 June 2008. Like a corporation, the foundation can hold title to assets in its own name. However, it can also make discretionary payments to the founder or beneficiaries, like a trust. As with the Stiftung, the foundation is mostly controlled by its bylaws. These bylaws do not have to be registered or publicly disclosed.

Perhaps the greatest advantage of the Panamanian foundation over the Stiftung is that the Panamanian version is relatively inexpensive to form and maintain. Another advantage is that Panama is in the U.S. Eastern time zone, making administration of the foundation from the U.S. easier. However, the time difference between the U.S.A. and Liechtenstein does have the advantage of being potentially frustrating to creditors in communicating with their local counsel.

Panama has a three-year statute of limitation for fraudulent transfer challenges to contributions to the foundation. If gifting is utilised to fund the foundation, there will be a three-year window available for creditors to attempt to void the gifts. Once past the three-year limitation, the assets are generally safe from creditors. Panamanian law specifically provides that the foundation assets may not be applied towards the debts of either the founder or any beneficiary.

As with the Stiftung, probably the best use of the Panamanian foundation is not to hold assets but rather to own an entity that is used as a management company. From a creditor's viewpoint, the management company will be owned by a Panamanian charity with three Panamanian residents as members of the foundation's council. The creditor will likely not see that the U.S. settlor has appointed one or more protectors to make sure that the council members carry out the purposes of the foundation, as set forth in the charter. Therefore it would be very difficult for a creditor to claim that the U.S. owner of the asset being managed has any ties to or control over the foundation.

I would be very pleased to provide you with further details should you be interested in setting up such an entity, and look forward to receiving further instructions.

Yours truly

John Platt

Optional extension
(Photocopiable worksheet 10.2)

This serves as a revision game to end the unit and the course. Students should work in small groups to find the answers to the 26 questions, mainly from the phrases studied in the SB, but also from the audio transcripts and students' own knowledge of the law systems of the world. As some of the questions are rather tough, you could say the winning team is the first to find 22 answers. Note that most of the answers start with the letter provided, and the number of lines in each word corresponds to the number of letters.

Answers

A asset protection   B beneficiary   C 'clean hands' doctrine   D discourse markers
E equity   F false friend   G good faith
H hybrid   I Islamic law   J Justinian code
K king   L Louisiana   M mixed systems
N notably   O overturn   P precedents
Q Quebec   R rendered   S *stare decisis*
T trust   U uniform law   V vast   W Western law systems   X tax haven   Y promissory estoppel   Z Zimbabwe

(SB p.114) Language Focus

Answers

1 **Word formation**

Verb	Noun	Adjective
globalise	globalisation	global
harmonise	harmony	harmonious / harmonised
enforce	enforcement	enforceable
unify	unification	unified
apply	applicability	applicable

2 **Synonyms**

   1 c   **2** d   **3** a   **4** b   **5** e

3 **Collocations**

   1 apply, enforce, render, recognise
   2 apply, enforce, harmonise, modernise, recognise

4 **Discourse markers**

   1 notably   **2** In addition   **3** Thus / Therefore
   4 however   **5** Therefore / Thus

Photocopiable worksheet 1.1

1	performance	a	a formal style of referring to legal documents
2	enforcement of contracts	b	a legal case which establishes a principle of law that other courts follow in similar cases
3	consideration	c	an act which interferes with a person's right to use and enjoy their land
4	negligently caused injuries	d	automatic responsibility as a result of owning or using something dangerous, such as explosives or a dangerous animal
5	strict liability	e	compensation for harm done, typically in money
6	vicarious liability	f	damaging somebody's reputation through slander (oral) or libel (written)
7	ultra-hazardous	g	decisions taken by higher courts which create a new legal precedent
8	products liability	h	evidence or opinions quoted from a person not in court, which is not admissible because the person cannot be cross-examined
9	nuisance	i	examination of a person's property and taking articles of evidence found during that examination
10	invasion of privacy	j	exemptions from penalties or legal requirements
11	defamation	k	fulfilment of contractual obligations
12	damages	l	harming a person as a result of lack of necessary care
13	crimes against public administration	m	illegal acts such as bribery, escaping from prison or perjury (lying under oath)
14	homicide	n	killing another person, including murder, causing accidental death and killing in self-defence
15	hearsay	o	legal procedures to ensure that parties fulfil their obligations
16	impeachment	p	legal responsibility for the harm caused by another person (e.g. a parent is responsible for a child's acts; an employer may be responsible for an employee's acts)
17	cross-examination	q	legal responsibility of manufacturers for harm caused by their goods
18	privileges	r	monitoring a person through e.g. closed-circuit TV cameras
19	constitutional and statutory limitations	s	so dangerous that strict liability will be imposed
20	search and seizure	t	something of value which both parties to a contract agree to exchange
21	incriminating statements	u	the act of discrediting a witness by showing that their evidence is false
22	electronic surveillance	v	the opportunity to question in court a witness for the opposing party in a trial
23	immunities	w	the right not to disclose certain types of evidence, such as confidential client–lawyer discussion
24	judicial opinions	x	things which are prohibited either by the constitution or by statutes (laws)
25	legal citation	y	violation of somebody's right to be alone
26	precedent	z	admissions of guilt by a defendant

Photocopiable worksheet 1.2

1 Stephanie, a talented junior lawyer, is a perfectionist. She can write beautiful English, but takes too much time checking for mistakes. She knows many rules of English grammar, but she doesn't like speaking English in public because she is ashamed of her mistakes. Her boss speaks English fluently, which makes Stephanie feel embarrassed. At meetings with native speakers, she prefers to let her boss speak.

2 Jung Hwan is a law student. He has to read a lot for his studies, but has great problems understanding written English. He checks lots of technical jargon in his law dictionary, but still doesn't understand what the text is trying to say. His listening is even worse: he understands lots of individual words, but cannot follow fluent speech at all. He has a very strong accent, which means that he is reluctant to speak.

3 Borys works in a large law firm. He speaks fairly fluently in English, but he makes lots of mistakes, including very basic ones. He can usually get his message across, but his boss is concerned that his carelessness in English creates a bad impression with international clients. His writing is terrible.

4 Mara is studying law and business administration. She has been studying English for years, but cannot get through a psychological barrier stopping her from speaking fluently. She always worries that she has misunderstood what the conversation is about, and that she will say something irrelevant or embarrassing. She knows lots of words, but forgets them when she wants to speak. By the time she has thought of the right word, the conversation has usually moved on to another topic.

a Don't be afraid of making mistakes. The biggest mistake is to say nothing. If you say nothing, people will surely think you're useless. Compared to that, grammar mistakes are nothing.

b Don't be ashamed of your English, especially in front of monolingual native speakers. Be proud that you're bilingual.

c Don't just learn complicated new words. Short words, even ones which you think you know, are also worth learning. There's a difference between recognising a word when you see it and being able to use it fluently. If you can't use it but ought to, it's worth learning.

d Don't try to translate from your own language when writing. Most sentences can be copied from other pieces of writing, with only small details changed. Keep a bank of useful phrases and sentences for writing and use them in your own writing.

e As you write, keep your sentences short and simple. Make sure every sentence has a subject at the beginning and a verb in an appropriate tense. When you've finished writing, check again for mistakes, or get a colleague to check with you.

f Learn some good interrupting phrases, like *Can I just say something?*. If you can use these fluently, you'll have time to think of the best way to continue.

g Learn words systematically. If you set yourself a target of ten words a day, you can easily learn 3,000 in a year. In other words, you could double your vocabulary.

h Listen as much as you can in English. Watch DVDs with subtitles in English, and then again without the subtitles. Find the lyrics to pop songs you like.

i Make a list of your mistakes so you can make sure you don't keep making them.

j Read as much as you can in English, not just for your work or studies. If you read for fun (e.g. novels, websites), don't spoil the fun by checking lots of words.

k Speak as much as you can in English. Find a friend who is also learning and chat together. It'll feel strange at first, but it's free and fun. Don't worry too much about mistakes, but experiment with new words and structures.

Photocopiable worksheet 2.1

Complete the sentences from the contract using the groups of words from the box so that the sentences contain the same information as the everyday English version.

1 The buyer must nominate when the goods will be shipped.

.... / .... / .... / .... / .... date .... / ....

2 The buyer must tell the seller when the vessel or vessels will probably be ready. The buyer must tell the seller more or less how much is going to be loaded onto the vessel. The buyer must do this at least two weeks before the goods are shipped.

.... / .... shall .... / .... / .... / .... / .... two .... / .... / .... probable .... / .... vessel(s) .... / .... / .... / .... quantity .... / .... / ....

3 As soon as the buyer has notified the seller when the vessel will probably be ready, the seller must nominate a port where the goods will be loaded.

Upon .... / .... / .... / .... / .... / .... , ... seller .... / .... / .... port .... / .... / .... / .... / ....

4 The deadline for shipping the goods is 22 May 2008.

.... / .... / .... / .... later .... / .... / .... / ....

at least two	give the seller	later than	loading of goods	of shipment
port for the	probable readiness of	probable readiness of	required no
shall nominate	shall nominate a	Shipment is	the approximate quantity
The buyer	The buyer shall	the date	to be loaded	Upon notification of
vessel(s) and of	vessel(s), the seller	weeks' notice of	22 May 2008

Now answer these questions.

5 Which version, the contract extract or the everyday English equivalent, contains the most ...
  a sentences?
  b indirect questions (starting with *when, how much, where*, etc.)?
  c nouns?
  d verbs?

6 What structure follows *as soon as*: a noun phrase (*something*) or a clause (*something happens*)?

7 What structure follows *upon*: a noun or a clause? Why do you think the contract extract uses *upon* instead of *as soon as*?

Photocopiable worksheet 2.2

Change the form of the words (1–15) below so that they make sense in this email of advice.

Subject: The termination of your contract with Drexler Inc.

Dear Mr McKendrick

Thank you for coming to see me on 30 May when we discussed the **1)** .... of your contract with Drexler Inc. I am writing to **2)** .... our **3)** .... and to confirm your **4)** ....

You told me that Drexler Inc. agreed to purchase a large quantity of goods (exact amount **5)** ....) from your firm, Export Threads. Under clause 2a of the contract, Drexler were to give you two weeks' notice of the date of **6)** .... so that you could arrange a port for the loading of goods. You were unable to arrange this because Drexler failed to let you know by the **7)** .... date. You now wish to terminate the contract.

The legal issue here is whether or not Drexler's breach is enough to allow Export Threads to terminate the contract without **8)** .... liable for damages. If the contract term in question can be shown to be a condition, you will be able to terminate the contract without fear of damages being awarded against you. If the term is simply a warranty, you will be able to claim damages to cover any costs you have incurred as a result of this breach, but may not actually terminate the contract.

Recent case law suggests that if you do choose to terminate the contract, and if Drexler **9)** .... decide to sue you, the courts would rule in your favour. Your contract involves a chain of sales, and in such cases, the need for **10)** .... is very important. You were unable to arrange the loading of the goods as a direct consequence of Drexler's breach of clause 2a, and this term would be interpreted as a condition.

I will write a letter to Drexler Inc. outlining the above and notifying them of your **11)** .... to terminate the contract. I will request **12)** .... from Drexler that they accept our interpretation both of the events and of the relevant law, and that your termination of the contract will not lead to any **13)** .... legal **14)** .... on their part. I will be in touch again **15)** .... Please do not hesitate to contact me if you have any questions.

With kind regards

Charles Dawe

---

1 terminate   **2** summary   **3** discuss   **4** instruct   **5** specify
6 ship   **7** agree   **8** be   **9** subsequent   **10** certain
11 intend   **12** confirm   **13** necessary   **14** act   **15** short

168

Introduction to International Legal English Photocopiable Worksheet 2.2   Photocopiable © Cambridge University Press 2008

Photocopiable worksheet 3.1

1 Medical negligence	**a** A businesswoman conspires with her competitors to keep their prices high.
2 Negligent damage to private property	**b** A careless driver accidentally kills a pedestrian.
3 Negligent misstatements causing financial loss	**c** A doctor mistakenly harms a patient by giving the wrong treatment.
4 Assault	**d** A (drunk) driver crashes after driving above the speed limit.
5 Battery	**e** A hooligan physically attacks and injures a victim.
6 Trespass	**f** A hooligan throws a brick at a victim, but misses.
7 Fraudulent misrepresentation	**g** A lawyer causes financial harm to his client by giving faulty advice.
8 Interference in contractual relations	**h** A manufacturer makes and sells food which contains harmful ingredients.
9 Unfair business practices	**i** A motorist drives too close to another car and scratches the side.
10 Wrongful death	**j** A party damages another's reputation by writing or saying untrue statements.
11 Fraud	**k** A party disrupts another party's ability to perform contractual obligations.
12 Conversion	**l** A party threatens to harm a victim at an unspecified time in the future.
13 Defamation	**m** A party tricks another party into signing a harmful contract.
14 Reckless driving	**n** A party wears a disguise in order to trick a victim into believing he is someone else.
15 Professional negligence	**o** A property owner irritates her neighbours by burning rubber tyres in the garden.
16 Nuisance	**p** A saleswoman takes deposits from customers who want holiday homes, but the homes don't actually exist.
17 False imprisonment	**q** A shop manager wrongly accuses a customer of theft, and locks her in his office for an hour.
18 Intentional infliction of emotional distress	**r** A thief takes and uses another person's property as his own.
19 Product liability	**s** A walker crosses a farmer's land and damages his crops.
20 Deceit	**t** An estate agent mistakenly tells a client that a property is structurally sound, but hasn't actually checked.

Photocopiable worksheet 3.2

A Complete the sentences using words from the box. Sometimes there is more than one possible answer.

> As cause caused causing Consequently result
> resulted results Since so Therefore to

1 Even though it was already moving, a passenger ran .... catch the train.

2 The man appeared to lose his balance, ... an employee of the railroad reached out to help him.

3 This act .... the package in the man's arm to fall onto the rails.

4 When it fell, the fireworks exploded, ... some large scales on the platform to strike and injure the plaintiff.

5 As a .... , the plaintiff sued the railroad.

6 The plaintiff claimed that her injury .... from the negligence of the employee.

7 Negligence is not a tort unless it .... in the commission of a wrong.

8 .... in this case the harm was not wilful, it had to be shown that the act had the apparent possibility of danger.

9 .... there was nothing on the outside of the package, there was no negligence.

10 It was the explosion which was the proximate .... of the plaintiff's injuries.

11 .... , the railroad was not negligent.

12 .... , the judgment of the appellate court was reversed.

B Now complete these sentences so that they describe the imaginary past – what would have happened if these events had been different. Follow this pattern:

If X **had / hadn't** *happened, Y* **would / wouldn't / might / might not have** *happened.*

Use sentences 1–12 above to help you remember the facts of the case.

1 If the train .... been moving, the passenger .... have run to catch it.

2 If the man .... lost his balance, the employee .... reached out to help him.

3 If the employee .... out to help, the man's package .... fallen.

4 If the fireworks .... , the scales on the platform .... the plaintiff.

5 If the plaintiff .... injured, she .... the railroad.

6 The plaintiff claimed that she .... injured if the employee .... negligent.

7 If, in this case, a wrong .... committed, it .... negligence.

8 If, in this case, the harm .... wilful, it .... necessary to show that the act had the apparent possibility of danger.

9 If there .... the words 'Danger! Fireworks! Do not drop!' clearly displayed on the package, there .... negligence.

10 If the fireworks .... , the plaintiff .... injured.

11 If the explosion .... the proximate cause, the railroad .... negligent.

12 If the Court of Appeals .... the railroad to be negligent, the judgment .... reversed.

Photocopiable worksheet 4.1

Match the crimes with the definitions.

1 armed robbery	**a**	a type of theft which does not involve burglary or robbery
2 arson	**b**	attempting to physically attack a person
3 assault	**c**	buying and selling illegal narcotics
4 battery	**d**	concealing the source of money obtained from crimes
5 bribery	**e**	creating a false document
6 burglary	**f**	deceiving somebody out of money or property
7 domestic violence	**g**	hiding evidence, threatening witnesses, etc.
8 drug trafficking	**h**	entering a building with intent to commit a crime
9 drunk driving	**i**	general term for taking another person's personal property without permission
10 embezzlement	**j**	giving money etc. to influence a public official
11 extortion	**k**	illegally trying to avoid paying taxes
12 forgery	**l**	intentional and malicious damage to or destruction of property
13 fraud	**m**	intentionally burning a building
14 homicide	**n**	killing somebody through an act or omission
15 insider dealing	**o**	obtaining money or property through indirect threats or intimidation
16 joyriding	**p**	operating a motor vehicle while under the influence of alcohol
17 kidnapping	**q**	repeatedly following and/or harassing a person with unwanted attention
18 larceny	**r**	stealing a car and driving it dangerously for fun
19 manslaughter	**s**	stealing from an employer
20 money laundering	**t**	stealing merchandise from a shop or business
21 obstruction of justice	**u**	striking a person with intent to harm
22 rape	**v**	taking a person against his/her will (or taking a child from the control of a parent or guardian)
23 shoplifting	**w**	using a weapon to take money or property by force or direct threat of violence
24 stalking	**x**	unlawful killing but without intent to kill
25 tax evasion	**y**	using confidential knowledge to give yourself an advantage when buying or selling stocks and shares
26 theft	**z**	using violence or threats to have sex without consent
27 vandalism	**aa**	violence or abuse against a member of the offender's own household (e.g. wife/husband and children)

Photocopiable worksheet 4.2

A Complete these fragments from Listening 2 using passive voice. After each fragment there is a paraphrase using active voice to tell you which verb to use and which tense (in **bold**). Note that the words in *italics* are not necessary in the passive versions.

(4.6) **1** According to experts, members of the public [...] .... that they must be more vigilant about discarding personal records ...
[*People* **are telling** members of the public that ...]

2 ... a wide range of crimes; for example, [...] obtaining other goods which criminals
....
[... privileges which *people* **might deny** criminals if they were to use ...]

(4.7) **3** Banks .... more accountable for losses which .... by so-called 'phishing' frauds.
[*People* **must make** banks more accountable for losses which so-called phishing frauds **cause**]

4 Phishing involves people .... by fake emails [...] into giving out bank or credit-card details to online fraudsters.
[Phishing involves fake emails **fooling** people into giving ...]

5 The term .... to describe the practice of creating look-alike websites ...
[*People* **also use** the term to describe ...]

(4.8) **6** The employees .... this week that they are at risk of identity theft ...
[*Somebody* **told** the employees this week that ...]

7 It's unclear whether the laptops .... because of the information they contain, or ...
[It's unclear whether *criminals* **are targeting** the laptops because of ...]

8 Fidelity has good news for those who ....
[Fidelity has good news for those whom *the situation* **has affected**]

(4.9) **9** It appears the data ....
[It appears *somebody* **encrypted** the data ...]

10 Two in five contained a whole credit- or debit-card number that .... to an individual.
[... a number that *thieves* **could link** to an individual.]

11 In the US, the practice .... as a real risk to consumers and businesses for many years.
[*People* **have recognised** the practice as ...]

B **(4.6– 4.9)** Listen again to check your answers – do you notice any differences?

Photocopiable worksheet 5.1

Match the two halves of these extracts from Listening 1.

1 I'll start off by **addressing** …	**a** … **through' to** the owners.
2 A corporation is a separate and distinct **legal** …	**b** … **the question**: what is a corporation?
3 This means that it can **do** …	**c** … the **debts**.
4 Its owners are not personally **liable** …	**d** … the day-to-day **operations** of the corporation.
5 A corporation may get sued and be **forced** …	**e** … **shortfall**.
6 The assets of the corporation may not be enough to **cover** …	**f** … **profits to** its stockholders.
7 The creditors cannot go after the stockholders to **recover** any …	**g** … **on** those dividends.
8 A board of directors is **responsible** …	**h** … **into bankruptcy**.
9 Officers **run** …	**i** … **for** overseeing the general affairs of the corporation.
10 The C corporation **distributes** …	**j** … **for** its debts and liabilities.
11 The stockholders **pay** income **tax** …	**k** … **entity**.
12 The corporate profits '**pass** …	**l** … **business** under its own name.

13 Corporations **enjoy** many …	**m** … **upon** the death of its stockholders, directors or officers.
14 The assets of the sole proprietorship or partnership cannot **satisfy** …	**n** … **up** and run than a sole proprietorship or partnership.
15 Creditors can **go** …	**o** … **to** technical formalities.
16 If a corporation **runs out** …	**p** … **to** self-employment **taxes**.
17 Earnings from a sole proprietorship are **subject** …	**q** … to **raise capital**.
18 The life of a corporation does not **expire** …	**r** … **the debt**.
19 A corporation has many **avenues** …	**s** … **of funds**, its owners are usually not liable.
20 Corporations cost more to **set** …	**t** … **meetings** and **recording minutes**.
21 A corporation can only be created by **filing** …	**u** … **losing** their personal liability protection.
22 A corporation must **adhere** …	**v** … legal **documents with** the state.
23 These include **holding** board and shareholder …	**w** … **after** each owner's personal bank account.
24 The stockholders **risk** …	**x** … **advantages over** partnerships and sole proprietorships.

Photocopiable worksheet 5.2

Here are four more techniques for understanding a statute, contract or other complicated legal document.

1 De-nominalisation

Nominalisation involves turning verbs and adjectives into nouns, in order to make your writing more formal and professional. De-nominalisation is the opposite technique, and makes writing easier for you and your clients to understand.

Change the six points (a–f) from subsection 1 so that they include more verbs and simpler language, as in the example. You may use the prompts in square brackets to help you.

a [decide, need, happen] _Whenever you decide what to do, you need to consider what will probably happen in the long term as a result._

b [try, respect, rights and expectations] ....

c [need, build up] ....

d [how, affect] ....

e [whether, want, behave] ....

f [must not, treat, shareholders, differently] ....

2 Parallel structures

Subsection 2 contains two sets of parallel structures.

a Underline two pairs of phrases linked by the word _or_.

b What is the relationship between the two pairs of phrases linked by _or_?

c Write the beginning of the sentence so that it contains only one use of _or_.

Where the .... **or** ....
.... _, subsection (1) has ..._

d The word _to_ near the end of subsection 2 relates back to an earlier mention of the same word. Find the earlier mention, and rewrite the end of the sentence in full.

... has effect as if the reference **to** promoting the success of the company for the benefit of its members were .... _._

3 Asking questions

Sometimes even stupid questions can lead to a better understanding of a complex text. Try to answer these questions about subsection 3.

a Does _this section_ refer to subsection 3, or to subsections 1, 2 and 3? What duty is imposed?

b What does it mean if _X has effect subject to Y_?

c What's the difference between _an enactment_ and _a rule_?

d Does _in certain circumstances_ refer to the verb _requiring_ or _to consider or act_? Does this make any difference to the meaning of the subsection?

e Who are the creditors of the company? In what circumstances might a director consider or act in the interests of creditors?

f Is there a difference between considering somebody's interests and acting in their interests? When might this difference be important?

4 Research

Many statutes have explanatory notes available online. Find explanatory notes to this section at http://www.opsi.gov.uk/acts/acts2006/en/ukpgaen_20060046_en.pdf to check what situations are especially relevant to subsections 2 and 3.

Photocopiable worksheet 6.1

1 Michael .... the firm four years ago and now .... a wide range of clients on information technology, communications, privacy, spam and intellectual property law, ... them in contentious matters in court.

2 He's currently .... a Master's of e-Law at Monash University.

3 I .... legal issues relating to information technology, ... and agreements, and I .... cases in court.

4 It's an extremely wide range of work, from .... software licence agreements to .... privacy and spam law to .... disputes about copyright ownership.

> advise on   advises   advising on   draft   drafting   joined
> litigate   negotiate   representing   resolving   undertaking

5 But I usually spend most of the day .... documents, ... agreements, ... clients and, of course, ... emails.

6 .... junior lawyers is also an important part of most days.

7 I spent much of my time .... scientific and technical documents to .... in what ways an invention was new and innovative.

8 I .... and .... patent applications to .... patents for the inventor.

> answering   determine   drafted   drafting   meeting with
> reading and analysing   reviewing   secure   submitted   supervising

9 I also had to .... patent drafts, which .... the basis for the patents that are .... by the patent office.

10 What I liked best was .... or .... patents.

11 I also particularly liked .... clients.

12 .... people was more exciting than .... all that research alone.

13 I enjoy being in the courtroom, ... a case and .... it to a satisfactory conclusion.

> advising   bringing   defending   doing   enforcing   form   granted   litigating   working with   write

14 And strangely enough, I also enjoy .... contracts.

15 Clients often .... us to .... tight deadlines.

16 I .... an affinity for commercial law.

17 I .... an internship during the summer at a big commercial law firm which .... in maritime law and carriage of goods by sea.

18 Things like .... charter party disputes, ... cargo claims and disputes .... bills of lading and contractual claims.

19 The challenge of shipping work is .... through a maze of different conventions, laws and regulations which .... the different areas.

> apply to   completed   concerning   drafting   had   handling
> meet   navigating   require   resolving   specialises

Photocopiable worksheet 6.2

Here are five techniques for making legal English easier for non-lawyers to understand. Try them out on the text in Reading 4.

1 Vocabulary

Think of plain English alternatives for these words and phrases.

Paragraph 3
a endeavour
b is bound to
c said
d to the best of his ability

Paragraph 4
e deviate from
f consent

Paragraph 9
g an indefinite period
h shall be expected
i provided that
j prior to
k where
l thereto

Paragraph 10
m in other respects
n domicile

Paragraph 11
o arising out of
p competent

2 Long sentences

Paragraph 3 contains two long sentences. Split them so there are four sentences.

a ....
b .... *also* ....
c ....
d *In particular,* ....

3 Positives and negatives

Look at paragraph 4 on page 68 of the SB, and the plain English version in Exercise 24. Both versions present the same information, but one presents it in the form of what is possible, and one presents it as what is impossible, with an exception.

a Which is which?
b Which structure is clearer?

4 Similarities and differences

Use these prompts to rewrite paragraph 9.

There are two options. The contract can either .... *or it can*
....

With both options, ...

The difference is that with the first option, ... *, while with the second option,* ....

5 Long subjects

What is the subject of the first sentence in paragraph 10? Try to rewrite this sentence in two ways. Which is clearer?

a .... *is governed by* ....
b *There is an* .... *which* ....
   Its provisions ....

Now do the same for paragraph 11. Which version is clearer?

c *If there are* ....
d *There may be* ....
   If that happens, ...

Photocopiable worksheet 7.1

1 Lease agreements for an indefinite ...	**a** ... agreement of the parties, or by a court of law.
2 ... by either party on three calendar months' ...	**b** ... be deemed terminated ...
3 Lease agreements for a ...	**c** ... by the law, ...
4 ... only in case of mutual ...	**d** ... consent.
5 The landlord shall have the right to ...	**e** ... definite term may be terminated ...
6 ... if the tenant uses the real property in ...	**f** ... notice.
7 The landlord shall have the right to terminate the lease agreement if the tenant transfers ...	**g** ... of public necessity under the procedure set by Ukrainian law.
8 ... without the landlord's prior ...	**h** ... of termination.
9 The landlord shall have the right to terminate the lease agreement if the tenant, due ...	**i** ... of the lease agreement if the landlord transferred the leased real property, ...
10 The landlord shall have the right to terminate the lease agreement if the tenant has not commenced any major ...	**j** ... payments for the use of the real property during three consecutive months.
11 ... where an obligation to do ...	**k** ... purchase of the land for public needs ...
12 The landlord shall have the right to terminate a lease agreement and claim the ...	**l** ... repairs of the real property ...
13 ... if the tenant does not make lease ...	**m** ... return of real property ...
14 In the event the landlord terminates a lease agreement, the lease agreement shall ...	**n** ... so was imposed on the tenant.
15 ... from the moment the tenant is notified by the landlord ...	**o** ... term may be terminated at any time ...
16 Pursuant ...	**p** ... terminate the lease agreement ...
17 ... the tenant shall have the right to demand termination ...	**q** ... the terms and conditions stipulated by the lease agreement or the designation of the real property.
18 ... and the quality of the leased property contravenes ...	**r** ... the use of the real property to another person ...
19 The tenant shall have the right to demand termination of the lease agreement if the landlord fails to comply ...	**s** ... to his/her negligence, creates a threat of possible damage to the real property.
20 According to Ukrainian law, an agreement on lease of the land shall be terminated in certain cases provided ...	**t** ... to the Civil Code of Ukraine, ...
21 ... namely compulsory ...	**u** ... violation of the agreement or the real property's designation.
22 ... and forced alienation of land on the grounds ...	**v** ... with the obligation to make capital repairs of the real property.

Photocopiable worksheet 7.2

Solve the anagrams to complete this email from Ms Fialová to Marta Cervera, sent as a follow-up to their discussion in Listening 2.

To: M Cervera

From: Jana Fialová

Subject: Buy-to-let in Prague

Dear Ms Cervera

It was very nice to talk to you this morning. It is excellent news that you are planning to **1) spraeuch** a property in Prague, and I can confirm that I will be delighted to deal with the **2) nocvnceaey**. Our conversation covered many aspects of the buy-to-let process, so please find below a summary of the most important points for your information.

Owing to the bureaucratic nature of property purchases in the Czech Republic, you can expect the process to take around four months from identifying the right property to **3) netmipcolo**. All transfers of real estate are recorded in the **4) dalstarac treegris**.

As we discussed, the requirement that foreigners must form a limited company in order to own property has been **5) eredalep**. However, you may still decide to **6) catpoinrore**, a process taking around six or eight weeks, as this may give you some tax **7) gedvsantaa**. For example, you would not be liable to pay **8) mapst utdy**, which is a property transfer tax normally **9) vileed** by the state on real estate sales. I must stress, however, that I am not in a position to give tax advice, so I strongly recommend that you discuss this with an accountant. I know of an excellent company **10) toinrmfoa** agent (www.bizformation.cz), who will be able to advise you of the advantages and disadvantages of incorporation.

Please email me a copy of all relevant **11) atnonodeticum**, so I can arrange translations into English and **12) ritsenoa** all the documents myself. I will also examine the standard form **13) asurepch atmregeen** that you have received from the estate agent and, if necessary, **14) errdtaf** it in order to ensure that it takes the form of a **15) edde**.

As the property is still under development, it is essential that uncompleted work is included in the purchase agreement, and I strongly **16) nmecedorm** that you keep some of the purchase money in **17) sworec** so that the developer pays a penalty if the work is not completed within a **18) atdiptesul** period. This would also protect you in the unlikely event that the developer goes **19) tkrbanup**.

I will also arrange for a full **20) ltiet cheasr** to be conducted, in order to identify problems with the **21) hcnai fo itelt**. There are many **22) earsucencnmb** which could prevent or delay the sale. For example, there may be an unpaid **23) enli** against the property, used as security for a loan, which would give the **24) eldlerhoin** a legal claim against the property. There may also exist **25) iettrsiverc tsencvnoa**, which could limit your use of the property, or **26) eatsneems**, which give others the right to use the property for a specific purpose.

Finally, I will ask my brother, Marek, to contact you to arrange a meeting. For your information, the website of his **27) negltti ncyeag** is www.praguelet.cz.

I look forward to receiving the documentation from you, which I will examine and arrange translation as soon as I receive written **28) iroatinmoncf** from you that you are definitely going ahead with the purchase.

Best regards

Jana Fialová

Photocopiable worksheet 8.1

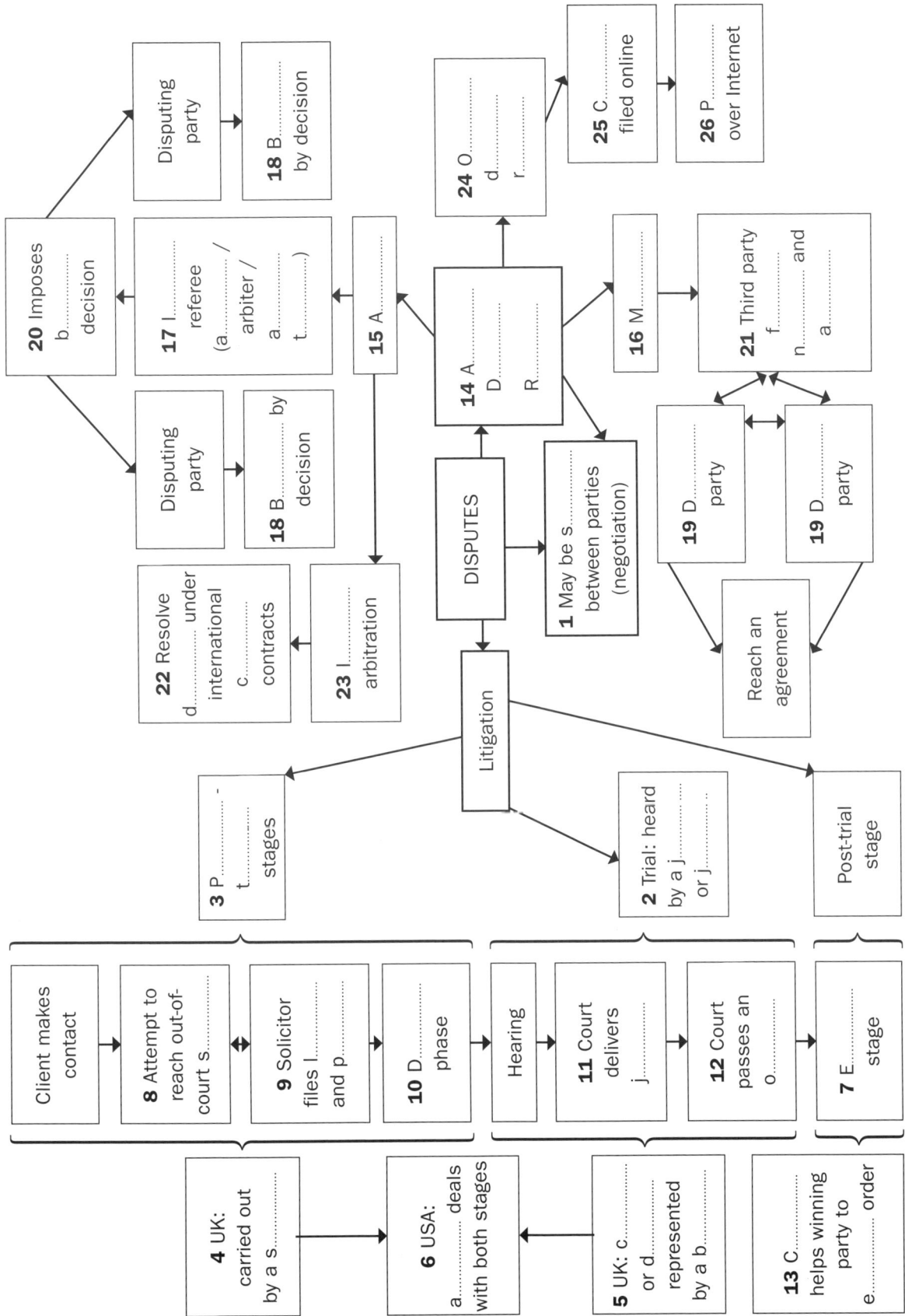

DISPUTES

1 May be s............. between parties (negotiation)

14 A............. D............. R.............

15 A.............

16 M.............

21 Third party f............. n............. and a.............

19 D............. party

19 D............. party

Reach an agreement

24 O............. d............. r.............

25 C............. filed online

26 P............. over Internet

20 Imposes b............. decision

17 I............. referee (a............. / arbiter / a............. t.............)

18 B............. by decision

Disputing party

18 B............. by decision

Disputing party

22 Resolve d............. under international c............. contracts

23 I............. arbitration

Litigation

3 P............. - t............. stages

2 Trial: heard by a j............. or j.............

Post-trial stage

Client makes contact

8 Attempt to reach out-of-court s.............

9 Solicitor files l............. and p.............

10 D............. phase

Hearing

11 Court delivers j.............

12 Court passes an o.............

7 E............. stage

4 UK: carried out by a s.............

6 USA: a............. deals with both stages

5 UK: c............. or d............. represented by a b.............

13 C............. helps winning party to e............. order

Photocopiable worksheet 8.2

✂

I have to say, it does look as …	**1**	**a**	… detail as possible.	
Could you tell …	**2**	**b**	… I need to establish the relevant facts.	
I'm not quite sure you …	**3**	**c**	… if you've got yourself into a rather serious situation.	
Before I can give you any advice, …	**4**	**d**	… me exactly what happened?	
Please do give as much …	**5**	**e**	… that this is what Ms Loushe has done?	
Try not to avoid any facts …	**6**	**f**	… to the facts.	
It's better I hear everything now in order …	**7**	**g**	… to avoid any unfortunate surprises later.	
It's probably best just to stick …	**8**	**h**	… what you suspect Ms Loushe of having done.	
I think you'd better tell me just …	**9**	**i**	… which may be uncomfortable.	
And do you have any proof …	**10**	**j**	… understand what Ms Loushe is alleging.	

From what you tell me, I have to advise you that if this does go to a tribunal, …	**11**	**k**	… for your firm's current financial troubles.	
Unless you were able to provide concrete evidence of the alleged theft, …	**12**	**l**	… generous offer of a settlement before this goes any further.	
I'm not entirely convinced that Ms Loushe can be blamed …	**13**	**m**	… her to take the case to a tribunal.	
If I were advising Ms Loushe, I would certainly be encouraging …	**14**	**n**	… it will be very difficult for us to put together a convincing defence.	
Your best chance of avoiding litigation is …	**15**	**o**	… that the dismissal was 'fair'.	
I think that first it might be useful for me to talk you through …	**16**	**p**	… the tribunal must then decide whether you have acted reasonably.	
To defend the case, we must show …	**17**	**q**	… to offer a generous settlement.	
I must warn you that, even if we are able to plead one of these five permitted reasons, …	**18**	**r**	… to which her lawyers allude in their letter.	
I hope you agree with me that it is in your best interests to make a …	**19**	**s**	… what is likely to happen should Ms Loushe decide to litigate.	
You may want to consider offering her the promotion …	**20**	**t**	… you'd have very little chance of avoiding substantial damages against you.	

Photocopiable worksheet 9.1

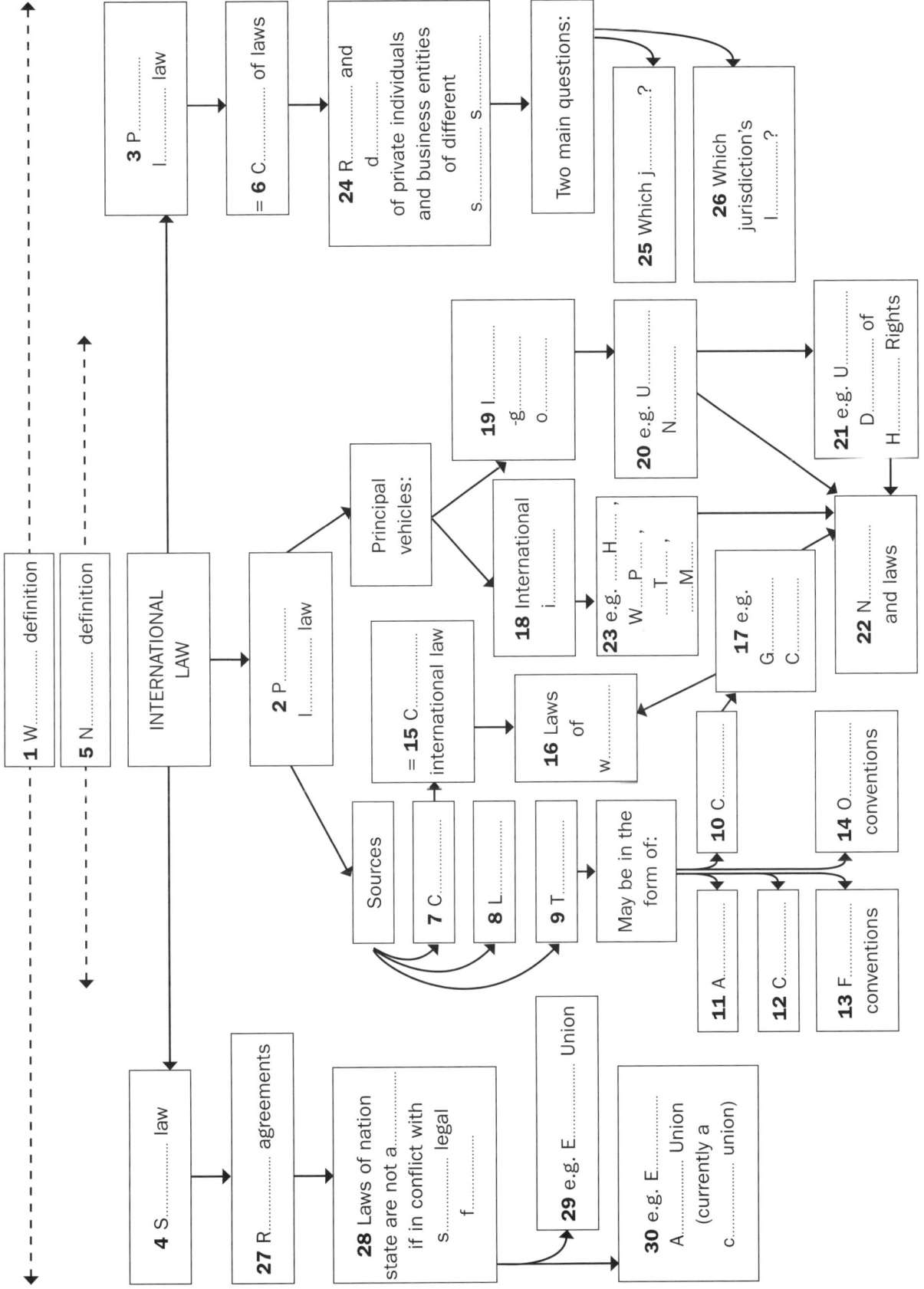

1 W................ definition

5 N................ definition

INTERNATIONAL LAW

3 P................
l................ law

= **6** C................ of laws

24 R................ and
d................
of private individuals
and business entities
of different
s................ s................

Two main questions:

25 Which j................?

26 Which
jurisdiction's
l................?

2 P................
l................ law

Principal
vehicles:

19 I................
-g................
o................

20 e.g. U................
N................

21 e.g. U................
D................ of
H................ Rights

18 International
i................

23 e.g. H................,
W................ P................,
T................,
M................

17 e.g.
G................
C................

22 N................
and laws

Sources

15 C................
international law

16 Laws
of
w................

7 C................

8 L................

9 T................

May be in the
form of:

10 C................

11 A................

12 C................

13 F................
conventions

14 O................
conventions

4 S................ law

27 R................ agreements

28 Laws of nation
state are not a................
if in conflict with
s................ legal
f................

29 e.g. E................ Union

30 e.g. E................
A................ Union
(currently a
c................ union)

Photocopiable worksheet 9.2

1 In each of the useful phrases for debates, there is one extra word. Find it and delete it.

a Let me to pick up on something my opponent said earlier.	**b** As I see it, there are three things we must need to consider. Firstly, ... Secondly, ... Finally, ...
c My opponent would claims that ... , whereas in fact it should be perfectly clear that ...	**d** My colleague has already mentioned that ... . I would like to be expand on the area of ...
e That argument may sound like convincing in theory, but I'm afraid the evidence simply does not support it.	**f** My opponent has correctly pointed you out that ... . What she/he has failed to mention is that ...
g My opponent gave a very persuasive response to my question, but unfortunately has failed to answer to it.	**h** This case rests on three assumptions, all of which, I have hope to demonstrate to you, are false.
i While it may be true that ... , I take my issue with the assertion that ...	**j** In answer to my opponent's first argument, I would argue that it is simply not relevant to the case in his hand.
k I would like to begin by addressing the general principles involved in, and then turn to the specifics of this case.	**l** My colleague has raised a number of important questions, and I would like now to address to one of those questions, namely ... .
m My opponent made three claims. I would like to address each one in a turn. Firstly, she/he tried to draw a parallel between ... and	**n** According to my opponent ... . But I would like argue that precisely the opposite is true.
o It should have be obvious to anyone who understands the subject of ... that	**p** Why isn't it the case that ... ?
q That's all very well, but we must consider about the wider issue, namely ...	**r** My opponent would have us to believe that ... , but there are serious flaws in that argument.
s I fail to see any logical or connection between ... and ...	**t** I am sure you will be agree with me that ...

2 Now sort the phrases into these three categories:

1	Organising your arguments
2	Making points
3	Arguing against your opponent's points

Photocopiable worksheet 10.1

1 Civil law may be defined .... that legal tradition which has its origin .... Roman law, ...
codified .... the Corpus Juris Civilis (the Justinian Code), and .... subsequently developed
.... continental Europe and .... the world.

around   as   as   as   in   in   in

2 Civil law relies .... declarations .... broad, general principles. Common law's principles appear
.... the most part .... reported judgments, usually .... the higher courts, ... relation
.... specific situations arising .... disputes that the courts have adjudicated.

for   in   in   in   of   of   on   to

3 A major difference .... common-law and civil-law systems is the heavy reliance .... case
law .... common-law systems. .... such cases, the courts interpret statute law .... the
development .... of case law.

between   In   in   on   through

4 .... the doctrine .... *stare decisis*, lower courts are compelled to follow decisions rendered
.... higher courts. Thus, precedent is .... the core .... common-law legal systems.

at   in   of   of   Under

5 .... arriving .... a decision .... a case, a court will first determine whether there are any
applicable statutory provisions. [ ] If there is no case law ....the statute, the court will place its
own interpretation .... the statute. If no statutes apply, the court will look .... previous case
law.

at   In   in   on   on   to

6 Although codified law (mainly .... the form .... statutes) is paramount .... both legal
traditions, it differs .... its importance. .... civil-law jurisdictions, priority is given ....
enacted law .... unenacted law.

in   in   in   in   of   over   to

7 Codes provide the core body .... law and are supplemented .... decisions .... individual
cases. Conversely, the opposite is true .... the common-law tradition, ... which precedent is
the major source .... law.

by   in   in   in   of   of

Photocopiable worksheet 10.2

Activity of placing one's wealth in a place out of reach from creditors, tax offices, etc.	a _ _ _ _ _ _ _ _ _ _ _ _ _
The assets of the foundation are held on behalf of a	b _ _ _ _ _ _ _ _ _
Rule of law that a person bringing a case must be free from unfair conduct in connection with that case	'c _ _ _ _ _ _ _ _ _' _ _ _ _ _ _ _
Words and phrases used at the beginning of a sentence to show the relationship between ideas	d _ _ _ _ _ _ _ _ _ _ _ _ _ _
System of courts that developed alongside law courts in England	e _ _ _ _ _
Word or phrase which looks similar to one in another language, but with an unexpected meaning	f _ _ _ _ _ _ _ _ _
The defendant has the burden of proof to show that the claimant is not acting in	g _ _ _ _ _ _ _ _
The Anstalt is a .... between a company limited by shares and a foundation.	h _ _ _ _ _
The most widely used form of religious law	I _ _ _ _ _ _ _ _ _
Codified body of Roman law	J _ _ _ _ _ _ _ _ _ _ _ _
In the late Middle Ages in England, litigants could petition the	k _ _ _
US state which has a civil-law system	L _ _ _ _ _ _ _ _
Jurisdictions which have elements of both common and civil law	m _ _ _ _ _ _ _ _ _ _ _
This discourse marker is used for emphasising	n _ _ _ _ _ _
In a common-law system, the legislature can .... case law through new legislation.	o _ _ _ _ _ _ _
Decisions made in earlier cases	p _ _ _ _ _ _ _ _ _
Canadian state which has a civil-law system.	Q _ _ _ _ _
A formal way of saying decisions are *made*	r _ _ _ _ _ _ _
Doctrine in common law that compels lower courts to follow decisions of higher courts	s _ _ _ _ _ _ _ _ _ _ _
An entity which holds assets for the benefit of certain beneficiaries	t _ _ _ _
An aspect of comparative law associated with HCC and UNIDROIT	u _ _ _ _ _ _ _ _ _
Common law is used in the .... majority of English-speaking countries.	v _ _ _
Collective term for common-law and civil-law systems	W _ _ _ _ _ _ _ _ _ _ _ _ _ _ _ _
Jurisdiction with low or zero rate of taxation	_ _ x _ _ _ _ _
Doctrine that prevents one party from withdrawing from a promise made to another party if the other party has relied on it and acted upon it to his detriment	_ _ _ _ _ _ _ _ _ y _ _ _ _ _ _ _
Country with a mixed common/civil-law system, based on South African law	Z _ _ _ _ _ _ _

Introduction to International Legal English Photocopiable Worksheet 10.2